SHIKITEI SANBA AND THE COMIC
TRADITION IN EDO FICTION

*Harvard-Yenching Institute
Monograph Series 25*

Shikitei Sanba and the Comic Tradition in Edo Fiction

ROBERT W. LEUTNER

Published by the Council on East Asian Studies, Harvard University, and the Harvard-Yenching Institute, and distributed by the Harvard University Press, Cambridge (Massachusetts) and London, 1985

The Harvard-Yenching Institute, founded in 1928
and headquartered at Harvard University, is a foundation dedicated to the advancement of higher education in the humanities and social sciences in East and
Southeast Asia. The Institute supports advanced research at Harvard by faculty members of certain Asian
universities, and doctoral studies at Harvard and
other universities by junior faculty of the same universities. It also supports East Asian studies at Harvard through contributions to the Harvard-Yenching
Library and publication of the *Harvard Journal of
Asiatic Studies* and books on pre-modern East Asian
history and literature.

Book design by David Horne

Library of Congress Cataloging in Publication Data

Leutner, Robert W.
    Shikitei Sanba and the comic tradition in Edo fiction.

    Bibliography: p.
    Includes index.
    1. Shikitei, Sanba, 1776–1822. 2. Novelists, Japanese
—Biography. I. Title.
PL798.2.Z5L48 1985   895.6'33 [B]   85–4173
ISBN 0–674–80646–8

FOR KATHY

Preface

I cannot recall precisely how and when I first heard about Shikitei Sanba, but in retrospect there seems to have been a certain inevitability to my choosing him as the subject of the dissertation on which this book is based. Like many of my fellow students at the time, I began my graduate study of Japan with a strong interest in the Meiji period, where we were sure there was to be found everything we might need to support, modify, or refute, as the case might be, the prevailing academic visions of what "modernization" was all about. Most of us soon came to realize that the Meiji Restoration, whatever its symbolic drama, was part of a historical process of indeterminate limits, and began to reformulate our questions while looking at earlier or later times.

I myself straddled 1868 at first, in a Master's thesis about the changes that came to the Japanese publishing industry with the importation of new printing technology and the explosion of demand for information about the outside world. It was then that I first caught a glimpse of the world of Edo—not just the world of Meiji waiting to be born, but one with its own special texture and richness. I came back to that world, finally, after a detour through the Heian classics and the study and translation of Ihara Saikaku. Better equipped philologically to deal with Edo Japanese in all its quirkiness and with a very different perspective on Japanese culture, I turned to *gesaku* fiction with the thought that it might be a means of approaching from the inside, in a sense, the world from which Meiji was to spring. That it indeed proved to be; but I hope I am not alone in thinking that this close look at Shikitei Sanba and his works demonstrates that the fiction of the late Edo period

is not just a curious cultural artifact, a body of source material for
the cultural historian looking for the "Tokugawa heritage," but is
also a literature of interest and considerable merit in its own right.

I chose Sanba as the subject of my dissertation because he
seemed not unrepresentative of the writers of his time and because
his masterwork, *Ukiyoburo*, struck me as a work of both charm
and artistry. I know him now as a writer who was not merely a
skillful craftsman but also a sensitive student of human nature. In
the aggregate, his works recreate with a startling vividness the world
of the Edo townsman, peopled with a great and varied crowd of
portraits from life. In the end it is the humanity of his subjects
that lingers in the mind's eye more than anything specifically
"Japanese" about them—a sign, perhaps, of the universality of his
vision and the sureness of his brush. Cultural attitudes about
fiction, the political climate, the isolation of Japanese culture, all
put forced limits on the range and depth of *gesaku* fiction, but,
within those limits, Sanba succeeded in producing a body of fiction that needs no apology. (What it needs most, of course, is to
be enjoyed. It is the nature of books based on dissertations to be
more solemn than enjoyable, but I hope the translations that
appear here will show that Sanba was not just a literary artist but
a humorist, and a good one.)

There are many people and institutions that in one way or
another made this book possible. First and foremost I must thank
Prof. William Sibley, now of the University of Chicago, for his
patient and supportive help as thesis advisor and friend. For, among
other things, their uncompromising rigor in matters of English and
Japanese, my thanks to Prof. Robert Brower of The University of
Michigan and Prof. Edward Seidensticker, now of Columbia University. Thanks also to Professors Roger Hackett and the late
Richard Beardsley of the University of Michigan for unstinting
encouragement. Colleagues and friends in Japan whom I should
like to thank include Professors Jinbō Kazuya, Honda Yasuo,
Ogatoa Tsutomu, Konishi Jin'ichi, and Shimura Kaichi, and the
staff of the Kokubungaku Kenkyū Shiryōkan. For their counsel,
intellectual stimulation, assistance of one sort or another, and
simple friendship during the years I have spent with Sanba, my
thanks to many, many people in Ann Arbor, New Haven, Iowa
City, and elsewhere, but most especially Michael Cooper, Chuck
and Shirley Cross, Aileen Gatten, Howard Hibbett, Andrew

Markus, Edwin and Rachel McClellan, John and D. Lee Rich, Mary L. Willett, and through Davenport College, Ivo and Marija Banac, Firuz and Caterina Kazemzadeh, the late Harry Scammell, Henry and Jane Turner, and others who gave "fellowship" a special meaning. A special world of thanks to Prof. John K. Fairbank, who set me on my present course long ago with his supreme assurance that any reasonable person should know something about East Asia. And, before all others, my thanks to my wife and my parents.

I am grateful also for financial support from the following sources: The Department of Health, Education, and Welfare (National Defense Foreign Language and Fulbright Dissertation fellowships); the Center for Japanese Studies, The University of Michigan; The University of Michigan (Horace G. Rackham Prize Fellowship); Yale University (Sumitomo Faculty Research fellowship); The University of Iowa (Old Gold fellowship).

Contents

SHIKITEI SANBA AND THE COMIC
TRADITION IN EDO FICTION

CHAPTER ONE

Introduction

In the last decades of the eighteenth century, the literary imagination took flight in Japan in a way it had never done before. In the place of the anonymous storytellers of the middle ages or, in more recent times, an isolated Ihara Saikaku or Ueda Akinari, there appeared in Edo (modern Tokyo) what was by comparison virtually an army of writers; by the 1850s, several generations of authors had produced a prodigiously large and varied body of fiction. The sheer dimensions of this explosion of imaginative writing are arresting in themselves, but what to modern eyes most distinguishes these authors from their predecessors is their clearly articulated awareness of themselves as members of a profession, practitioners of a craft with its own developing traditions. That their vision of themselves and of their relationship to society seems so well defined is partly a matter of historical accident, since we are almost bound to know more about them and their times than is the case with earlier writers. Still, it is clear that these men brought to their work attitudes toward writing and the concept of authorship itself that were new to the culture.

This book is about Shikitei Sanba (1776–1822), a writer whose works and the shape of whose career mark him as squarely in the mainstream of late Edo fiction. Sanba is remembered today as a humorist, and principally for *Ukiyoburo* (The bathhouse of the floating world, 1809–1813), parts of which appear in translation beginning on page 137 of this volume. *Ukiyoburo* made Sanba's reputation, but it is only one of a number of his works in the *kokkeibon* (comic or funny book) medium whose quality and historical importance recommend them both for enjoyment and as objects

1

of study. These books naturally form a principal focus of this study, although they represent only a small proportion of the hundred or more fictional works Sanba wrote. His particular achievements as a humorist set Sanba apart from his contemporaries, but his career as a whole makes him an exemplar, a representative writer of his time and place. One purpose of this book will, therefore, be to use Sanba's life and works as a guide to the world of the Edo writer and to the values and social and economic forces that shaped the fiction of his day.

Sanba and his fellow writers called themselves *gesakusha*, makers of *gesaku*, or "playful compositions," and with few exceptions they bore the title proudly. In its early appearances in Chinese sources, the term *gesaku*, usually applied to poetic compositions in *shih* form, suggested both an author's attitude toward his writing and the nature of the work itself. These meanings survived intact in later Japanese usage: whatever the nature of the piece, whether written in Chinese (as the earliest works labeled *gesaku* invariably were) or Japanese, the writer approached his work in a spirit of play, and the piece itself was meant to be amusing. By implication, the writing of *gesaku* was a diverting amusement for an otherwise serious man, but unlike other pastimes appropriate to the literatus—calligraphy, painting, the tea ceremony, or, indeed, serious poetry or prose in Chinese—the witty final product was intended to provoke laughter or a wry smile.

This use of the term *gesaku* flourished for several generations in Japan after its earliest appearances in the mid-eighteenth century, well into a period when the original type of the *gesakusha*, the high-status amateur writing for a restricted audience of like-minded friends, had long since been replaced by that of the professional writing for the broadest possible popular audience. Sanba, in spite of his undeniably plebeian origins and the unabashedly commercial nature of much of his writing, clung tenaciously to his *gesakusha* persona; while he did as much as any writer of his time to expand the bounds and to enrich the content of *gesaku* fiction, he maintained with what must have been at least half-conscious irony that, from first to last, he was dedicated to preserving and enhancing the *gesaku* tradition as established by the writers of the 1770s and 1780s.

But Sanba was not alone in his efforts to foster the impression that *gesaku* was an art with a pedigree. Its spiritual line of descent was from Chinese antecedents, and so, even in their choice of pen names, for instance, the *gesakusha* were at pains to suggest their affinities with the Chinese gentleman-amateur model: for the most part, fiction was published under names that looked and sounded Chinese, if in actual fact they were often of Japanese invention. Names ending in *-dō* (hall) or *-tei* (pavilion), perhaps the commonest of *gesakusha* pen names, called to mind the figure of the scholar of means retired from worldly concerns; *sanjin* (man of the mountain) and *-an* (hermitage), the even more unworldly existence of the hermit in full retreat from everything but art and contemplation. When the *gesakusha* wrote comic verse in Japanese (*kyōka*), he usually identified himself with a wholly Japanese name, but when he turned to fiction he most often chose a name of unmistakably Chinese aspect.[1]

The wholesale commercialization of fiction after the 1780s threatened the amateur ideal but never completely undermined it, however few true amateurs there may have been among the first rank of writers. While the fiction of the early 1800s was very different from that of a generation before, and while writers of samurai-class origin had been largely superseded by commoners, Sanba and his contemporaries continued to portray themselves as *gesakusha* of the old sort. Although they were transparently eager for the financial rewards of fiction writing, they maintained a conventional pose of contempt for their publishers' greedy ways; and, although they catered happily to their readers' taste for romance and adventure, they lamented the disappearance of urbanity and wit from *gesaku* fiction. The expansion of the audience for fiction meant that the *gesakusha* was no longer writing for a coterie of people like himself but instead for a faceless audience whose tastes and degree of sophistication he could no longer instinctively divine. Yet, in introductions and prefaces, authorial asides and afterwords, the *gesakusha* frequently addressed his audience directly and intimately, thereby encouraging the illusion that writer and reader were still members of a circle of initiates.

While much *gesaku* fiction by Sanba and his successors may be devoid of explicit humor, and while, from the author's point of view, writing was no longer "play" but a profession, the "playfulness" implicit in the term *gesaku* never wholly disappeared; it survived in the give-and-take that the unpredictable obtrusiveness of the author fosters. There was an exhibitionistic, self-advertising impulse in early *gesaku* fiction that was born of contradictory desires: the writer's objective was to entertain and amuse, but he was unwilling to put his reputation at risk by appearing to be simply a jester or a buffoon. The result was a form of writing that constantly forces upon the reader an awareness of its artificiality and tentativeness, of the fact that it is, after all, only the offhand creation of someone who just happens to be adept at amusing literary entertainments—cousin, perhaps, to the virtuoso punster or singer of bawdy ditties at a party in the pleasure quarter. What to modern eyes is the not altogether pleasing intrusiveness of the author in later *gesaku* fiction is in part the result of attempts to preserve something of the distance between the author and his work that the amateur ethic of an earlier generation required. Whether he announces his presence directly in asides to the reader or indirectly in eruptions of wordplay or flights of seemingly irrelevant erudition, the later *gesakusha* is at constant pains to remind the reader that the world he has created in his fiction is his creation and his alone, one from which he can remove himself at will, by ceasing to be simply a narrator and taking on some wholly different persona. This refusal on the part of the writer to take himself wholly seriously, or even to pretend to to do so, is one of the charms of *gesaku* fiction; it is also a barrier to its appreciation by modern readers whose expectations of fiction have been shaped by the Western novel and short story.

The vast body of fiction published in Japan in the century or so preceding the Meiji Restoration of 1868 has been little studied, in Japan or abroad. One reason for this neglect is surely the modern reader's disappointment at the *gesakusha*'s failure to apprehend the potential of fiction as an instrument of psychological or social analysis owing to his studied refusal to admit to any great seriousness of purpose. But there are other reasons as well. One has to do with historical accident: As the dominant tradition in fiction, *gesaku* was bound to become the kind of writing against which the aspiring Western-style novelists of the 1880s and 1890s felt it necessary to rebel in order to free themselves to understand and assimilate the new styles; their tendency to denigrate or simply to ignore *gesaku* has colored subsequent generations' vision of the earlier kind of writing. Then, too, from the point of view of many scholars, *gesaku* fiction is neither here nor there: it is not so old that age alone and the mere fact that it has survived might make it a worthy object of study; and its role in the development of modern fiction seems minor and indirect. Works of the period are neither old enough nor difficult enough to be taught in the schools as classics, yet they are still far enough from the modern world linguistically and culturally that they cannot be read with ease and pleasure without special study. Ironically, the very fact that many species of fiction written in this period often closely approach modern novels in superficial aspects of form and content makes them hard to like: the surprise of recognition soon wears off, to be replaced by a growing sense that the object at hand is simply a strangely defective and primitive sort of novel rather than a piece of fiction from a wholly different tradition that can be appreciated only on its own terms.

The sheer volume of fiction produced from the 1790s onward is a further impediment to its systematic study. Shikitei Sanba's fictional works total over one hundred, and he produced in addition a large number of works that today would be called nonfiction. His contemporary, Jippensha Ikku (1765–1831), is credited with over four hundred books of all kinds, and other writers of the period were nearly as prolific.[2] Not all works of *gesaku* fiction were of any great length—many complete, separately published works were of modern short-story length—but the new works appearing annually in Sanba's day often numbered into the hundreds.[3] While a few works by a relatively few authors have by scholarly consensus been accorded the status of a canon of representative pieces of *gesaku* fiction, the fact that the fiction of the period goes so generally unread means that there is no real consensus, scholarly or otherwise, as to which other works and which other writers might be worth further study; indeed there is little agreement, when the issue is joined at all, on what standards might be—or have been—invoked to separate the wheat from the chaff.

Only a small proportion of the fiction of the period has been reprinted in the carefully edited and annotated scholarly editions that make full appreciation possible; many more works are available in modern printed editions dating from the late nineteenth and early twentieth centuries, but these versions are often textually unreliable and, for the most part, do not reproduce the illustrations that are so integrally a part of the fiction of the age. The rest are available only in the original editions, rare and difficult of access, often defective, and, in any case, difficult to read without a thorough familiarity with Edo-period[4] calligraphic styles and publishing conventions. The acknowledged masterpieces of major writers are readily available in good editions, but such works are by definition unrepresentative, and generalizations based solely upon such a biased sample of the fiction of an age (or of an author) are suspect.

The apparently popular, commercial nature of all but a few kinds of *gesaku* fiction no doubt also contributes to the disfavor in which it has so often been held. By the early 1800s, it is clear, fiction had a very large following. Sales in the easy-to-read, heavily illustrated *kibyōshi* and *gōkan* genres seem often to have reached 10,000 copies per title; best sellers sold perhaps twice that over a span of several years in print, and reached an even wider audience through used-book dealers and flea markets.[5] Books of the *yomihon* type, which required a relatively higher level of education to read than other varieties of fiction and which were too expensive for most readers to buy outright, were rarely published in printings of more than 1,000 or 2,000 copies, but their readership was multiplied to an incalculable degree by a nationwide network of commercial lending libraries, of which there were 655 recorded in Edo alone in 1808.[6] It appears that *gesaku* fiction in Sanba's day and afterwards was on the way to becoming a truly popular fiction for a mass market. The fact that after the 1790s it was evidently the practice to pay writers for their manuscripts according to their previous sales records bolsters the impression that fiction was becoming a commodity, a commercial rather than an artistic enterprise.

Evidence indeed abounds that writer and publisher alike were keenly attuned to shifts in public taste, that fads and market demand rather than individual inclinations tended to dictate what kinds of books an author wrote. Much of Sanba's non-comic writing, and that of his contemporaries, is characterized by techniques and devices familiar to anyone who knows something of mass-market fiction in the West, from the nineteenth-century English "penny dreadful" to the westerns, crime stories, and drugstore romances of today: formulaic plots, for instance, and stereotyped characters; exotic settings, violence, romantic love, and illicit liaisons; an almost scholarly attention to historical detail or to the fine points of the behavior and language of a contemporary subculture, whose effect is to lend a spurious authenticity to a fiction

otherwise highly romantic and unrealistic. Yet, for all these indica-
tions that later *gesaku* fiction might best be discussed in juxtaposition to modern popular fiction, it should be noted that the actual
size of any imagined mass market for *gesaku* was considerably
smaller than its equivalents in the West, in both relative and absolute terms. In England in the early nineteenth century, for instance, when a recognizable mass audience for fiction first took
shape, the weekly and monthly periodicals that were the primary
medium for fiction often attained circulations of 50,000 or more,
not in the aggregate but individually; this in a population of perhaps 6 million. Given an estimated population of 30 million in
Japan at this time, even an unusually popular *gōkan* selling an extraordinary 20,000 copies looks like a book for a discerning elite;
how much more so a *yomihon* in an edition of a mere 2,000, no
matter how aggressive the lending libraries might have been in cir-
culating their stock. [7]

No writer can be called wholly representative of his generation,
but, in surveying the whole of Shikitei Sanba's career, one garners
what is probably a fairly accurate picture of what fiction was like
in his time and what it meant to be a writer. His works include
examples of virtually every current genre of fiction; although he is
remembered as a *kokkeibon* author, the bulk of his output consisted of titles in a considerable variety of other popular forms.
In this respect he is representative, since most of his contemporaries were active in many different kinds of fiction. Like most of
his fellow writers, Sanba was a member of the urban middle class,
and with them he shared the tastes and personal style of the *Edokko,* the self-confident and slightly jaded "son of Edo" who could
conceive of no better world than his own sophisticated city. Edo
in his time was, like Tokyo today, the cultural and political capital
of Japan, and increasingly its economic nerve center as well. There
are few of his works that do not take Edo as their implicit, and
often explicit point of reference; *gesaku* fiction in general was historically and spiritually at home in Sanba's city.

Sanba's principal medium throughout his career was that of the
kusazōshi, [8] quintessentially an Edo form. The term *kusazōshi* is
virtually untranslatable—it suggests something like "books of little
consequence"—but applies to a succession of different kinds of
fiction published in visually similar formats beginning in the early
eighteenth century. The main representatives of the *kusazōshi*

medium in Sanba's day were known as the *kibyōshi* and the *gōkan*. The *kibyōshi* (yellow-cover, so called because the dominant color on the cover of late-eighteenth-century *kusazōshi* was either a blue that faded quickly to a greenish yellow or, later, yellow from the start) as a distinct species of writing developed in the late 1770s out of an earlier tradition of heavily illustrated books in similar format (*akahon*, "red books"; *kurobon*, "black books"; *aobon*, "blue/green books") that seem to have been aimed primarily at a juvenile audience.[9] In the hands of writers like Koikawa Harumachi (1744–1789), Hōseidō Kisanji (1735–1813), Shiba Zenkō (1750–1793), and Santō Kyōden (1761–1816), the *kibyōshi* became increasingly a medium for adult satire, while retaining the physical appearance of the earlier *kusazōshi* genres, in which the text and dialogue were fitted into the white space in and around the visually dominant illustrations that covered each page. In its short-lived heyday, the *kibyōshi* aimed its satire, mainly in the form of parodies, lampoons, and fantasies, at the Chinese classics, popular historical myths and heroes, Japanese classics of all kinds, preposterous, greedy, or pompous behavior wherever found, and ultimately political affairs. Political satire, however, was regarded as off limits by the Tokugawa shogunate (one of its natural objects), and as official punishments were meted out in the early 1790s to political satirists—most of them samurai *gesakusha* who should have known better—there appeared among *kibyōshi* authors a backing away from satire in general. The *kibyōshi* gradually became a medium devoted in large part to politically inoffensive retellings of historical tales, updated fairy tales, and illustrated novelistic versions of popular *kabuki* plays and puppet dramas (*jōruri*). A fad for tales of vengeance that began shortly after 1800 signaled the end of the *kibyōshi* as a vehicle for satire and the beginning of its transformation into a species of juvenile adventure literature.

The *gōkan* soon succeeded the *kibyōshi* as the primary representative of *kusazōshi* tradition. The term *gōkan* itself means simply "bound-together volumes," and refers to works in basically the old *kibyōshi* format consisting of three to ten or more volumes bound together as one or two larger volumes. Sanba regarded himself as the originator of this new fashion in *kusazōshi*; while it now seems clear that the *gōkan* originally developed simply as a more convenient and less costly way to bind and distribute multi-volume *kibyōshi,* the popularity of Sanba's works in the new format seems to have been a major factor in its survival and in its eventual domination of the field of illustrated fiction. The *gōkan* of Sanba's era continued the trend visible in the *kibyōshi* toward works more and more obviously directed at a juvenile audience (or an undemanding adult one). Most contain large doses of physical violence well suited to dramatic pictorial representation in the illustrations that dominate every page, the text, as in the *kibyōshi,* occupying spaces above, below, and within the art work.

The next most common sort of work among those Sanba published is the *kokkeibon.* It is here that most studies of Shikitei Sanba begin and end, not only because of the immense popularity his *kokkeibon* enjoyed in their day but also because it is in these works that he most clearly reveals his skills as a writer, his sensitivity to the nuances of behavior and speech, and his sense of humor; here, too, are the works that earn for him an important niche in history for helping show the way toward the realistic rendition of dialogue in fiction and for helping legitimize the literary treatment of the middle and lower classes and their ordinary, daily concerns. Or, to put it another way, Sanba's *kokkeibon* are simply better and historically of greater interest than his work in other media. In spite of the fact, then, that *kokkeibon* account for perhaps only a fifth of Sanba's published works, this study, like most others, will accord these works a certain centrality and discuss his other writing generally from the point of view of the light it sheds on the skills and attitudes he displays in his *kokkeibon.* Sanba himself, one suspects, would be more than happy to be regarded today as first and foremost a *kokkeibon* author, given his vision of himself as a guardian of the comic tradition in fiction and given, more specifically, the role assigned him by his contemporaries and successors as the spiritual representative in his day of the school of comic writing associated with Hiraga Gennai (1728–1779), who then as now was regarded as the originator of the *kokkeibon* in the mid-eighteenth century.

Sanba published only a small number of *sharebon,* books of "style" or "wit" that dealt with the people and customs of the pleasure quarters, perhaps because by his time the form had already begun to be dominated by decidedly unfunny, melodramatic love stories instead of the satiric treatments of the elegant misbehavior of pleasure-quarter dandies that had earlier been the norm.

The *sharebon* of Sanba's day exhibit a tendency to lay their primary stress on the romantic entanglements of the inhabitants and
habitués of the pleasure quarters, and consequently lack the sparkle
and wit Sanba admired in early *gesaku* fiction. These late, melodramatic *sharebon* (appropriately called *nakihon*, "weepy books")
were the precursors of the *ninjōbon*, the "books of human senti-
ment" that would be the forte of Sanba's erstwhile student Tamenaga Shunsui (1790–1843). From the point of view of his
development as a writer, Sanba's *sharebon* are interesting as works
where he was experimenting with solutions to the problems of
writing convincing dialogue that would stand him in good stead
in *Ukiyoburo* and his other *kokkeibon;* they also reveal his interest at an early date in portraying members of the lower social
orders in Edo, characters previously rarely seen in the *sharebon.*

Sanba published only one *yomihon* ("book for reading," as opposed, presumably, to the illustration-heavy *kibyōshi* and *gōkan*)
while he was alive, and left the manuscript of another barely
finished at his death. The earlier effort was a self-admitted failure.
Both the *sharebon* and the *yomihon* were part of the traditional
repertoire of the *gesakusha*, and Sanba was bound to try his hand
at both kinds of writing; but his lack of formal education and
probably his ingrained dislike of unqualified humorlessness prevented him from producing a successful *yomihon.*

Sanba's works, taken as a body, the good with the bad, help
give shape to our notions of what *gesaku* fiction in general consisted
of; a survey of his personal life and professional career gives greater
specificity to our picture of the social and professional world of
the early-nineteenth-century writer. Biographical sources dealing
with Sanba's life are disappointingly few and of uneven quality,
but it is clear that in some respects he was highly representative of
his generation of writers. As a member of the *chōnin* (urban merchant or artisan) class, Sanba was typical of his fellow writers,
who, unlike previous generations of *gesakusha*, were as a group
overwhelmingly by birth and culture of the middle class. Their
social and economic position meant for Sanba and his fellow
writers that it was not only desirable but often necessary that
writing be a paying proposition, since few could have diverted
their energies away from more usual moneymaking pursuits to
indulge a passion for writing unless they had hopes, at least, of
being paid for their efforts. The large-scale commercialization of

fiction after the 1790s was both a cause and a result of increasing *chōnin* domination of the *gesakusha* ranks.

One aspect of the artistic life of early-nineteenth-century Edo that emerges very clearly as one studies Sanba's literary activities and attempts to reconstruct a picture of his daily life is the striking degree to which all the arts we think of as typical of merchant-class culture were interrelated. Popular fiction, the performing arts (*kabuki*, puppet theater, and professional storytelling), and the art of the great *ukiyo-e* printmakers all fed on one another. They are inextricably linked in Sanba's books, of course, but in his daily life also we find the same confluence of interests. Print artists were among Sanba's closest friends; while they illustrated his books and those of other writers, their preferred medium was that of the *kabuki* print. Both their prints and the illustrated novelizations of *kabuki* plays by Sanba and others helped fan public enthusiasm for the theater, which in turn helped Sanba sell his books. Sanba no doubt was a regular theatergoer with backstage entrée, but the painting and calligraphy exhibitions he attended and sometimes organized also frequently involved theater people as patrons, as subjects of the paintings or comic verse and prose on display, or as honored guests. Sanba's oldest and most constant friendships seem to have been with people associated in one way or another with the vigorous revival of *rakugo* and allied storytelling arts that coincided with his most active years as a writer—a fact that is of extreme importance to understanding Sanba's *kokkeibon*, many of which, *Ukiyoburo* among them, were strongly influenced by the art of the stage storytellers.

Sanba and other writers were often involved with the graphic and performing arts more intimately than simply as connoisseurs or observers: both Sanba and Ikku occasionally illustrated their own books; Kyōden was an illustrator of note before he turned to writing; and Shunsui, at several times in his life, took to the stage as a raconteur. Sanba's earliest patron and mentor, Utei (or Tatekawa) Enba (1743–1822), was not only a *gesakusha* but also a *rakugo* performer and impressario. Sanba's milieu and that of his contemporary writers was clearly not purely literary. Just as occasional verse loses much of its meaning when divorced from the context in which it was written, much *gesaku* fiction becomes unintelligible when it is uprooted from the cultural context upon which it was so often a kind of commentary. A twentieth-century

Western student of *gesaku* fiction can not hope ever to know enough about the time and place in which it was written to appreciate it the way its original readers did, but even a sketchy knowledge of who a writer like Sanba was, who his friends were, and how he spent his time helps considerably to make the world of the *gesakusha* a more familiar place.

For a number of reasons—his reputation as a humorist probably chief among them—Shikitei Sanba has not received the quantity or quality of scholarly attention in Japan that has been paid other Edo-period writers like Santō Kyōden, Takizawa (or Kyokutei) Bakin (1767–1848), and, of course, such earlier luminaries as Saikaku and Chikamatsu. The first book-length study in Japanese devoted exclusively to Sanba's life and works, Honda Yasuo's *Shikitei Sanba no bungei,*[10] did not appear until 1973. Still, Sanba's claim to an important place in the ranks of the writers of his period has long been recognized by Japanese literary scholars, and he has been the object of regular scholarly attention since the beginning of modern literary studies in the Meiji period.

The earliest scholarly and critical treatments of Sanba and his works shared with other Meiji-period studies of Japanese literature a tendency to judge their subject almost entirely according to Western literary standards. This was a period when much intellectual energy was expended on attempts to find one-to-one correspondences between the Japanese and Western literary traditions, in order both to formulate a "modern" critical approach to the native literature and to demonstrate that the Japanese need not be ashamed of their own literature. The implicit assumption that Western literary standards and categories were absolute provoked rash attempts to identify Japanese counterparts to the acknowledged literary titans of the West: Chikamatsu, for instance, was soon being touted as "the Japanese Shakespeare," and a project was begun to prepare a word-by-word concordance to his dramatic texts.[11] Sanba's satiric writing was compared variously to that of Addison and Steele, Fielding, Dickens, Gogol, and Cervantes;[12] his works in categories other than the *kokkeibon* were largely ignored, partly because his other principal medium, the *gōkan,* was generally regarded as subliterary and also because of the scholars' tendency to identify any given writer with only one kind of fiction, no matter how active he may have been in other fields.

This was also the period, of course, when author-critics like

Tsubouchi Shōyō and Futabatei Shimei were struggling with the problem of developing a graceful and easily understood form of written Japanese suitable for novels on the Western model. Sanba was one of the writers to whom they turned for help in their quest, since of all late-Edo-period writers it was he who had devoted the most effort to finding ways of representing real speech in print. Shōyō's suggestion that Futabatei try modeling his prose on the language used by the great contemporary *rakugo* storyteller San'yūtei Enchō in relating his anecdotes proved to be misguided, since writing convincing dialogue involves far more than simply transcribing speech. Sanba's writing turned out to be a useful guide, since he himself had, more than half a century before, worked out ways of translating from one medium to another the storytellers' sensitivity to the rhythms, vocabulary, and syntactical patterns of actual speech.[13] To what extent the ways Sanba and other writers of his period found to write convincing dialogue influenced modern fiction is an exceedingly difficult question to answer, but there can be little doubt that their efforts simplified the task facing the aspiring novelists of a later generation.

The second phase visible in Japanese studies of Sanba's work is characterized by efforts to redefine the objectives of literary scholarship. Scholars like Yamaguchi Takeshi and Mitamura Engyo, basing their work on close reading of vast amounts of *gesaku* literature and careful consideration of non-literary source material, were no longer interested in describing the works of Sanba and his contemporaries from the point of view of literature as defined in the West, but rather in redefining the concept of literature itself by expanding and altering it to include forms and genres that did not fit into Western categories.[14] Yamaguchi began what has by now become a somewhat over-hallowed and sterile "scientific" tradition of combing the corpus of Edo fiction for the models and precursors written by other authors that are presumed to lie behind and explain, seemingly, any given work, but he also, by virtue of his vast erudition in his field, was able to put together an authoritative body of detailed commentaries on a huge number of significant works of the period. Mitamura's interests ranged far beyond literature itself, and his comprehensive study of the *kokkeibon,* published in 1936, has yet to be surpassed in breadth and depth of insight. He was the first to demonstrate the all-important link between most varieties of *kokkeibon* writing and the oral storytelling arts, and in addition brought to bear in his study a considerable sensitivity to the historical and social context of the *kokkeibon* that has set a high standard for subsequent scholarship. The basic research and insightful analyses of Yamaguchi, Mitamura, and Ebara Taizō, who was among the first to expand the range of work being done on Sanba to include works other than his *kokkeibon*,[15] provided a solid foundation for more sophisticated later studies. In the postwar period, an impressive number of articles and chapters in general works have appeared that deal with many different aspects of Sanba's writing: the nature of his humor, the linguistic aspects of his methods of recording speech, his *gōkan,* certain of his individual works in various genres, bibliographical topics, and others.[16]

This book could not have been written without constant reference to *Shikitei Sanba no bungei,* the definitive study of Sanba's life and works by Honda Yasuo, who has not only drawn together virtually everything that has been learned about Shikitei Sanba and his works over the past several generations of study, but has also managed the feat of looking carefully at practically everything Sanba published (most of which has yet to be reprinted in easily accessible modern editions, let alone studied). As a result, he has been able to provide plot summaries and descriptions of all but a very few of Sanba's works. Honda's most valuable contribution, perhaps, is his well-grounded insistence that neither Sanba nor his writing can be talked about intelligently unless it is recognized that *Ukiyoburo* and his other *kokkeibon* account for only a fraction of his total literary output. Sanba was at his best as a humorist, but it is only when his accomplishments in other fields of writing are taken into consideration that a study of his career becomes meaningful as one approach to deepening our understanding of the *gesaku* tradition in Japanese literature.

CHAPTER TWO

Childhood and Early Career

It was perhaps only natural that Shikitei Sanba should have been tempted to try his hand at the writer's craft, for the world of books and publishing was his by birthright and upbringing. He was the eldest son of a master wood-block carver named Kikuchi Mohei,[1] and both Sanba, then known as Kikuchi Taisuke,[2] and his brother were sent in their early teens into apprenticeships with book and print publishers. Sanba published his first books while working in a publishing house in his late teens; he was married twice, both times to publishers' daughters; and he continued to be formally connected with publishing enterprises until his middle years. His brother, too, although not a writer, was engaged in the book trade, and his name appears alone or jointly as publisher of several of Sanba's major works, including the first two books of *Ukiyoburo*.[3] While Sanba's early environment was probably not self-consciously "literary," he grew up surrounded by the world of commercial publishing, and it was not a great leap from the business of printing and publishing books to that of writing them, particularly in a time and place where the writer of books for commercial publication was only beginning to be perceived as an independent artist rather than as only one of a number of specialized craftsmen employed by the publisher on a par with illustrators, carvers, printers, and bookbinders.

Detailed biographical information about late-Edo-period *gesakusha* is difficult to come by. Many authors are known only by their pen names, and there are many others whose real names are known, but about whom little else is certain. The broad outlines of Sanba's life, however, are reasonably well known. Two major contemporary sources of basic information survive: Takizawa Bakin's treatment of Sanba in his *Kinsei mono no hon Edo sakusha burui*,[4] and a chapter in a collection of short biographical sketches of six major Edo authors entitled *Gesaku rokkasen,* compiled originally by Bokusentei Yukimaro (1793-1853) and edited and expanded by his disciple Iwamoto Sashichi (Darumaya Kattōshi).[5] A fragment of Sanba's own diary for 1810 and 1811, published as *Shikitei zakki,*[6] also survives and provides a brief but enlightening glimpse of Sanba's day-to-day existence during one of the busiest and most productive periods of his career, although it contains little by way of intimate self-revelation. Further bits and pieces of Sanba's life, mostly in the form of dates, friendships, and associations, can be gleaned from introductions, colophons, and other brief notices in his works and those of others.

Direct documentation of Sanba's birth is lacking, but indirect evidence favors 1776, the 5th year of the An'ei year period (1772-1780), as the year of his birth; the most conclusive source is a note in Sanba's hand in his copy of a work by Koikawa Harumachi that reads, "This year Sanba born," referring to the An'ei 5 publication date in the colophon.[7] Of the circumstances of Sanba's family very little is known, but some deductions may be made.

How and why Sanba's father, Mohei, became a wood-block carver are unanswerable questions. He is described in several sources as having been the son, by a concubine, of an official of the Tametomo Daimyōjin Shrine in Hachijōjima, an island off the coast of the Izu Peninsula south of Edo.[8] The circumstances of his birth and the fact that they seem to have been public knowledge suggest that he was probably reasonably well educated.

Further evidence about Sanba's family background is found in his mention of having an aunt who was in service to a "great lord" in Edo.[9] This fact does not, by any means, imply that Sanba's family was itself of samurai rank. It suggests, rather, that at least one side of his family, perhaps his mother's, consisted of *chōnin* of wealth, status, and connections enough to place a daughter in service to a household of rank. This practice was not uncommon among socially ambitious merchant families eager to give a daughter a chance to acquire social grace and polish, and reflected status as well, all useful in later marriage arrangements after her period of service ended.[10]

On very scanty evidence, then, it may be guessed that Sanba

grew up in a reasonably prosperous merchant- or artisan-class home that differed from thousands of others only in the fact that his father's craft was central to the business of producing books. A wood-block carver necessarily had not only business connections with publishers, but also personal contact with illustrators and authors as well in the course of preparing printing blocks. As an author who worked primarily in the heavily illustrated *kibyōshi* and *gōkan* genres, Sanba no doubt benefited from his father's connections with *ukiyo-e* artists and illustrators, which may help account for the fact that Sanba's first book, published when he was only eighteen, was illustrated by Utagawa Toyokuni, who was even then among the illustrators in greatest demand. The associations with *ukiyo-e* artists that Sanba in effect inherited from his father went beyond purely professional dealings: he numbered Toyokuni and other artists among his close personal friends, and, at least during the period covered by *Shikitei zakki,* he frequently both organized and attended exhibits and other celebrations in honor of print artists.

The world of the printed book and the publishing trade was a natural part of Sanba's childhood, and he had become an avid reader by his early teens. When he was still a child, he often visited his aunt in her quarters in the mansion of the "great lord" she served:

Since I liked reading [he related some time late in his career], every time I went I picked up and read the books that were always scattered around the place. The other serving ladies who happened by and saw me thought it very impressive that I should be reading at so early an age, and told me that, if I was already such a literary genius, what might I be when I grew up? By the time I was thirteen or fifteen, I had read all sorts of dramas as well, and, by the time I was sixteen or seventeen, I had resolved to become a writer.[11]

Sanba's reading habit was no doubt reinforced when he entered into an apprenticeship with a book publisher. The surviving sources disagree about which publisher he served, but, once again, Sanba's habit of jotting things in the books in his library comes to the aid of the scholar. In his copy of *Ta ga sode nikki,* a *sharebon* published in 1785, he wrote:

This book was published in the spring of my ninth year by Gangetsudō. . . . Gangetsudō was my wife's father; his real name was Horinoya Nihei (formerly Okuraya Kinbei, later Nihei, finally Horinoya). From the winter of my ninth year to the fall of my seventeenth, I was raised in this house, and I owe this man an immense debt of gratitude.[12]

It was undoubtedly the fact that Sanba for a time styled himself "Nishimiya Taisuke" that led Takizawa Bakin to assume Sanba had been apprenticed to Nishimiya Shinroku; but *Gesaku rokkasen* explains that Nishimiya, who published many of Sanba's early works, merely "bestowed the name on him as a token of their warm friendship."[13] In any case, Sanba's apprenticeship to the book dealer Gangetsudō ended in his seventeenth year, just about the time he "resolved to become a writer."

Sanba acted on his resolve almost immediately. *Gesaku rokkasen* records Sanba's recollection of the beginning of his writing career:

At eighteen, I was independent, and wrote and published my first book, a *kibyōshi* entitled *Tentō ukiyo no dezukai.* When I began to write that book, I worked on the manuscript even after I had gone to bed, with my hands sticking out from beneath the bed clothes. After I finished the manuscript, I decided I had to have a pen name, and so I wrote three names I thought appropriate on little pieces of paper, crumpled them up in my hand, and tossed them in the air. I then picked one of them up. The name written on it was Shikitei Sanba, and so I decided to use that one.[14]

Sanba's living situation at this time is unclear. He calls himself "independent," but no surviving source provides any indication of where he was living or how he was supporting himself. He may have simply returned to his father's house upon completing his formal apprenticeship, but, if that was the case, then his use of the term *independent* seems strange, since he would have merely exchanged the dependency of an apprenticeship for dependency upon his father. Bakin, furthermore, asserts that Sanba and his father never lived together,[15] although he would not necessarily have known about a brief period early in Sanba's career when he was living with his family. All sources agree, however, that at some point Sanba became the adoptive son-in-law of the book dealer Yorozuya Tajiemon (Rankōdō) of Yamashitachō.[16] It is possible that Sanba's move directly from his apprenticeship to employment under Tajiemon led, after a few years, to his adoption and marriage.

Wherever Sanba was living at the time, the publication of *Tentō ukiyo no dezukai* (The heavenly puppeteers of the floating world)[17] and of a second *kibyōshi* entitled *Ningen isshin nozoki karakuri* (A mechanism for peering into the heart of man)[18] during the same publishing season of 1794 marked the beginning of his writing career. His output thereafter rarely dropped below two or three titles a year, but it was to be some time before he achieved anything but a modest reputation as an author. (Bakin was unaware that Sanba had published anything before 1796 or 1797).[19]

While few of the products of Sanba's brush during the first decade or so of his career are of any remarkable quality, or more than marginally distinguishable in style and content from those of other writers, Sanba used these years to polish his writing skills and to establish a working style. Marriage and responsibility in the Yorozuya establishment gave him the confidence, respectability, and means to develop his connections with other writers, artists, and the theater; and the very typicality of many of his works during this period makes them useful as examples of certain categories of *gesaku* literature of the late Kansei (1789-1800) and Kyōwa (1801-1803) eras, despite the tedium they often induce in the modern reader.

Tentō ukiyo no dezukai seems not to have "raised the price of paper," as best sellers have long been said to do in Japan, but, when seen in the context of Sanba's later works and of its contemporary *kibyōshi* in general, even this first effort of Sanba's contains many elements that would characterize his later style and approach to his work.[20] The book is built around the simple conceit that human behavior is controlled, puppet-like, by the stars, to which Sanba attributes decidedly human personalities. While, by and large, "good" stars have the upper hand in the general scheme of things, Sanba's story focuses on one "evil" star who manages by treachery and mischief to arrange the replacement of the "good" stars in charge of a number of different human beings by "evil" stars, and thereby succeeds in bringing to ruin, or almost to ruin, a number of previously "good" souls before he himself is brought back under control by the King of Heaven (Tentō-sama).

There are three tendencies already visible in this earliest of Sanba's published works that would be highly evident in much of his later writing. The first is seen in the fact that *Tentō ukiyo no dezukai* is obviously and closely modeled on previously published works by other writers. It is not a plagiarism, however, but rather a careful attempt to work minimal changes on conceits, themes, and plot elements that had already been proved by others to be commercially successful. This sort of reliance on established formulas and the reworking and exploitation of currently popular plot types and themes recurs again and again throughout Sanba's career, even in *Ukiyoburo*, his acknowledged masterpiece. Second is Sanba's tendency to subordinate careful plotting and continuity to a loose, almost fragmented structure consisting of a series of vignettes or word-pictures of unrelated characters, representative types drawn largely from among the middle-class "little people" of Edo. A third characteristic of his later writing seen in *Tentō ukiyo no dezukai* is Sanba's interest in the theatrical arts, revealed here in his choice of a controlling conceit or metaphor drawn from the puppet theater.

The work upon which Sanba seems to have modeled *Tentō ukiyo no dezukai* was a popular *kibyōshi* by Santō Kyōden entitled *Shingaku hayasomegusa*, published in 1790.[21] In Kyōden's story, the King of Heaven breathes out human souls like soap bubbles. (The opening illustration shows the King of Heaven, haloed and dressed in flowing robes, holding a small bowl and blowing bubbles from a pipe.) The hero of the story, Ritarō, has been protected from birth by a "good" soul, but, in his eighteenth year, an "evil" soul enters Ritarō's body and takes control. Ritarō thereafter leads the life of a classic Edo reprobate and is disowned, whereupon he enters upon a life of crime. Finally he encounters by chance a famous teacher named Dōri-sensei, who takes him home and reveals to him the truths of Shingaku, the popular moral philosophy originated by Ishida Baigan whose popularity, encouraged by the *bakufu*, had reached fad proportions by the late 1780s.[22] Dōri-sensei, clearly modeled on the Shingaku teacher Nakazawa Dōni (1725–1803),[23] explains that good and evil spring from within the human heart, and, at the moment Ritarō accepts this truth, the son of the ousted "good" soul returns to the scene, vendetta fashion, to avenge his father and to reclaim Ritarō, who is forgiven by all and becomes a model young man.

The parallels with Sanba's story are obvious: the control of human behavior by outside agents, the plotting and temporary ascendancy of evil forces, description of the degradation brought about by possession by evil, and the ultimate triumph of the good soul or star. That Sanba not only was familiar with Kyōden's work but probably even had it in front of him as he wrote is suggested by the appearance in both works of a punning verse that computed the number of one's souls according to which of the five elements ruled the year of one's birth.[24] (Sanba was to use the verse again, in a radically different context, in *Ukiyoburo*.) In its basic conception and some of its details as well, Sanba's story is clearly modeled on Kyōden's; Honda shows that Sanba's star-as-puppeteer conceit was also far from original. The fundamental notion of man-as-puppet had been explored at length in works by Hōseidō Kisanji in 1786[25] and Shiba Zenkō in 1792.[26]

While a tendency to steal material from other writers was particularly evident in Sanba's case, it was far from uncommon in the work of many of his contemporaries. From the point of view of literature as art, the reliance of the *gesakusha* on formulas, on minor and timid variations on best-selling themes, and on imitation rather than originality betrays either a lack of imagination and talent or a craven surrender to commercialism. From the point of view of literature as entertainment, however, these tricks of the *gesakusha*'s trade are wholly understandable. Sanba and his colleagues were not engaged in private quests after the Great Japanese Novel; they were entertainers. A wise popular writer in early-nineteenth-century Japan would no more tamper with a successful formula just for the sake of originality than would a television executive today who had an eye on the ratings. What Sanba was doing in *Tentō ukiyo no dezukai* was simply trying to grab a small share of the market by combining the basic formula of Kyōden's immensely popular *Shingaku hayasomegusa* with inspirations that appealed to him in other best sellers. A writer who takes this sort of approach to his work runs the risk, of course, of falling into mere mechanical imitation, instead of producing a book that satisfies his audience's demand for a certain predictability combined with a dash of surprise and novelty.

Sanba's lifetime preoccupation with the portrayal of stock or standard character types drawn from the urban population also makes its first appearance in *Tentō ukiyo no dezukai*. The use of character types—in this case, the Drunk, the Lying Courtesan, the Greedy Borrower, the Confucianist, the Disobedient Wife, the Dissolute Son, and others—to illustrate a theme was not, of course, Sanba's invention, but rather a convention of long standing in Edo fiction first exploited by Saikaku in works like *Honchō nijūfukō*

(Twenty cases of unfilial conduct in Japan) and turned into a genre of its own by Ejima Kiseki and his imitators with the eighteenth century *katagimono*, or "character sketch" books.[27] One of the failings of *Tentō ukiyo no dezukai* is precisely the extreme fragmentation of structure that resulted from Sanba's decision to offer a series of examples of the results of possession by an evil spirit rather than to concentrate on the career of a single victim, as Kyōden chose to do. As Sanba matured as a writer, he learned to suppress this tendency toward fragmentation in his *kibyōshi* and *gōkan* and instead used his *kokkeibon* as vehicles for presenting what amounted to series of character sketches.

But, while the character sketches in *Tentō ukiyo no dezukai* were perhaps out of place, structurally speaking, and while as a general technique they were nothing new in popular fiction, they nevertheless exhibit characteristics that would reappear in the best of Sanba's mature writing, most particularly his reliance on carefully reproduced natural speech rather than description to develop his characters, and a tendency to portray commonplace people in nondescript, everyday settings rather than to concentrate on the extreme examples (like immensely wealthy playboys or their favorite courtesans disporting themselves in the pleasure quarters) favored by other writers from Saikaku onward. Kyōden's Ritarō in *Shingaku hayasomegusa* is a caricature, a model young man who reaches nearly absolute depths of degradation and then, freed from possession, reclaims his position as an exemplary son. Sanba's victims, by contrast, are people of no particularly outstanding virtue or wealth to begin with, possessed simply of common decency and middling social position; and their sins are not depravity and thievery, but rather the petty failings of drunkenness, greed, mendacity, or a tendency to talk back to one's mother-in-law. While, even in his mature works, his characters remain "types" and rarely take on a sharp individuality, it was minor differences among unexceptional people that would always interest Sanba, and it was his skill at portraying these minor differences, largely through the medium of direct discourse, that made his best work very good indeed.

Beyond the basic conceit of the gods as puppeteers controlling man's behavior, and a few passing remarks in the introduction, *Tentō ukiyo no dezukai* can not be said to show any real connection with the dramatic arts. But it is significant that in his first book Sanba revealed, however tentatively, an interest in the theater that would be a source of inspiration for a large proportion, perhaps even a majority, of his later works. To judge from the emphasis he put upon it in his reminiscence in *Gesaku rokkasen*, drama accounted for much of Sanba's reading in his childhood, and it is little wonder that he found a conceit drawn from the puppet theater a congenial one for his first attempt at writing for public consumption.

Between the appearance of *Tentō ukiyo no dezukai* in 1794 and the end of the decade, Sanba published some fifteen known works, an average of about three a year.[28] Most of them were *kibyōshi* sharing many characteristics with his first work, but this period also saw the publication of Sanba's first *sharebon* and of several works that foreshadowed major trends in his later writing.

A large proportion of the *kibyōshi* Sanba wrote in this early period were based on themes connected with Shingaku in one way or another. Like Kyōden, upon whose works he continued to model his own, Sanba used the ultimately commonplace philosophical sentiments of Shingaku and the figure of the Shingaku teacher simply as mechanical devices enabling him to present what amounted to negative examples of proper moral behavior. This sort of mock-didactic stance in mounting satires of disreputable or pompous behavior had been common since at least the time of Saikaku; Sanba was no innovator. It would seem, also, that the tendency of Sanba and his contemporaries to stick closely to the combination of a pious tone and harmless vignettes of foolish, lecherous, impecunious, or merely petty behavior was in part attributable to a sensitivity to the efforts of the *bakufu* to raise the general moral tone of Japanese life during the period of the Kansei reforms in the early 1790s. While the government's publication-control edicts focused on *sharebon* and other works of alleged erotic content as being particularly harmful to public morals, it was clear to writers and publishers alike that the *bakufu* was keeping a watchful eye on all forms of publishing, even if its vigilance was known occasionally to relax. As a result, prudence dictated a reliance on themes, plots, and forms of satire that were as unobjectionable as possible. The retreat into harmlessness taken by Kansei-period *gesakusha* resulted in an unwillingness to explore further the kind of broad and biting social satire, supported by erudition and wit, that had been pioneered by Hiraga Gennai[29] and continued for a time by Kyōden and Zenkō. The Shingaku-based *kibyōshi* by Kyōden, Sanba, and others were hardly didactic tracts; yet they refrained from directly satirizing the simple-minded pieties of Shingaku, since the Shingaku movement furthered values and behavior that were too close to the government's own vision of what was good for the lower orders.

In 1795 and 1796, Sanba published *Go Taiheiki Shiraishi-banashi* (A tale from Shiraishi: A chronicle of great peace played on a *go*-board)[30] and its continuation, *Katakiuchi Shiraishibanashi* (A tale of a vendetta in Shiraishi).[31] Together these works formed a two-part version in *kibyōshi* format of a popular *jōruri* play first performed in 1780.[32] The final product was little more than a re-telling of the main outlines of the play's plot (a vendetta carried out by two sisters, one a country girl and the other a high-ranking Edo courtesan, to avenge the death of their father), with selected bits of dialogue reproduced verbatim. The text was accompanied by the usual extensive *kibyōshi* illustrations. A large number of Sanba's later books, particularly in the *gōkan* format, were of this type. Most of them represent a largely mechanical job of putting down on paper the highlights of a play's plot and coordinating this abbreviated text with the flashy illustrations that visually domi-nated the finished product, which was intended to be a kind of "*kabuki* on paper" that recreated the theatergoing experience on the printed page.[33]

Whatever the literary merits of works such as these—it is doubt-ful whether they should be regarded as creative works of fiction at all—they were to occupy a major place in Sanba's writing activities year after year, probably because they brought him regular income at the cost of a small expenditure of creative energy. Sanba may have been encouraged to keep turning out these simple condensa-tions of *kabuki* and puppet plays by the gratifying sucess of *Go taiheiki Shiraishibanashi* and its companion volume, his first ef-forts in the field: they were reprinted at least four times, once fif-teen years after his death,[34] but this publishing history probably says more about the continuing popularity of the play itself than about the inherent quality of Sanba's work.

Sanba published his first *sharebon* in 1798, a one-volume work entitled *Tatsumi fugen* (Women's words from the southeast),[35] which was the first to deal with life in the unofficial pleasure quar-ter (*okabasho*) of Furuishiba in the Fukagawa area of Edo, on the far side of the Sumida River to the southeast of the shogun's castle. Honda suggests that the publication of *Tatsumi fugen* was a symbolic declaration of the twenty-two-year-old Sanba's wish to be regarded as a full-fledged *gesakusha,* the *sharebon* having been seen since the first days of its existence as the medium most expressive of the gentleman-dilettante stance embodied in the term *gesaku* as first used.[36] Certainly *Tatsumi fugen* was an elegant production with all the trappings appropriate to a work by an established *sharebon* writer, whether or not Sanba was attempting to adopt the persona of an elegant gentleman of leisure. The work contains, in addition to Sanba's own introduction, a preface by the *yomihon* and *sharebon* master Shinrotei[37] and an afterword signed by a disciple, Rakusanjin Bashō.[38] To outward appearances, at least, it seems that Sanba had, at a surprisingly early age, achieved a reputation sufficient not only to merit an introduction by an established, older writer, but also to attract at least one aspiring writer eager to identify himself as his student. In this connection, it might also be noted that a *sharebon* by Umebori Kokuga (1750–1821) published the same year as *Tatsumi fugen* contains an introduction by Sanba—further evidence of his growing reputation.[39] *Tatsumi fugen* was a physically impressive book. Not only was its frontispiece by the *ukiyo-e* master Kitagawa Utamaro, but it was in color, a rarity in *sharebon.*[40] If for no other reason, this work is worthy of note as the earliest work by Sanba deemed to be of enough significance or quality to appear in standard modern collections of late Edo fiction.[41]

The setting of *Tatsumi fugen* is the Mikawaya house in the Furuishiba quarter in Fukagawa (thinly disguised as the "Nikawaya" of "Furuichiba" in "Futagawa" in Kamakura; a tradition of setting Fukagawa stories in Kamakura was begun by Kyōden[42] and would be followed later by Tamenaga Shunsui).[43] The plot revolves around the affairs of the courtesan Otoma and her "suitors," Tōhei, Kinosuke, and Chōgorō, with emphasis on the wiles and ruses Otoma uses, cynically or not, to ensnare each of her lovers. Like an embarrassingly large number of Sanba's works, *Tatsumi fugen* is indebted almost to the point of plagiarism to earlier works, principally *Fukagawa haiken* (1782), a *sharebon* by Hōraisanjin Kikyō,[44] and several *sharebon* by Santō Kyōden for specific plot elements and devices;[45] but it is now generally agreed that the imitative aspects of the work are overshadowed by recognizably Sanba-like touches that point forward to the best of his later work.[46]

In particular, Sanba's decision to set his story in Furuishiba allowed him to stake out a new world of characters hitherto ignored by *sharebon* authors. While the classic *sharebon*, true to its name, concentrated on the elegant and rarefied customs, tastes, and language of the Yoshiwara, the world of *Tatsumi fugen* was populated by characters drawn from the middle and lower reaches of Edo society. A number of earlier *sharebon* had been set in Fukagawa, beginning with *Tatsumi no sono* (The garden of the southeast) in 1770,[47] but these works had tended to focus on Nakachō, the most elegant of the *okabasho* of Fukagawa; they were written with the Yoshiwara as a point of reference, an ideal to which the only marginally different dialect, slang, customs, and clientele of Nakachō were compared. Sanba, however, chose to write with little reference to the Yoshiwara, and to concentrate instead on the people and customs of Furuishiba, one of the least respectable of the unofficial Fukagawa districts, both because the idea of a *sharebon* on such an unlikely subject was likely to attract readers,[48] and because, it may be surmised, the world of Furuishiba was simply closer to Sanba's experience and taste than the more exclusive Nakachō.

While *Tatsumi fugen* borrows heavily from earlier works by other authors (Yamaguchi Takeshi speaks of it as "an expression of Sanba's usual habit of imitation"),[49] it differs significantly from its models by virtue both of its setting and of Sanba's particular gift for capturing, through painstaking attention to the nuances of natural speech, the essence of his lower-middle-class characters. Sanba had, of course, learned the importance of natural and lively rendering of dialogue from Santō Kyōden. But he used techniques borrowed from Kyōden neither to create positive or negative models of how to behave in the pleasure quarters nor simply to record accurately examples of what constituted proper pleasure-quarter wit, but rather to recreate on paper a corner of society that was much closer to the real world of the Edo townsman than the special atmosphere of elegance and stylized humor that infused the world of the traditional *sharebon*. The world of *Tatsumi fugen* does not end at the walls of the Nikawaya; Sanba provides generous glimpses as well of the lives his characters lead outside the world of commercial sex. This sort of extension of the field of vision of the *sharebon* had, as might be expected, been attempted previously by Santō Kyōden (in *Kokei no sanshō*, 1787),[50] but Sanba's concentration on a lower stratum of society, combined with the higher degree of attention he pays to his characters' "outside" lives, makes *Tatsumi fugen* a decidedly different sort of *sharebon*.

In 1806 and 1807, Sanba published *Sendō shinwa* (Profound tales of a boatman)[51] and *Sendōbeya* (The boatman's quarters),[52] sequels to *Tatsumi fugen* which are traditionally classed as *sharebon* but which all but dispense with traditional *sharebon* concerns, focusing instead on the continuing tribulations of the characters introduced in *Tatsumi fugen* outside the pleasure quarter itself. While he probably did not have sequels in mind when he wrote *Tatsumi fugen*, this trilogy stands as an early example of the multivolume "serial" *sharebon* (*tsuzukimono no sharebon*), also known as *nakihon* ("weeping book," a reference to the concentration of the form on the emotional trials of pleasure-quarter life), out of which the novel of life in and around the pleasure quarters now known as the *ninjōbon* would later develop. Sanba cannot, however, be credited with having invented the serial *sharebon* or the *nakihon; Sendō shinwa* and *Sendōbeya* are best seen as a belated effort to cash in on a new fad begun by others (principally Umebori Kokuga).[53]

A quick survey of the works Sanba published in 1798 and 1799 yields the impression that, though still only in his early twenties, he was gaining rapidly in self-confidence and was increasingly interested in experimenting with new forms of writing he had not yet tried. Several of Sanba's *kibyōshi* from these years seem to show, at least in their outlines, that he was becoming dissatisfied with the general blandness that had overtaken fiction in the cautious atmosphere induced by *bakufu* censorship. One is a slightly demented adult fairy tale populated by the foxes, badgers, demons, and other beasts and monsters that had formerly appeared with great regularity in the old *akahon* and early *kibyōshi;* annoyed at their displacement by the cloying, sentimental moral tales of present-day *kibyōshi,* they avenge themselves and assuage their boredom by conjuring into existence a new pleasure quarter whose innocent patrons become the objects of various bewitchings and humiliations.[54] Another is constructed around a peculiar plot that combines elements of the Urashimatarō and Dōjōji Temple maiden legends, but is set in the contemporary and very plebeian world of Fukagawa.[55] This sort of interweaving of plot elements, characters, and settings from different historical or legendary worlds is a technique borrowed from the *kabuki* and puppet theaters; in general outline this work, in its use of a Fukagawa setting, is particularly reminiscent of the later *kabuki* plays of Tsuruya Nanboku and his colleagues, like *Sakurahime azuma bunshō* (1817)[56] and *Tōkaidō Yotsuya kaidan* (1825), which similarly exploited the dramatic possibilities of juxtaposing and interweaving radically different historical, legendary, and social "worlds." These two *kibyōshi* of 1798 seem to lie closer, in their exuberance of style, content, and conception, to the first-generation *kibyōshi* of Hiraga Gennai, Shiba Zenkō, and the early Kyōden than to the conservative works of the late Kansei period. In this connection, it is perhaps noteworthy that, at around this time, Sanba was considering calling himself Shiba Zenkō II.[57] (Zenkō had died in 1793.)[58] Sanba held back, however, feeling that he was not yet ready to claim such distinction, and fearing that he could only sully his respected model's name with his own inferior imitations.[59] In any case, Sanba is not known ever to have used the name Shiba Zenkō; his modest hesitation may have been genuine, or he may, perhaps, have been confident that his talent was such that he could attract readers even without adopting the name of the then famous but now nearly forgotten Zenkō.[60]

Another of Sanba's early works worth a passing glance is *Yakusha gakuya tsū* (A connoisseur's guide to the actors' green room, 1799),[61] the first book he published in the "middle-size" *chūbon* format that would be the standard one for his later *kokkeibon*. This work is divided into two parts. The first is a series of portraits of thirty-six popular *kabuki* actors by Toyokuni and Kunimasa, accompanied by laudatory comic verses (*kyōka*) by famous contemporary poets. The second part, separately entitled *Yakusha hiiki katagi* (Portraits of actors' patrons), is a loosely structured story, little more than a series of sketches of the members of a *kabuki*-mad family who constitute a living catalogue of various kinds of theater addiction. Sanba explicitly acknowledges that this work is modeled on the early-eighteenth-century "character pieces" of Ejima Kiseki.[62] It is of interest for several reasons. First, it gives evidence of Sanba's continuing and ever-developing affection for the theater and his interest in it as a source for his writing. Second, it shows that, even at twenty-three, he had begun to form strong connections with the established masters of comic verse; Sanba's interest in *kyōka* never went beyond that of a serious amateur, but the composition of comic verse and intercourse with professional *kyōka* poets would, throughout his career, be both a diversion and a way of gaining entry into literary and artistic circles that might otherwise have been closed to him. Third, the second half of this work clearly foreshadows in format and content a number of Sanba's *kokkeibon* and suggests once again that Sanba was consciously attempting, at this time in his career, to revive satiric or comic attitudes that had for some time been dormant.

Late in 1798 or early in 1799, Sanba published a work that signaled very clearly an intent to capture in his writing something of the irreverence and wit that had characterized the best of the early *kibyōshi* by Harumachi, Kyōden, and others. *Kyan taiheiki mukō hachimaki* (Swaggering headbands: A chronicle of urban knight-errantry in a peaceful realm)[63] was the first *kibyōshi* to be published in many years that dared to deal, even obliquely, with current events—in this case, a brawl between two municipal fire brigades in Edo the previous autumn. The actual incident upon which Sanba based his story was presumably of little historical significance, since no record of it seems to survive except in the commentaries on *Kyan taiheiki* itself in sources like *Gesaku rokkasen* and Bakin's *Sakusha burui*. But, since the *bakufu* had for decades made very clear its stern disapproval of literary or dramatic treatments of contemporary events, Sanba evidently felt compelled to set his treatment of this trifling outburst of rowdiness far back in the historical past, in the fourteenth-century world of the *Taiheiki*, the classic semi-historical "Chronicle of Grand Pacification" that dealt with the grand events of the chaotic transition between the Kamakura and Ashikaga shogunates. The juxtaposition of the petty squabbles and proud bravado of the fire brigades and the stirring heroics of the *Taiheiki* must have been comic in itself (the illustrations depict the noble warriors of the *Taiheiki* battles grandly brandishing ladders, hooks, axes, and other "weapons" of the firefighter's calling). But Sanba turns the story into lunatic burlesque in its climactic scene by suddenly transferring the action to a theater stage, where a curtain[64] is pulled aside to reveal, in the grand *kabuki* manner, a ludicrously anachronistic array of legendary military heroes (among them Yoshitsune,

Benkei, and Tametomo of the twelfth century; Asahina Yoshihide of the thirteenth; the fairy tale hero Kintarō; and Watōnai, a hero of Chikamatsu's play, *Kokusen'ya kassen*), who rush forth and scatter the attacking forces.

How *Kyan taiheiki* was received by the reading public, how critics like Bakin regarded it, whether Sanba was proud of it—all are unanswerable questions, since contemporary observers speak not of its reception or its quality, but only of its consequences. On the 5th day of the 1st month of 1799, members of a fire brigade allied to one of the brigades satirized in Sanba's book attacked and ransacked the houses of both Sanba and the publisher of *Kyan taiheiki*, Nishimiya Shinroku. However the *bakufu* viewed the book itself, it could not overlook this breach of the peace, and not only the offending firefighters but Sanba and his publisher were summoned to judgment. The firefighters were sentenced to terms in jail as the principal offenders; Sanba, as the prime instigator of the quarrel, was sentenced to manacles for a period of fifty days; Nishimiya Shinroku was heavily fined.[65]

Sanba's seven weeks in manacles proved to be a turning point in his career. The punishment—light by prevailing standards, perhaps, but still a harrowing and uncomfortable experience—left Sanba chastened and demoralized, but also brought him his first real fame. Long after the event, he still spoke of it with considerable circumspection:

When *Kyan taiheiki* came out, it angered certain people, and I ran afoul not only of their ire, but of that of the authorities as well. I received a not insignificant punishment, and caused both my publisher and my father a great deal of pain and trouble. In the end, however, thanks to the benevolence of the present regime, I was pardoned. After that, although my father from time to time told me to give up the writer's trade, I refused to abandon it, and, after a year or so, I began publishing again. As a result of that incident, in fact, my fame had increased greatly, and lately, ever since the success of my *Ikazuchitarō*,[66] I have been blessed with a good reception by the public.[67]

Sanba and Nishimiya were punished, it would seem, not for any breach of the *bakufu*'s censorship laws, but simply as the instigators, however unwitting, of a brawl. While in legal terms their experience is nothing more than a good example of the *bakufu*'s approach to the maintenance of public order, it also stands as one more example of the perils faced by the writers and publishers of the period.

It is interesting to speculate about the directions Sanba's satiric urges might have taken had *Kyan taiheiki* not resulted in the firefighters' counterattack and the government's consequent involvement as guardian of the public peace. It was not the content, but rather the indirect consequences of *Kyan taiheiki* that aroused official hostility; Sanba, however, preferring to err on the side of safety, could easily have seen his punishment as a judgment against the acceptability of topical satire. In fact, he never again wrote anything that dealt satirically with current events or recognizable contemporary individuals or groups.

Generally speaking, however, the years during which Sanba was active as a mature writer, embracing the Kyōwa, Bunka, and part of the Bunsei eras (1801–1829), were marked by little overt government interference with writing and publishing, and the censorship process was a formal routine that seems to have weighed lightly on the producers of popular fiction. The writers of the period were free, within limits dictated more by common sense and instinct than by government fiat, to experiment with new literary forms and subject. As Sanba grew into a somewhat chastened and responsible adulthood, he participated in and sometimes led the general broadening, if not yet the deepening, of the concerns of the *gesaku* writer.

CHAPTER THREE

The Mature
Professional

For several years after his encounter with Tokugawa justice over his involvement with the hot-tempered firefighters, Shikitei Sanba published little, and much of what he did produce was markedly different in character from what he wrote before or after. The fact that he published nothing at all in 1800 was no doubt a direct result of his unpleasant experiences of the year before, compounded perhaps by his father's urgings that he give up writing altogether. It would be a mistake, however, to attribute the changed character of his work in the next few years entirely to the lingering effects of the *Kyan taiheiki* episode, for, harrowing as that experience was, it was merely the beginning of a series of events and involvements that were, in the end, probably of greater importance to him personally and as a writer.

The complexity of Sanba's domestic and business affairs alone in this period would, in fact, account for his diminished creativity in the half-decade or so following 1799. It is unclear what Sanba's living arrangements were at the time of the *Kyan taiheiki* incident, but, by 1802, he had taken up residence in the Yorozuya household. His marriage to the daughter of the house, and his adoption as heir, presumably took place prior to that date, but not, it would seem from accounts of the firefighters' attack, before 1799. In 1803 or 1804, his wife died and he severed his connection with the Yorozuya family. In 1804, he took on the responsibility of supporting the widow of his former master, Gangetsudō Horinoya Nihei. One source says that he moved to Yokkaichi in the Nihonbashi district, where he opened a used-book store; Sanba himself says that he was living in a different neighborhood near Nihonbashi in the spring of 1806, when a great fire that destroyed large areas of central Edo burned him out of his home and destroyed his library (perhaps a reference to his stock of used books for trade). Some time later in 1806, he established himself in Honkokuchō 4-chōme, and it may have been at this time that he married the daughter of Horinoya Nihei, whose shop was in that neighborhood.[1]

While it is impossible to pin down more precisely Sanba's movements and the nature of his relationships with the families of his two wives between 1800 and 1805, he was obviously unsettled in one way or another during this period of his life. If his marriage to the Yorozuya daughter took place shortly after the *Kyan taiheiki* incident, it may be presumed that he entered that family under something of a cloud, and her death shortly thereafter could hardly have contributed to his peace of mind. He then found himself almost immediately burdened also with the unexpected responsibility of looking after the widow of his former master, an unavoidable duty that must have been thrust upon him because the second Horinoya Nihei, his future wife's brother, was either under age or incompetent.[2] It is possible that being thus brought back into close contact with the Horinoya family, which included a marriageable daughter whom he had known from childhood, resulted in emotional complications for Sanba; Bakin seems to hint that there were reasons other than simply the death of his bride that caused his relationship with Tajiemon's house to be severed.[3] Whatever his lingering feelings about his fifty days in manacles may have been, this was a time in Sanba's life when he might well have been unable to find either the time or the emotional energy necessary for writing much original fiction.[4]

Of the twelve or so titles Sanba published in the years between 1801 and 1805, only six can by any stretch of the definition be called original, creative works, and, of these, only one, the first book to be formally included among his *kokkeibon,* seems worthy of much praise; it will be discussed at greater length in Chapter 4. The remaining works, all *kibyōshi,* are interesting only as further examples of Sanba's "habit of imitation," although one dating from 1805 marks the beginning of a long series of similar works in the category known as *katakiuchimono,* "vendetta pieces," that would account for a large proportion of his later output.

While the more interesting of Sanba's works from this period

cannot be classed as imaginative fiction, they include some that reveal his approach to the craft of writing. These "nonfiction"
works are a miscellaneous lot, but in many ways they mark his
final emergence as an authentic *gesakusha*. They suggest that Sanba
was using these years as a kind of rest period after his first burst
of creativity, during which he let his imagination lie fallow and devoted himself instead to reading, editing, and the establishment of
a network of friendships with older, more experienced authors.

Two of these books are perhaps best classed as reference works,
in spite of the fact that they contain many elements of parody.
Kusazōshi kojitsuke nendaiki (*Kusazōshi:* A burlesque chronicle),
published as a three-volume *kibyōshi* in 1802, is a history of light
fiction from the seventeenth-century *kanazōshi* forward.[5] *Shibai
kinmō zui* (Illustrated encyclopedia of the theater), an illustrated
compendium of detailed information about the Edo *kabuki* theaters, is a five-volume *hanshibon* published in 1803.[6]

The main text of *Kusazōshi kojitsuke nendaiki* consists of a
retelling of the story of Hachikatsugihime, "Princess Pot-on-her-
head," a well-known *otogizōshi* tale.[7] Each successive set of facing
pages is written in the style of a progressively more recent period
and illustrated by Sanba himself in a corresponding, chronologically
appropriate style. The work also contains a more straightforward
presentation in tabular form of a wealth of information about
authors, publishers, and publishing practices during the golden age
of the *kibyōshi,* from the mid-1770s to the early 1790s.

As one of a relatively small number of contemporary critical
works on the subject of popular fiction, *Kusazōshi kojitsuke nendaiki* continues to be of practical value to the student of late Edo
literature, but its appeal at the time no doubt lay not in its useful-
ness as a literary-historical document but in the wit of its conception and the skill of its execution. Sanba takes care not only to
mimic the writing style of each successive age of Edo fiction, but
also to have Princess Pot-on-her-head undergo adventures appropriate to the kind of fiction of each successive age. While he was
not a great artist, his illustrations in the successive styles of paint-
ers like Hishikawa Moronobu and Torii Kiyomasa of the early
eighteenth century through Katsukawa Shun'ei and Utagawa
Toyokuni of the early nineteenth are more than merely competent. He clearly devoted much time and effort to the historical,
bibliographical, and critical apparatus of the work, consisting of

lists and charts of publishers' seals, writers' names, dominant themes of successive periods of fiction, and comments on changes in illustration styles.

It would seem that one of Sanba's major diversions during his enforced withdrawal from publishing must have consisted of many long, thoughtful hours of reading and compiling information about his *gesakusha* predecessors and their work; *Kusazōshi kojitsuke nendaiki* bears every mark of having been prepared with great thoroughness, care, and affection for its subject matter. For any reader who is even moderately familiar with Edo fiction and able to distinguish stylistic variation through the haze of the language of the period, this work is without peer as a concise and amusing review of the development of Edo prose style; it reminds one forcefully that the Edo period was, indeed, of over two centuries' duration, and that no single generalization can be applied to the whole range of Edo popular fiction.

Shibai kinmō zui similarly presents much material of unquestionable authenticity in parodic form. Sanba organizes his information along the lines of the monumental *Wakan sansai zue* of 1713, a classified encyclopedia in 105 volumes on Chinese and Japanese subjects. Here the onstage and offstage worlds of the theater are treated as two "countries," each with its own geography, climate, history, customs, architecture, and so on. While both *Shibai kinmō zui* and *Kusazōshi kojitsuke nendaiki* can be described as parodies, their object seems to have been neither to denigrate the originals being parodied nor to score any discernible satiric point, but rather simply to raise an appreciative chuckle at their novel blends of form and content. One is reminded of Sanba's *Tatsumi fugen,* an earlier experiment with new wine in an old bottle.

Evidence of Sanba's efforts to form personal and professional associations with other *gesakusha* is visible in two other works published under his name in this period. *Kyōkakei* (A key to comic verse), which appeared in two parts in 1803 and 1805, is a guide to the Edo schools of *kyōka,* the preferences and verse-grading techniques of *kyōka* judges, and other *kyōka* miscellany.[8] *Kyōgen kigyo* (Mad words, beguiling prose), published in 1804, is a two-volume collection of humorous congratulatory messages and advertising texts by well-known writers, collected as a *festschrift* of sorts in honor of the writer and *rakugo* raconteur Utei Enba.[9]

The world of comic verse composition and competition that Sanba treats in handbook form in *Kyōkakei* seems to bear little direct relation to the style or content of his fiction. From some time prior to the compilation of this work, however, Sanba must have been an active participant in *kyōka* competitions, since he lists himself among the judges in *Kyōkakei;*[10] and, throughout his later career, attendance at competitions and other social functions involving *kyōka* seems to have been one of his major diversions. He is not, however, numbered by modern scholars among the major *kyōka* poets of his period.[11] Takizawa Bakin was not fond of Sanba, and so his criticisms must perhaps be discounted to some extent, but his assessment of Sanba's poetic abilities agrees with the scholars' judgment:

From the time he moved to Yamashitachō, Sanba frequented the Kyōkadō and studied comic verse under Magao, who, always pleased by flattery, would invariably praise Sanba to others and call him a genius. But perhaps because he was simply insufficiently talented to write good *kyōka*, Sanba left behind not a single celebrated verse; still less was he capable of composing comic verse in Chinese. One might assume that he at least composed *haikai*, but this writer has never seen a single such verse by him. He was, it seems, a *gesakusha* and nothing more. He was like Hsieh Chao-che of the Ming, who was called a genius but never read a book.[12]

Whatever the quality of his verse, Sanba seems to have been a welcome guest at parties in honor of artists and poets and other gatherings where *kyōka* were composed, to judge from the regularity with which he attended (and sometimes organized) such events during the period covered by *Shikitei zakki.* He may have been in demand more for his ability to produce witty, spontaneous verses than for the enduring quality of the final product, but then it would seem that *kyōka* was as much a social phenomenon as a literary one. In this respect, *Gesaku rokkasen* ranks Sanba with Utei Enba, one of the acknowledged *kyōka* masters:

At painting and calligraphy exhibitions, only Sanba and the late Enba managed to compose poems on the spot, based on the paintings, to give to others in the party; there was none to equal them.[13]

In any case, *Kyōkakei* is further evidence of Sanba's determination to provide himself with all the credentials of the traditional *gesakusha.* (In its broadest sense, the notion of *gesaku* was associated from the beginning not only with prose fiction, but with *kyōka* and the related comic verse form known as *senryū;*[14] in the passage quoted above, Bakin uses the term *gesakusha* almost scornfully, perhaps because he preferred to think of himself and others he considered his real equals as genuine *bunjin,* men of letters.) Its publication formally marked his entry into a literary circle presided over by Ōta Nanpo (1749–1823) and his literary disciple Shikatsube no Magao (1753–1829).[15] By this time Nanpo, known as Yomo no Akara and Shokusanjin in *kyōka* circles, was a trusted *bakufu* official often absent from Edo, but had behind him a long career as a prominent *sharebon* and *kibyōshi* author and teacher of both *kyōka* and *kyōshi* (comic verse in Chinese).

More than almost any other writer of the period, Ōta Nanpo embodied the old *gesakusha* ideal, and seems to have had the sort of personality that somehow naturally invites respect and admiration; no doubt his high official status also contributed to the esteem in which other writers held him.[16] While there is no particular evidence that Sanba's writing was directly influenced by Nanpo's, merely to be able to spend time in his celebrated presence and, more often, in that of Nanpo's old friends Magao and Enba must have been a heady and inspiring experience for Sanba.[17]

If Ōta Nanpo's presence hovers in the background of *Kyōkakei,* it is the spirit of Nanpo's own teacher, Hiraga Gennai, that pervades *Kyōgen kigyo.* Gennai's satires and fantasies and the descriptive passages of his *sharebon* had long since become the standard and the model for compositions in the humorous, playful prose style known as *kyōbun;* the texts and essays in *Kyōgen kigyo* are written for the most part in the *kyōbun* mode, and it seems to have been Gennai who first made such pieces a part of the *gesakusha*'s repertoire.[18]

The first part of *Kyōgen kigyo* consists of advertisements and other examples of *kyōbun* prose by a group of writers who gathered to celebrate Utei Enba's sixtieth birthday in 1803. The majority of the pieces in this section are by Enba himself, but also represented are such notables as Santō Kyōden, Shikatsube no Magao, the *kyōka* poet and *yomihon* author Rokujuen, and the *yomihon* author Shinra Manzō (or Banshō).[19] The last named, whose preface opens the collection and who seems to have been the host for the part for Enba, was, like Ōta Nanpo, a literary disciple of Hiraga Gennai; his preface, in fact, is signed "Fūrai Sanjin," and

"Shinra Manzō" is another of Gennai's pen names either granted
him by the master himself or appropriated by him after Gennai's
death. Both the content of *Kyōgen kigyo* and the role of Shinra
Manzō in its compilation speak of Hiraga Gennai's continuing spiritual presence as a kind of patron saint of *gesaku* literature well
into the 1800s.

In his preface to the second part of *Kyōgen kigyo*, which consists
entirely of his own advertisements and *kyōbun* exercises, Sanba
specifically acknowledges Fūrai Sanjin as his style model.[20] The
kyōbun style in which Sanba's pieces are composed, the so-called
"Hiraga manner" (*Hiragaburi*), is a playful, almost self-satirizing
prose exploitation of the standard devices of classical poetry, as
modified by their adaptation in *jōruri* ballad and by the addition
of daily life and popular culture as sources of vocabulary and ideas
upon which conceits may be built and wordplay may operate; it
is, in fact, the prose equivalent of *kyōka.* Many of Sanba's pieces
in this collection are examples of the most intricately constructed
variety of *kyōbun* prose; they are the despair of the translator, for
their considerable charm and their content are so thoroughly
bound up in allusions to classical literature and Edo theater culture, puns, and ornamental language that some of them cease to
exist as coherent utterances as soon as the translating process is
begun. The same sort of statement might be made, of course,
about other, more dignified species of Japanese literary expression.
But somehow a translator is willing to plunder a Japanese original
if it is manifestly great art to begin with; he feels merely silly con-
structing elaborate English similes to translate puns involving bean
cakes, patent medicines, dumplings, or hemorrhoids. One of Sanba's pieces in *Kyōgen kigyo,* for instance, is a kind of *kyōbun* ode
to the "ten great men" of contemporary *kyōka,* an exhaustive
catalogue of every conceivable pun and manipulation involving the
number ten.[21]

It is by no means the case, however, that all *kyōbun* prose is
dependent to an untranslatable degree upon what W. G. Aston
called "puns and other meretricious ornaments of style."[22] *Kyōbun* is by definition an artificial, mannered style, but its light-
hearted and playful spirit will often survive translation reasonably
well. The introduction to "The Men's Bath" and "The Women's
Bath" from *Ukiyoburo,* translated in the Appendix, will stand as
examples of Sanba's less intricate *kyōbun* style. On the other

hand, any student of Edo literature who has undertaken to read Tamenaga Shunsui's *Shunshoku umegoyomi* has encountered, in its introduction, and probably recoiled from, a representative piece of *kyōbun* of the most extreme sort. Shunsui's use of a seemingly interminable series of elaborately contrived plays on the special language of astrological almanacs to establish the setting and mood of his melodramatic novel stands in a direct line of descent from one variety of *kyōbun* composition practiced by Sanba and his predecessors and colleagues.

The fact that many of the *kyōbun* exercises by Sanba and others in *Kyōgen kigyo* are advertisements should not be taken as evidence of the commercialization of *gesaku*, although it certainly demonstrates that *gesakusha*, and in particular the *kyōka* poets, were far from contemptuous of the world of commerce. It seems doubtful that Gennai's endorsements and advertisements were the result of purely mercenary arrangements. Even a generation and more later, when writing had become a commercial enterprise for many authors, Sanba's occasional references in his diary to requests for endorsements or short bits of advertisement treat them little differently from similar requests from his artist-friends, for example, for a few lines of "appreciation" in *kyōbun* style to be written on painted fans executed for presentation to friends or acquaintances.[23] Perhaps in the case of Gennai and other early writers, the composition of short bits of humorous prose or a verse or two for advertising purposes was simply another aspect of the *gesakusha*'s determinedly playful and condescending attitude toward writing. For Sanba and his contemporaries, such writing, whether done simply as a favor or for value received, was probably a manifestation both of this older *gesakusha* spirit and of a recognition of the benefits of self-advertisement: a fan or scroll prominently displayed in a shop, or a flyer printed for distribution to customers, that bore a witty text by Sanba not only helped sell the shop's products but kept Sanba's name before the eyes of the reading public.

Whatever the inspiration for advertising texts like those in *Kyōgen kigyo* may have been, Sanba occasionally produced works that were unambiguously commercial. Two of them date from this period of his life: *Wata onjaku kikō hōjō* (On the marvelous efficacy of the cotton warming plaster: An announcement," 1802)[24] and *Myōdai no aburaya* (Oil seller by ordination, 1804).[25] The first is a three-volume *kibyōshi* extolling the virtues of a kind of medicated sticking plaster sold as a sideline in Yorozuya Tajiemon's book shop. The second, a single-volume *kibyōshi,* is a loosely plotted tale of how the oil merchant Toraya Sosaburō entered his trade at the command of an oracle. The story is interrupted by short texts describing Toraya's cosmetic and pharmaceutical products.

   In spite of the miscellaneous and, on the whole, unimaginative nature of his writing at this time, it would appear that far from being driven from the field by his unhappy experience with *Kyan taiheiki,* Sanba instead committed himself even more strongly to his chosen career in the years following the incident. By his own account, *Kyan taiheiki* and its aftermath brought him widespread public attention for the first time, and, indeed, soon thereafter we see him in print as a recognized junior member of the most exalted of *gesaku* circles. Sanba no doubt still kept the low profile expected of youth; his willingness to undertake the editing of *Kyōgen kigyo* and *Kyōkakei* looks very much like the eagerness to please of a young newcomer happy to do the dirty work in return for approval and acceptance by his elders.

   There can be little doubt that Sanba's new associations and friendships were exciting and profitable for him both personally and professionally. The world in which he found himself revolved around *kyōka.* However difficult it may be today to grasp the attraction of that verse form, to be an active member of one of the prestigious *kyōka* clubs of Edo in the years around 1800 was to be part of what was probably the most cosmopolitan, intellectually open, and socially varied subculture in Japan. Within the *kyōka* circle, social class distinctions were blurred, if not quite wholly irrelevant. Even a few women were in evidence. Perhaps more remarkable was the intellectual mix. In addition to playwrights, actors, and artists, there were visible among the leading *kyōka* enthusiasts representatives of nearly every academic and philosophical school—the various competing strains of Confucianism, *kokugaku,* and Dutch learning—and of the new breed of thinker concerned with agrarian reform and technological innovation whose interests transcended traditional academic allegiances.[26]

   The *gesakusha* Shinra Manzō (1754-1808), for instance, who used the name Takezue no Sugaru in *kyōka* competition, is far better known as Morishima Chūryō, under which name he published a number of scientific and geographical studies; he thus took Hiraga Gennai as his mentor not only in literary matters but in Dutch studies and science as well. He was a close associate of Hayashi Shihei (1738–1793), the scholar who in a celebrated incident in 1791 earned the wrath of Matsudaira Sadanobu and a turn in prison for publishing *Kaikoku heidan* (On the defense of a maritime nation), an essay calling attention to Japan's woeful lack of defense against potential Western attacks by sea. Morishima himself, who had been born into the distinguished Katsuragawa family of Dutch scholars and physicians, became an advisor to Sadanobu shortly after Hayashi's arrest.[27]

The others whose work appears in *Kyōgen kigyo* were men of similarly varied talents and interests. Santō Kyōden was by then the foremost writer of popular fiction in Edo; he had earlier made a name for himself as an *ukiyo-e* artist and illustrator, and ran a successful tobacco shop. Utei Enba was a successful carpentry contractor until middle age, when he turned to a new career as a *rakugo* storyteller and impresario; in the late 1780s and 1790s, he was a tireless promoter of *rakugo* as a legitimate entertainment medium, and put the art on a professional footing for the first time. He also produced a number of *sharebon* and *gōkan*.[28] Ishikawa Masamochi (1753–1830), appearing here as Rokujuen, the name he used when writing fiction, but known as Yadoya no Meshimori in *kyōka* circles, was by hereditary calling the keeper of an inn for visitors coming to Edo to transact business with the shogunate, but was deprived of his livelihood and banished from Edo for alleged corrupt business practices. Upon his return, he became a pillar of the *kyōka* establishment, noted particularly for his influence in the provinces, and was said to have had three thousand disciples around the country. Masamochi was also a *kokugakusha* of considerable repute. His father, though also an innkeeper by calling, had achieved renown in a wholly different field as the *ukiyo-e* master Ishikawa Toyonobu (1711–1785). Shikatsube no Magao, Sanba's teacher and patron, studied *kyōka* with Ōta Nanpo and fiction-writing with Koikawa Harumachi; Magao was accomplished enough in the field of traditional poetry to be granted a teacher's certificate by the Nijō school in Kyoto, and liked to appear at *kyōka* gatherings wearing the ceremonial court cap to which that distinction entitled him.[29]

This circle that Sanba joined in his mid-twenties, organized around *kyōka* and the *kyōka* clubs or teams of Edo, was the closest thing then existing to a literary establishment, but it would seem to have been more than that. It is difficult, in fact, not to see here something that in modern terms would be called an avant-garde, consisting in early-nineteenth-century Japanese terms of people actively engaged, whether they were aware of it or not, in nothing less than a redefinition of Japanese culture. Many of them had, either personally or through open association and friendship, placed themselves in opposition to the rigid orthodoxies of the shogunate, and some had been punished for their defiance. Others, like Ōta Nanpo and Morishima Chūryō, maintained their ties with the world of *gesaku,* in many ways a slightly disreputable one, while making themselves useful to the shogunate. While *kokugaku* was, by 1800, a branch of learning with a respectable pedigree, its reexamination of the literary tradition and the heightened awareness of "Japaneseness" it fostered were revolutionary in their implications, and were in a way complemented by the more obvious heterodoxy of those who were struggling to understand and interpret the exciting and sometimes threatening new world of European culture that was the exclusive purview of the *rangakusha,* the "Dutch scholars."

The *kyōka* movement itself was subversive to the traditional social order insofar as it involved poets and poetasters of all but the lowest social classes. It contributed to the formation of a new urban culture in Edo that was in the way of becoming a cosmopolitan, national culture shared by an intelligentsia scattered throughout Japan in other big cities and in smaller provincial towns. The "madness" (*kyō*) of *kyōka* and *kyōbun* and the "playfulness" (*ge*) of *gesaku* were for many simply identical with frivolousness; for some, however, they implied conscious rejection of tradition, orthodoxy, and what they perceived as the stifling and perhaps dangerous small-mindedness of the official vision of Japanese society.

However much some of the *kyōka* poets may have consciously seen themselves as innovators in other ways, with respect to literature they made no such claims. By Sanba's time, *kyōka* and *kyōbun* were on their way to becoming just two more forms of literary expression surrounded and shaped by the machinery of schools and discipleships so characteristic of the arts, literary and otherwise, in Japan. Having made himself part of the *kyōka* establishment and having steeped himself in *gesaku* lore while preparing *Kusazōshi kojitsuke nendaiki,* Sanba reentered the competitive world of popular fiction-writing in 1805; it is not surprising that he marked the occasion with a strong call to his audience and to his fellow writers for a return to what he thought of as the legitimate, "classic" tradition in *gesaku.*

The beginning of the mature phase of Sanba's career is symbolized by *Oya no kataki uchimatakōyaku* (A father avenged: a plaster on the inside of a thigh),[30] a *kibyōshi* published in 1805 that was the first of a dozen or more vendetta stories he was to publish in the next few years. Sanba's lessened productivity in the years immediately after 1800 was due in part to his unsettled domestic situation and in part to involvements with the *kyōka* circle, but in the preface to this work and elsewhere he offers an additional explanation of his own: an utter lack of interest in the burgeoning vogue for *kibyōshi* with vendetta-based plots. In his preface to another *kibyōshi* that he published in 1805, he remarks:

Of late, vendettas have robbed the *kibyōshi* of its humor, and for three years now I have not picked up the writer's brush. . . . It is my wish that all of you who are still imbued with the spirit of Edo forswear the vendetta and its seriousness. Shatter it in all its brittleness, I say, with a return to the style of Harumachi and Kisanji.[31]

But, during the same publishing season, Sanba succumbed to popular demand, or seemed to, and presented *Oya no kataki uchimatakōyaku* to his public. The beginnings of the vendetta fad in *kibyōshi* are usually identified with a work by Nansenshō Somabito published in 1795,[32] but it seems to have been only after 1803 that it reached proportions Sanba could no longer ignore.[33] Sanba had published a vendetta story in 1798,[34] but this work of 1805 marks the real beginning of his participation in the *katakiuchimono* (vendetta piece) boom. Sanba makes very clear his attitude toward vendetta stories in his introduction:

Publishers are all like plasters stuck on the inside of a thigh: They attach themselves first to one side and then the other, adhering to every passing fashion, paying heed neither to duty nor to principle. . . . "It's just a fad! Ah, just give it time, give it time"—but my solitary laments are simply a self-imposed burden of regret over my own lack of ability, and are more foolish by far than these vendetta books themselves. But he who would disparage the barbarian commits a barbarism; one should always "follow the customs of the place." If the vendetta is in fashion, then I shall imitate everyone else, submit to the publisher's urgings that I write a vendetta story, and at long last take up my brush again, even though a plot that is all seriousness is an affront to the spirit of playfulness implicit in the word *gesaku*. . . . Indeed, the writer, too, is like a plaster stuck on the inside of a thigh.[35]

As its more than faintly ridiculous title suggests, *Oya no kataki uchimatakōyaku* was hardly meant to be taken seriously; it seems to have been a parody, a determined effort to kill off the genre by exaggerating to a ludicrous level its melodramatic and mechanical conventions.[36] Nevertheless, Sanba evidently found himself unable to resist the insistent pressure from his publishers, most often that of his old friend and patron, Nishimiya Shinroku, for in the next few years *katakiuchimono* of the conventional sort account for nearly half the titles he published.[37] (In 1808, he published no less than seven vendetta stories.)[38] In spite of himself, he had become another frantic author "splitting his head and wracking his soul, spending sleepless nights awake in his bed in search of new methods of exacting vengeance, unusual ways of killing people, pathetic encounters, and perilous escapes."[39]

Upon resuming an active writing career, Sanba found himself almost immediately in the unexpected position of starting a new fashion of his own with the publication in 1806 of what is sometimes regarded as the first example of the new *gesaku* "genre" or format known as the *gōkan. Ikazuchitarō gōaku monogatari* (The story of the villainous Ikazuchitarō) was the longest work he had published to date, consisting of ten of the usual small five-leaf *kibyōshi* volumes bound in two larger volumes of five each. It seems that, even prior to the publication of this work, *kibyōshi* of three to five volumes in length had occasionally been bound together as single volumes by the owners of commercial lending libraries, who had found that loose volumes had a tendency to disappear; *Ikazuchitarō*, however, was the first work to be issued by the publisher in what would become the standard *gōkan* format (multiple volumes in a set of one or more larger volumes), and to be explicitly labeled *gōkan* on its cover. Whether or not this work of Sanba's was technically the first *gōkan*—there are a few dissenting opinions[40]—he prided himself on having originated the form:

In the spring publishing season of 1806, we put on sale the ten-volume *Ika-zuchitarō gōaku monogatari* in two parts, bound in two separate volumes. It was very well received by the public, and met with great success. The book wholesalers soon found that the *gōkan,* which required far less by way of expensive covers, was much easier to produce, and so by the following year all of them, without exception, were dealing in *gōkan.* Even now, in 1810, the *gōkan* maintains its popularity. I may sound like a wrestler who talks only of his victories, but it will be a source of pride for me for the rest of my life that it was I who began the vogue for the illustrated *gōkan;* the memory will sustain me in a dignified old age.[41]

Sanba seems to have found the *gōkan* well suited to him; between 1806 and 1822, he produced seventy or more books in this format, which account for well over half the titles he ever published.[42] Even these figures do not really indicate the extent to which *gōkan* dominate his total output, however, given the fact that each *gōkan* title represents anywhere from three to ten or more *kibyōshi*-size volumes; they average perhaps six or seven volumes, compared to the standard three volumes of the later *kibyōshi.* With the exception of *Ukiyoburo* and his two *yomi-hon,* probably none of Sanba's works in other formats approaches his average *gōkan* in length of written text. In terms of the actual amount of writing involved, then, Sanba's *gōkan* account for a large proportion of all the words he ever wrote and published. Clearly, if sheer volume were the sole criterion, Sanba should be known best not as a *kokkeibon* author, but for his *gōkan.*

The very speed and regularity with which Sanba turned out *gōkan* after 1806 raise the suspicion, indeed, that they may not represent his best, most original work. Something over 40 percent of his *gōkan*—28 titles in all[43]—are based closely on *kabuki* or *jōruri* dramas, works that, like his *Go taiheiki Shiraishibanashi* of 1795 (discussed in Chapter 2), usually amount to little more than heavily illustrated plot summaries or simplified retellings of high-lights of popular plays and whose publication seems often to have been timed to coincide with the openings of new plays or new mountings of old favorites. Many others of Sanba's *gōkan* are ven-detta stories, a genre in which we know he wrote with little enthu-siasm, and many of the remainder seem to have been historical tales that, like the vendetta tales, were highly formulaic and de-rivative; if, as seems likely, most of his *gōkan* were hastily written hack work, it is little wonder that it is usually not for them that he is remembered today, despite their popularity at the time.

It is ironic that, at this time in Sanba's life, when he seems to have been actively working at developing a sense of himself as a proper *gesakusha* of the old school—associating with an earlier generation of writers, studying his predecessors' work, and looking for stylistic models to follow—he should also have shown himself to be more than ever before a writer with a keen eye on the marketplace. Unlike Takizawa Bakin, who was equally attuned to changes in his readers' tastes and careful to write marketable books, but hated himself for having to sell the products of his brush,[44] Sanba not only saw nothing wrong with writing for money, but seems to have reveled in pandering successfully to the popular taste.

In a summary in *Shikitei zakki* of his publishing activities between 1806 and 1810, for instance, Sanba notes carefully which of his works were "big hits" (*ōatari*), which were average (*seken nami*) sellers, and which were "misses" (*hazure*), and particularly how they fared against Santō Kyōden's competition. For 1809, he ranks a work by Kyōden as the season's best seller, but puts two of his own in second and third place, and, when the following year one of his works takes first place ahead of two by Kyōden, his joy is evident.[45] Interestingly, if perhaps predictably, Sanba's comments on his and Kyōden's works never include critical judgments of their literary merit, originality, or social worth, but focus instead only on how well they were received by the reading public. Then again, even Takizawa Bakin, the most thoughtful contemporary critic of *gesaku* fiction, seems to have been inclined to judge a book in terms more of its popularity than of its quality as a work of art; his ultimate criterion was still popular acceptance rather than artistic integrity.[46]

Sanba's decision to give in to his publisher's repeated requests for vendetta stories and his first burst of productivity in the new *gōkan* format mark the beginning of a new phase in his career; from this time forward his publishing record shows clearly that he was writing primarily, if not exclusively, with the mass market and his potential income in mind. There seems to be no direct evidence surviving to indicate precisely what sums a popular writer like Sanba could command for a *gōkan* of average length. Successful *yomihon* authors, however, were paid well for their manuscripts: at first, 5 *ryō* seems to have been the going rate for a five-volume work; later, writers like Bakin and Kyōden are said to have commanded 7 *ryō* and sometimes as much as 15 *ryō*.[47] It may be assumed that the going rate for a *gōkan* of five or six volumes in length was lower, considering how much less written text was involved and the added expense to the publisher of paying for illustrations as well, but no records exist to tell us how much lower.[48] Still, a year like 1810, when he published no less than ten *gōkan* titles, must have been a profitable one for Sanba, even if for his *gōkan* he received just a fraction of the prevailing rate paid for *yomihon* manuscripts. In any case, Bakin asserts that Sanba and Kyōden were the only writers who succeeded in establishing a flourishing household by means of their writing income only, testimony enough to the size of Sanba's earnings.[49]

In spite of the fact that, by 1810, Sanba had learned that he could make a decent living through his writing, he evidently was not willing to trust entirely to his brush for his livelihood, for in that year he made arrangements to assure himself a more reliable income by setting up shop as a dealer in cosmetics and patent medicines in Honchō 2-chōme, a few blocks north of Nihonbashi. Sanba's shop opened originally on the 26th of the 12th month of Bunka 7 (early in 1811 by the Western calendar) as the exclusive Kantō outlet for Senpō Enjutan (Immortals' Formula Longevity Pills), the product of a Kyoto pharmacist named Tanaka Sōetsu.[50] The following year, Sanba added to his stock a makeup base of his own devising called Edo no Mizu (Water of Edo), which sold unexpectedly well and seems to have ensured the success of the shop.[51]

Many if not most of Sanba's works dating from 1810 and beyond carry advertisements for his shop and its products, sometimes only on the last page of a volume, but often as prominent insets on interior pages; sometimes, too, Sanba signed his introductions, "by Shikitei Sanba, in the Enjutan shop in Honchō."[52] He was obviously more than willing to take advantage of the increasing popularity of his books and the prominence of his name to draw patrons to his shop. It may indeed have been simply a desire to capitalize on his growing fame that prompted Sanba to open his shop, much as celebrity and greed in our own day continue to generate fast-food chains and clothing lines carrying well-known names from the worlds of show business and sports. Another parallel might be found in the reliance of writers like Charles

Dickens and Mark Twain on lecture fees to supplement their incomes. The institution of the lecture circuit did not exist in Japan, however, and so, while their European and American counterparts could earn sizable amounts of money reading from their own works, Sanba the patent medicine huckster and Kyōden the tobacconist could turn only to business activities wholly unrelated to their writing.

There were probably reasons other than simple need that compelled a successful writer like Shikitei Sanba to enter a non-literary trade. Most important, perhaps, was the fact that the very idea of earning a living as an independent writer was still a relatively new one in the early 1800s. Bakin says that it was only in 1795 or 1796 that the custom was established—by Kyōden and himself, he claims—of paying authors a fixed fee for their manuscripts,[53] although an earlier example of a cash payment for manuscripts may be found in the money Kyōden received in 1790 for the three *sharebon* whose publication in defiance of the ban resulted in his punishment.[54] Prior to that time, two different sorts of writer-publisher relationship seem to have prevailed. The first was that established early in the century by publishing enterprises like the Hachimonjiya in Kyoto, wherein the writer was little more than a highly specialized employee of the publishing house, working under an informal, exclusive contractual agreement to supply a certain number of manuscripts per year for some sort of recompense, ranging from simple room and board to an agreed-upon stipend in cash or kind.[55] The other, perhaps more typical of Edo in the 1770s and 1780s, when the ideal of the high-status *gesakusha* writing for his own amusement still prevailed, seems not to have involved cash payments at all; rather, the author was rewarded, if a book sold well, with gifts from a grateful publisher—a selection of newly published books or prints, bolts of fabric, or other items of value, or simply an evening's entertainment in the pleasure quarters or at the theater.[56]

By Sanba's time, however, a system of cash payment for individual manuscripts seems to have become the norm. Acting as an independent agent, the author either sold completed manuscripts to interested publishers or contracted in advance to write a book tailored to the publisher's requirements; in the latter case, the writer seems to have received a cash advance, followed by a further payment upon completion of the manuscript. If the book turned out to be a best seller, the author was rewarded further, but more often by entertainment than by cash.[57] These arrangements may be seen as "anticipating the modern system of advance and royalties"[58] only in a limited sense, since the publisher's formal obligation seems to have ended with a lump-sum payment for the completed manuscript, and "royalties" were paid only out of a sense of gratitude (and even then were more symbolic than concrete). Nevertheless, the writing of fiction had become a profitable enterprise.

To count on a regular income from the sale of book manuscripts, however, was a risky business: An author who missed a major shift in popular taste, whose creative powers failed him for a season, or who otherwise slipped from public favor could expect difficulty in peddling future manuscripts. At several points in his career, Sanba bitterly broke off all intercourse with artists (among them his old friend and collaborator, Toyokuni) who failed to complete the illustrations for his works promptly; their willful dilatoriness, in his view, kept him from publishing quickly enough to capitalize on new trends in fiction, giving an unnecessary edge to the competition (usually Kyōden).[59]

While Sanba's decision to become a shopkeeper was partly a matter of economic necessity—he had probably remarried by this time, and a source of income more reliable than writing would have been desirable—it may also be seen as an expression of his identity as a member of the urban merchant class. What interested Bakin about Sanba's and Kyōden's earning power as writers was not simply that their incomes were enviable, but that they had been able to "build up an estate."[60] Both writers invested their earnings from writing and exploited their reputations to establish businesses (in Kyōden's case, a pipe and tobacco-pouch shop)[61] that would ensure the prosperity and continuity of their houses independent of their fortunes as writers.

The fact that Kyōden and Sanba supplemented their writing incomes by running unrelated businesses does not mean that they should not be recognized as two of the earliest independent professional writers to appear in Japan. The writing of imaginative fiction and other varieties of prose remained their principal occupation, and in no way can either of them be described as having been principally a merchant for whom writing was merely a profitable avocation. They were, however, *chōnin*, and, to the

merchant-class townsman, income alone could never be an index
of social status; it was rather the possession of a flourishing family
business that conferred respectability and a social identity on one's
house. It happens that Sanba's son ultimately became a moderately successful author in his own right,[62] but the fact remains
that writing, necessarily a matter of individual talent and inclina-
tion, was not in principle a "family business" that could be passed
on to one's descendants. Sanba's decision to open his shop was
thus based not only on financial considerations but also on his
sense of duty as a *chōnin* to provide his family with the dignity
that only a "family business" could offer.

Sanba's family background and his demonstrated entrepre-
neurial abilities, both as a writer attuned to shifts in popular taste
and as a shopkeeper, mark him as a creature of the Edo merchant
class. In this respect, he is representative of his and later generations of Edo writers. Unlike the first generation of *gesakusha*
active in the An'ei, Tenmei, and early Kansei eras, who were predominantly of samurai extraction,[63] these later writers, as a group,
were mostly of the urban middle class.[64] Most of them were probably merchants first and writers second, since few could hope to
challenge the popularity of men like Sanba, Kyōden, and Ikku.
They were, thus, amateurs, in the sense that they were unable to
make a profession of writing, but, to the extent that any of them
aspired to full-time writing careers, it must be assumed that their
attitudes toward their craft differed from those of the gentleman-
dilettante *gesakusha* who had gone before them.

What the ascendancy of the *chōnin* author after the 1790s really
signifies in literary-historical terms, however, is very difficult to
say. Its causes were manifold and interrelated: the withdrawal of
many samurai writers from active publishing as a result of the
Kansei reform movement, the spread of literacy and a corresponding expansion of the non-elite reading population, and the commercialization of the enterprise of writing, which not only attracted
greedy novices but also, no doubt, legitimized what otherwise
would have been seen (from a merchant-class perspective) as a
frivolous, unprofitable waste of time. The results of *chōnin* domination of popular literature are far harder to specify. If Sanba's
works are in any way representative, one could point, in terms of
content, to the appearance of greater numbers of books that
dealt with the lower orders of society, and with the largely *chōnin-*

supported *kabuki* theater; in terms of style, the *chōnin* author may have favored a general simplification of vocabulary, grammar, and syntax, an avoidance of overly erudite allusions, and increased attention to the problems of reproducing the actual living speech of the urban middle class. It might be argued, too, that the increasing reliance of later *gesaku* fiction on the conventional morality of *kanzen chōaku* ("encourage virtue, chastise vice") in predictable formulations is a sign of its middle-class origins. But all these developments, if they indeed have anything to do with social class at all, probably say more about the nature of the audience for fiction than the class of its authors. In the final analysis, the emergence of the non-elite author is probably more significant as a social phenomenon than as a literary one.

By 1810, Sanba had achieved a great deal. He had already published close to seventy books, over a third of which he had produced in a remarkable outburst of creative energy in the previous three years. In his twenties, he had been through a series of upheavals in his private life—arrest and punishment, the death of his first wife, and a disastrous fire—but by now, at thirty-four, he was a writer of considerable reputation, the head of a stable household, and a respectable shopkeeper. The first book of *Ukiyoburo* had appeared the year before, to great acclaim; it had been labeled *zenpen*, "the first book of two," but, when the second book appeared in 1810, it was called *nihen*, simply "Book Two," a clear signal that *Ukiyoburo* was to be an extended project, unlike anything he had previously published. *Ukiyoburo* was not his first *kokkeibon*, but it was the work that established his reputation as a comic writer, and hereafter the *kokkeibon* became a regular part of his repertoire, though never to the exclusion of *gōkan*, which continued until his death to dominate his annual publishing activities.

Sanba was not an assiduous diary keeper, but in *Shikitei zakki*, dating from 1810 and 1811, he left a partial record of his activities during this busy period of his life. According to the first entry in this work (not so much a diary as a series of "random jottings," as its title implies), he had kept a similar journal earlier in his career. It was lost in the conflagration of 1806, and so we lack his own perspective on that important time in his life. But, by drawing on *Shikitei zakki* and scattered anecdotes preserved in *Gesaku rokkasen* and elsewhere, it is possible to put together a portrait of

Sanba in the mature phase of his career, although that portrait must remain frustratingly incomplete.

There is little reason to think that the life Sanba lived after 1811 was markedly different from that recorded in *Shikitei zakki.* He continued to live at the same location in Honchō, and advertisements for his shop appear in most of his later works. Proof is meager and scattered, but it appears that his friends and associates remained fairly constant, despite periodic quarrels. The only major change in his living situation seems to have been the birth of his only child, Toranosuke, in 1812.[65] He may, however, have suffered from increasingly serious bouts of poor health, to judge from the fact that in several later years his annual publishing output dropped to only two or three titles.[66] Indeed, as early as 1810, his health showed signs of deteriorating: in the third month of that year (after the spring publishing season had passed, during which he had published a record fourteen books) he was stricken with dropsy, and in the ninth month suffered a crippling attack of gout. He did not fully recover until early in 1811, and notes that this prolonged illness, which coincided with the period when he must have been making the final arrangements for the opening of his shop, kept him from writing and left him heavily in debt.[67]

In spite of his earlier efforts to establish friendships and associations with other writers, Sanba seems not to have been an active member of any definable literary "circle." His real intimates, instead, were a miscellaneous group of friends chosen not for their literary interests but for sheer congeniality. His friendship with the aging Enba seems to have remained a close one, but the men he himself describes as being good friends included artists like Toyokuni and his pupil Kunisada, and a restaurateur named Masuya Kuhei; his companions for evening drinking parties or expeditions to shrine festivals in the spring of 1811 were most often his literary disciples Ekitei Sanyū,[68] Tokutei Sankō,[69] and Kokontei Sanchō,[70] and a male geisha with a checkered past named Kamiya Isaburō.[71] Sources other than *Shikitei zakki* suggest that he also numbered among his close friends Sanshōtei Karaku and other *yose* storytellers active in the current revival of *rakugo*.

Sanba had occasional social contact with his major competitor, Santō Kyōden,[72] but, according to Bakin, as a rule "he had no intercourse with Kyōden, Bakin, and their circle, and was said to have a particular loathing for Bakin, whom he saw almost as an enemy, perhaps because Sanba had an uncharitable aversion to anyone better than he."[73] Bakin, for his part, was irritated beyond measure by the popular acclaim Sanba enjoyed. He seems to have been unable to understand how someone so clearly unlettered and uncouth as Shikitei Sanba could not only have the temerity to call himself a writer but achieve such conspicuous success in that profession. Long after Sanba's death, he grudgingly conceded that

Sanba's calligraphy was not unskillful, in an honest and straightforward way; he had not studied painting, but was extremely accomplished at it. While he was unschooled, he was a gifted man, and so in composing, for instance, his introductions, he was able to manipulate citations from the classics, and could easily have been thought a scholar of Chinese.[74]

But earlier, when Sanba published in 1810 a *yomihon* entitled *Akogi monogatari,*[75] Bakin had been so incensed at this invasion of his territory that he immediately wrote a long, bitter essay for private circulation about that book.[76] His critique consisted largely of a detailed and sneering catalogue of Sanba's sins against proper *yomihon* style. Most of his criticisms revolve around Sanba's faulty grasp of Chinese vocabulary and syntax, and seem on the whole justified, despite their frequent pettiness. Whether or not the degree of venom Bakin indulged in was justified, the public was not taken with *Akogi monogatari,* and it sold extremely poorly.[77] Perhaps as a result, Sanba never published another *yomihon,* although he left one in manuscript that was published posthumously in 1825.[78]

During his most productive years, Sanba must have been busy indeed. Between 1808 and 1814, he averaged ten or eleven new titles per year, most of them *gōkan* of five or six volumes,[79] and, to judge from *Shikitei zakki,* he expended a good deal of time and effort responding to requests and commissions for *kyōka* and a bit of *kyōbun* prose as advertising or as "appreciations" of the work of artists or actors, and for his calligraphic services as a well-known writer. Because he was lacking in self-discipline, however, Sanba seems to have spent these years in perpetual battle against publishers' deadlines. He almost prided himself, it appears, on his ability to write under pressure: Many of his works are prefaced with remarks to the effect that they were written "on urgent request" or "in response to the publisher's urgings" in the span of

a few days and nights.[80] Whether we are meant to admire Sanba
for his virtuosity or excuse him for any lapses due to haste is impossible to tell. At any rate, a picture emerges of frantic writing
marathons alternating with periods devoted to days and evenings
drinking and going on excursions of one sort or another with
friends.

Sanba's journal entries in the spring of 1811 provide a glimpse
of his erratic working style.[81] The end of the 3rd month saw him
finishing the introduction to Book Three of *Ukiyoburo* and attend-
ing to the purchase of glass bottles for his Edo no Mizu and other
business matters. The 1st day of the 4th month was devoted to
shrine visits with his disciple Tokutei Sankō, accompanied, presumably, by alcoholic refreshment. The 2nd was occupied with
business—redesigning the Edo no Mizu label to read positively,
"Helps your powder stay on," instead of, "Keeps your powder
from coming off," and distributing promotional flyers—and with
doing a large number of fan inscriptions. On the 4th, he made a
visit to his brother's grave on the hundredth day after his death;
Sanba's entry for the day includes two long, mocking diatribes,
one against the Nichiren sect (for referring to the founder of the
sect as "the great *bodhisattva* Nichiren"), the other against an incompetent neighborhood calligrapher and sign-painter. Between
the two is the parenthetical explanation, "Tonight, as always,
writing while drunk."

Sanba devoted the following week mostly to advertisements
and fan inscriptions—as many as thirty in a day—after a final
drunken evening with his friend Isaburō on the 5th of the month.
The 10th and 11th disappeared in send-off festivities for an agent
of the Kyoto pharmacist whose "long-life pills" Sanba was market-
ing, but he was back at work on the 12th cranking out fan and
scroll inscriptions. The 16th through the 20th he devoted again to
partying: an excursion to Ōji (with a drinking stop at the Ōgiya,
the famous restaurant in that town mentioned in *Ukiyoburo*, I.1),
an overnight stay with his disciple Tokutei Sankō celebrated with
drink and *kyōka*, followed by shrine visits and a second night at
Sankō's; on the 19th, Sanba attended a party to ratify his reluctant reconciliation with the illustrator Katsukawa Shuntei, and he
concluded his week of revels with an impromptu party on the evening of the 20th with Tokutei Sankō, Ekitei Sanyū, and Utagawa

Kunisada. The following week was spent on another batch of advertisements and inscriptions and, evidently, the first part of Book Three of *Ukiyoburo,* which he finished and sent to the publisher on the last day of the month.

Bad weather and a cold kept him housebound during the first week of the 5th month, but he spent the 5th and 6th days receiving visitors for the dolls' day festival. By the 8th, Sanba's publisher was pressing him for the remainder of Book Three of *Ukiyoburo,* and Sanba records that he wrote late into the night. The next evening, Tokutei Sankō and Ekitei Sanyū joined him to help with the final stages of the work and to compose an afterword. Sanba retired finally at dawn, but was up again by 10 o'clock to finish by noon some overdue advertising texts. That afternoon, a gift arrived to commemorate the first anniversary of the death of the restaurateur Masuya Kuhei; exhausted by several days of non-stop writing and too little sleep, Sanba wept in private over this pathetic reminder of a good friend and drinking companion, once alive but now a box of rice cakes, nothing more. [82]

Gesaku rokkasen draws the following portrait of Sanba at work, which is reminiscent of "the Master's" own account in *Shikitei zakki:*

When the Master was writing a book, there were times when he completed an entire manuscript of six or seven, or even eight or nine parts in three days and three nights. . . . Early in the Bunka era, when *gōkan* and *yomihon* were popular, Sanba and Toyokuni and others like them were under constant pressure from various publishers to come up with drafts and manuscripts. When they were struggling to meet a previously agreed-upon deadline that was fast approaching, they would go to the publisher involved and borrow a room for five days or seven days at a time, and complete the story or illustrations there. On any given day, one of them might be in a second-floor room, and then the next day the other would move into a guest room in one of the wings. . . . Things sometimes reached a point where even then they could not manage, and they would find themselves hounded by a publisher whose deadline they had missed. In such cases, they would simply go into hiding somewhere, and appear at the publisher's later, when they had finished. [83]

The nature of the principal medium in which Sanba worked during these years—the illustrated *gōkan*—put him under pressures that went beyond simply juggling his time to maintain a constant flow of manuscripts. Completing the text was only one step in the

production of a *kibyōshi* or *gōkan;* Sanba seems often to have
been actively involved in the illustrating process as well, arranging
for the services of artists and supervising their work. Given the
number of stages through which a work passed before its final
publication—negotiation of terms of payment with the publisher,
writing, preparation of a clean copy of the text (Sanba sometimes
farmed this task out to disciples or friends), illustration, preparation of the blocks, and proofreading—each *gōkan* must have
represented many hours of labor and much emotional energy,
particularly in cases where he had to work with artists who either
were slow in their work or had different conceptions of how a
story might be illustrated. (In at least one case, Sanba relates, he
himself reworked illustrations that were not to his liking.) [84]

Considering the pace and complexity of his work as a popular
writer, it is little wonder that what evidence there is suggests that,
when Sanba relaxed, he did so aggressively and with the help of
liberal amounts of alcohol. He himself regarded his dropsy and
gout as attributable to heavy drinking, [85] and the prominence he
gives to drunks and drinkers in his *kokkeibon* and the care with
which he portrays their types and habits suggest that he spent a
good deal of time in their company.

While his drinking may have contributed to the decline of his
health, Sanba's relationship with alcohol seems not to have been,
on the whole, a destructive one. And he did not, like Jippensha
Ikku, find pleasure and inspiration in travel. (He is known to have
left Edo only once, for a brief sojourn in the nearby countryside
of Kazusa after the disastrous fire of 1806.) He was devoted instead to the circumscribed but richly textured world of the
Edokko, for whom the delights of life in Edo were inexhaustible.
Sanba's entertainments—the theater, *kyōka* parties, excursions to
local temples and shrines, the company of raconteurs and witty
friends—were typically urban, and were of the sort that revolved
naturally around the consumption of *sake.* If drinking sometimes
undermined his productivity, it was also the universal lubricant
of the world in which Sanba was most at home and from which
he drew inspiration for the best of his work, the portrayals of the
ordinary people of his city in *Ukiyoburo* and others of his *kokkeibon.*

Takizawa Bakin has left the only contemporary sketch of Sanba's personality that is not a conventional hymn of praise from a

disciple. Brief as it is, it still presents Sanba as a personality of some complexity:

His personality was marked by a certain bitterness; one often heard that, when drunk, he was prone to disputation. In no way did his character resemble that of a man of letters, but neither, for that matter, was he like a merchant. Though he often behaved like some swaggering "knight of the streets" [kyan-kaku], it is said that once he reached the threshold of old age he foreswore drunkenness and devoted himself to making a living. One thing about him worthy of praise: his father Mohei being very fond of sake, Sanba for some years sent him every month three pieces of silver as drink money. [86]

Sanba's drinking need not concern us further, but it is interesting to note the prominence Bakin gives it in his assessment of Sanba's character; interesting, too, how Sanba fulfilled his filial obligation to Mohei—it would seem that his affection for alcohol was an inherited one.

In spite of the popularity of his works, the length and productivity of his career, and his gregariousness, and despite the fact that he attracted to himself as many as fourteen or fifteen writers eager to call themselves his pupils,[87] Shikitei Sanba can not be said to have founded a "school" of popular fiction, or even to have exerted a significant direct influence on later writers. One of his literary disciples, Tamenaga Shunsui (known as Sanro during the time of his apprenticeship under Sanba), achieved real prominence as a writer, but his relationship with Sanba was brief and seemingly uncomfortable for both parties; Shunsui later studied under Ryūtei Tanehiko, the acknowledged master of the gōkan, and it seems that, in both cases, he may have been as interested in gaining approval to reprint his teachers' works—he ran a small publishing and book-lending concern briefly—as in studying the writer's trade.[88] Sanba's successful exploitation of the techniques of the yose storytellers in his kokkeibon may have encouraged Shunsui to draw upon his own skills as a professional raconteur when he began to perfect his ninjōbon style, and his tutelage may be visible in some small way in Shunsui's kyōbun and in those parts of his ninjōbon that are reminiscent of gōkan in their intricate plotting; but none of Shunsui's works seems to be particularly identifiable as having been written under Sanba's influence, except in inconsequential ways. Sanba's other disciples and his son Toranosuke, who styled himself Shikitei Kosanba (Little Sanba), left a small body of work reminiscent of their teacher and father, but none achieved any notable reputation as an independent author.

Sanba's achievements as a writer lay more in the area of the adaptation and refinement of techniques and style pioneered by others than in real innovation. The success of his *kokkeibon*, particularly *Ukiyoburo*, was due not to any radical innovation but to Sanba's consummate mastery of the skills required of a comic writer and to his decision, while still adhering to the existing conventions of the genre, to treat a broader segment of his society than had previously been attempted. Even if Sanba's writing exerted considerable influence over that of his contemporaries and successors, it would be virtually impossible to detect, since his work was not by nature groundbreaking (except in terms of its quality), and his influence would not be distinguishable from that of his predecessors and contemporaries, individually and collectively.

Having chosen to work within the traditional confines of *gesaku* fiction as defined by Fūrai Sanjin, Santō Kyōden, and others, Sanba could not be a revolutionary, but neither was he simply a mindless tiller of already well-ploughed fields. He was conscious both of his considerable strengths as a writer and of his limitations, and was well aware of what a popular writer must and must not do if he wished to remain popular. "What is lacking in *gesaku* . . . is any serious confrontation with life," writes Donald Keene, quoting Nakamura Yukihiko, one of the leading modern interpreters of late Edo fiction;[89] Sanba would no doubt have agreed, and then gone on to say, "And so it should be." One certainly sometimes misses in even the best of his work an acknowledgment that life is more complex than its surfaces; indeed he may have been not only uninterested in but incapable of writing with anything other than the simple entertainment of his audience in mind. On the other hand, one aspect of his genius was knowing not only his audience and its expectations but also his own limitations; he was careful not to let his reach exceed his grasp, and devoted himself instead to perfecting the kind of writing he was most comfortable with—a sure sign of his professionalism.

An anecdote related by Bokusentei Yukimaro is highly revealing of Sanba's attitudes toward his craft and of his quiet but almost defiantly proud dedication to his kind of art:

One time when I was talking with the Master [Sanba], I told him, "The other day, I heard a friend . . . doing a recitation of the 'Suetsumuhana' chapter of *The Tale of Genji,* and it occurred to me that might be a good thing to base a novel on."

The Master replied, "I don't suppose there is any writer who hasn't, at one time or another, turned to *The Tale of Genji* for help in his writing, because it is, after all, the greatest work of pure fiction ever written. But the *gesakusha* should not concern himself unduly with such difficult things. If you are thinking of giving fiction-writing a try, you mustn't spend your time lapping up recitations of bits and pieces of *Genji.* If you get carried away listening to parts of *Genji* or the *Shui-hu chuan*—well, it's certainly the business of the popular writer to pick good subjects and write about them knowledgeably— but if you get too wrapped up in *Genji,* you'll wind up with nothing but a warmed-over *Genji* full of unpleasant-sounding anachronisms. The popular writer's belly wants simpler fare, like the things the man in the *oden* stall jabs on a skewer—eggplant, *konnyaku*—or the popped rice they sell at New Year's: four coppers for this, four for that! Your real job is mixing together that sort of thing."

The Master clapped his hands together and laughed. I find his words amusing even now as they come back to me. [90]

Sanba died on the 6th day of the intercalary 1st month of the 5th year of Bunka (1822), and his ashes were buried in the precincts of the Chōgen'in, a subsidiary temple of the Unkōin in Fukagawa. [91] It is probably safe to assume that he had been in ill health for some time, since his output had dropped to only a few short works in each of the three years before his death. [92] (Bakin's assertion that Sanba began to lead a more temperate existence once he reached "the threshold of old age" may refer to this period of declining health; if so, Sanba's reformation may have been a matter more of necessity than of choice.) Toranosuke was only ten years old when his father died, and so was unable to succeed to the headship of the house, but Sanba's old friends and disciples rallied round to help keep the medicine shop in business, and were able to pass on a thriving enterprise to the heir when he came of age. [93] With the help of his friends, Sanba's dream of assuring the prosperity of his descendants was thus at last realized; he had long before guaranteed himself a different sort of personal immortality through the labors of his brush.

CHAPTER FOUR

The *Kokkeibon* and Shikitei Sanba

At just about the same time that he capitulated to the fad for vendetta stories, complaining all the while that it had "robbed the *kibyōshi* of its humor," Shikitei Sanba began in earnest to exercise his talents in a new medium. The *kokkeibon,* by definition immune to the epidemic of "seriousness" that had overtaken the world of the *kusazōshi,* proved to be the sort of writing with which Sanba was most obviously at home and which would earn him his lasting reputation. He did not, of course, abandon the *kusazōshi* genres: on the contrary, in spite of his professed distaste for them, they continued to dominate his output until his death.

The history of the *kokkeibon* has been explored in detail by Japanese scholars, and Donald Keene has given the subject a survey treatment in English.[1] The term *kokkeibon* itself seems not to have been used in its modern sense until perhaps the 1820s; prior to that time, the works now so designated were referred to simply as *chūbon,* but the establishment of the *ninjōbon* as a second kind of fiction published in the same *chūbon* format required the adoption of more specific terminology.[2] In any case, by the time Sanba turned his attention to it, the humorous *chūbon* or *kokkeibon* already had a pedigree of sorts. Its origins are usually traced to a species of comic writing known as *dangibon,* popular in the middle decades of the eighteenth century, which were parodies of the sermons presented on street corners and in other public places by itinerant moralists in an oratorical style very close to vernacular speech. The content of the *dangibon* was highly varied, borrowing as it did from other oral arts in addition to the sermons that were its original model; but the form adhered more or less to the style

60

of these vernacular sermons. The combination of satire and plain, conversational language would be one of the primary general characteristics of the later *kokkeibon*. A second element in the developing *kokkeibon* tradition was the satiric *kyōbun* prose of Hiraga Gennai and his lesser contemporaries. The influence of both the *dangibon* and *kyōbun* traditions is visible in Sanba's *kokkeibon*, but of far greater immediate importance in the development of the later *kokkeibon* was the influence of the *sharebon*.

Because its primary concern was the pleasure quarter, its rituals, and the poses of its habitués, there is a tendency among Westerners and modern Japanese alike to regard the *sharebon* either as a peculiar form of pornography or as little more than an overripe and decadent reworking of themes and topics already thoroughly explored by Saikaku and his fellow *ukiyozōshi* authors. Its concentration on the fine points of elegant behavior in the pleasure quarters, on the subtle distinctions between the true connoisseur (*tsū* or *tōrimono*) and the poseur (*hankatsū*, "half-*tsū*"), and on the argot of the denizens of the quarter do indeed set the *sharebon* apart as a very specialized sort of literature that is difficult for modern readers to understand, much less to appreciate. By the 1790s, however, the *sharebon* had become an item of mass consumption, or at least was no longer aimed at a restricted audience of connoisseurs. Books in the genre had become a staple stock in trade for the commercial lending libraries (*kashihon'ya*) and a major source of profit to publishers,[3] possibly because the *sharebon* had broken out of its earlier mold and was no longer a genre designed to appeal solely to actual or potential patrons of the pleasure quarters, but had instead become increasingly a means whereby people who could not, for financial or other reasons, emulate the pleasure-quarter *tsū* in his accustomed haunts could at least savor at a vicarious remove the atmosphere of his romantic world. Though the *sharebon* no longer dealt exclusively with the superficial arcana of the pleasure quarter, but now also more broadly and deeply with the personal, non-professional relationships among courtesans, patrons, entertainers, and brothel-keepers, it was still restricted in its subject matter. If even late representatives of the genre seem to modern eyes to be overspecialized and decadent, it is largely because the *sharebon* was concerned primarily with describing and evoking the mood of a small corner of Japanese society that was itself peculiarly specialized and decadent.

The narrowness of its focus does not detract from the fact that the *sharebon* was virtually the first species of prose fiction in Japanese literary history that attempted to describe its chosen world largely through the medium of realistic dialogue. True, the dialogue itself is often laden with slang, puns, and obscure references to current popular songs and fashions in dress that impart to it a certain stiltedness and cloying preciosity; these features of *sharebon* prose are not, however, flourishes and decorations derived from purely literary traditions, but rather are offered as examples of the living speech—however self-conscious and contrived it may have been—of the pleasure quarter.

The subject matter and humor of the later *kokkeibon* differ greatly from those of the *sharebon,* but the vast majority of *kokkeibon* written after about 1800 are equally dependent on dialogue rather than descriptive prose. The mechanical conventions used by the *sharebon* author to represent dialogue were similar to those seen in contemporary dramatic texts: each speech was set off with a single half-bracket or by the full or abbreviated name of the speaker or some other identifying symbol; short descriptions, much like stage directions, of the speaker's movements, appearance, or emotions appeared within or between speeches, written in a double line of smaller characters. These conventions were borrowed virtually intact and put to identical use by *kokkeibon* authors. In both forms the conclusion of a speech could be marked by the quotative particle *to,* but it was signaled in many cases only by the insertion of a "stage direction" or a half-bracket or other symbol marking the beginning of a speech by another character. The half-bracket "quotation mark" was used exclusively to set off passages of actual speech, never to mark internal monologues; thus the modern reader is spared the difficulty of distinguishing between speech and thought (or certain kinds of adverbial clauses that can look like quotations), which often makes reading earlier varieties of fiction that use only the particle *to* to mark both kinds of expression such a frustrating task. Indeed, internal monologues have no place in either the *sharebon* or the *kokkeibon:* in both kinds of fiction we can deduce the motivation or mental state of a character only from what he says or does.

Writing of the emergence of the dialogue-based *kokkeibon,* Takizawa Bakin bears contemporary witness to its similarity to the *sharebon:*

Since the prohibition of the *sharebon,* there has appeared something called the *chūbon,* consisting of "books" [*hen*] of one or two volumes each that contain very amusingly written, silly vignettes highly reminiscent of the "floating world impressions" [*ukiyomonomane*] performed by mendicants. . . . Though they do not deal with brothels and rakes, they are nevertheless a variant of the *sharebon.*[4]

Not only did Bakin perceive the fundamental similarity between the *kokkeibon* and the *sharebon,* but his reference to *ukiyomono-mane* impressionists is also very important to an understanding of the development of the *kokkeibon. Ukiyomonomane,* literally "imitation of the floating world," was one of a number of different kinds of oral storytelling practiced in the entertainment districts of Edo and other cities; the *ukiyomonomane* artist's speciality was the portrayal of various familiar stock figures of Edo life—the rustic tourist, the drunk, the country samurai, the self-styled "retired gentleman," the dissolute heir, and so on— through careful mimicry of the dialects, speech habits, and physical mannerisms of his subjects. This art, which seems to have remained far less formalized an entertainment than the similar *rakugo,* appears to have been practiced in Edo in the environs of the Asakusa Temple from some time in the last quarter of the eighteenth century, flourishing side by side with the other "oral arts" (*wagei*) of the period, all of which seem to have participated in a general movement toward professionalization catalyzed by the arrival from Osaka in 1798 of the great *rakugo* raconteur Oka-moto Mansaku.[5]

Bakin did not necessarily mean that the new *kokkeibon* were all based on the *ukiyomonomane* artists' routines; he was probably using the word simply as a slightly opprobrious term for all the various arts that specialized in oral caricature. In any case, it is clear that he saw a strong connection between the comic *chū-bon* and the arts of vocal mimicry and storytelling. That there was, indeed, an important association between oral artists and *chūbon* authors is certainly borne out in Shikitei Sanba's career.

A number of Sanba's *kokkeibon* are very explicitly related to contemporary oral storytelling modes. Foremost among them, of course, is *Ukiyoburo,* whose genesis Sanba himself described as follows:

One evening in Utagawa Toyokuni's lodgings, we listened to Sanshōtei Karaku telling *rakugo* stories. . . . Beside me that evening, laughing as hard as I was, sat a publisher. Greedy as ever, he suddenly asked me if I would put something together based on these stories of the public bath, leaving out the parts about the licensed quarter and emphasizing the humor in commonplace people and events. I agreed to try.[6]

Namaei katagi (Portraits of drinkers, 1806)[7] is even more directly related to oral storytelling, as Sanba reveals in a preface:

This work was originally a single evening's amusement, written as a present for Sakuragawa Jinkō, but, on the urgings of the publisher, I turned it into a book. I hope that you will keep Jinkō's mannerisms in mind as you look at it; its true meaning will then reveal itself, and it will be far funnier than if you were simply to read it.

I have been listening to Jinkō since my childhood. . . . He is accomplished at imitating physical mannerisms, and a master of mimicry. I have long loved him. It is for these reasons that I offer him this book.[8]

It would appear that Sanba intended *Namaei katagi* originally to be used as a performance text (*daibon*), or at least as a source of ideas for performance, by the raconteur and impressionist Sakuragawa Jinkō, a disciple of the *kibyōshi* author and *rakugo* artist Sakuragawa Jihinari.[9]

A third work with direct and obvious connections to the world of the raconteur is *Inaka shibai chūshingura* (*The Treasury of Loyal Retainers* on tour in the countryside, 1813-1814),[10] which is not really an original work by Sanba at all but rather a reworking and expansion by him of a story or cycle of stories performed by the *rakugoka* Asanebō Muraku, a pupil of Sanshōtei Karaku. Sanba explained in his introduction that Muraku had intended to publish his own version of the stories himself, but found that he lacked both the time and the skill, and so turned his drafts over to Sanba for rewriting and elaboration.[11]

In 1815, Sanba compiled and annotated a collection of miscellaneous documents and souvenirs relating to the history of *rakugo* and allied arts entitled *Otoshibanashi chūkō raiyū* (The origins and course of the *rakugo* revival)[12] that dealt particularly with the period of the *rakugo* revival of the late 1790s and early 1800s. This compilation is further evidence of Sanba's abiding interest in the oral storytelling arts, and is a major primary source for the study of the early roots of modern *rakugo*. The figures of

Sanshōtei Karaku, whose stories were one of the inspirations for *Ukiyoburo*, and Sanba's old friend and mentor Utei Enba loom large in *Otoshibanashi chūkō raiyū*, the former as the first Edo raconteur to follow Okamoto Mansaku's lead in elevating *rakugo* from the status of an occasional amateur entertainment to that of a professional performing art, and the latter as a storyteller himself, an organizer and promoter of *rakugo* performances and fan clubs, and author or compiler of a number of *hanashibon*, collections of short *rakugo* stories.

Jippensha Ikku, too, seems to have had a good deal of intercourse with the world of storytelling. One of his early *kokkeibon*, for instance, was a partial continuation of *Kyūkanchō* (first book published in 1805),[13] a work by Mantei (or Kannatei) Onitake (1760–1818)[14] that is said to have been derived directly from *ukiyomonomane* routines on the general subject of the rustic visitor to Edo; this work was, in fact, subtitled *ukiyomonomane.* Ryūtei Rijō (1778?–1841), author of the immensely popular *Hanagoyomi hasshōjin* (Eight laughers: A blossom calendar, 1820),[15] which recreated on paper the world of the amateur theatrical entertainment known as *chaban kyōgen*, was himself a raconteur, a pupil of the *rakugo* artist Ryūtei Riraku.[16] Tamenaga Shunsui was also a sometime storyteller; early in his career, as a pupil of Ryūtei Rijō, he performed as Tamenaga Masasuke, and toward the end of his writing career he mounted the *yose* stage again under the name Kyōkuntei Kinryū[17] as a reciter of *ninjōbanashi*, "tales of human feelings," a variety of story closely related to the *ninjōbon*.[18]

It is clear that Sanba and other late-Edo authors of dialogue-based fiction maintained intimate contacts with performers of *rakugo* and related arts. It should not be assumed, however, that Sanba's *kokkeibon* are merely transcriptions or recreations of *rakugo* or *ukiyomonomane* routines: they are all, to greater and lesser degrees, the products of a conscious process of literary composition, and they have their ultimate roots not in an oral but in a literary tradition. Sanba borrowed topics and characters, and acquired a sensitivity to the rhythms of the spoken language from the storytellers, but he learned his basic techniques for writing realistic dialogue and bringing his characters to life from the *sharebon* and *dangibon* traditions.

Honda Yasuo has shown beyond much doubt, however, that these earlier dialogue-based genres themselves had also been deeply affected in their formative stages by the oral entertainments of their day.[19] The *dangibon* was explicitly modeled on the sermons of street-corner moralists, but it appears that early *dangibon* authors like Jōkanbō Kōa, who wrote *Imayō heta dangi* (Bumbling sermons for the present day, 1752), the earliest classic of the genre, were themselves raconteurs who not only wrote but also performed their mock sermons. Many of them also entertained professionally in an oral medium known as *kōshaku,* which in its original form consisted of recitations of military and historical tales and fables. Adopting the poses of legitimate *kōshaku* narrators or *dangi* preachers, humorists like Kōa and Fukai Shidōken would preface their routines with appropriate bits of historical or moral texts and then wander off into irreverent, rambling commentaries on contemporary life and manners, interspersed with punning *rakugo*-like routines, imitations of famous actors, and oral caricatures of the habitués of the entertainment districts.[20] One of the classics among early *kokkeibon* is Hiraga Gennai's *Fūryū Shidōkenden* (An up-to-date biography of Shidōken, 1763),[21] a whimsical account of how the great *kōshaku* artist Shidōken was guided into his calling by a fictional teacher of morals named Fūrai Sennin. This work reflects the close relationship between the burlesque versions of *kōshaku* and *dangi* recitation—"Fūrai Sennin" is depicted as a *dangi* sermonizer—and shows moreover that Hiraga Gennai was profoundly impressed with Shidōken's skills as a storyteller and impersonator. Gennai had a respect bordering on reverence for Shidōken, who seems to have been unusually advanced in years at the height of his career, and he seems to have regarded himself as the elderly Shidōken's special patron or protector.[22] ("Fūrai Sennin" is an obvious reference to Gennai's *gesaku* pen name, Fūrai Sanjin).[23]

The most outstanding formal characteristic of the classic *sharebon* and the one that links it most closely with the later *kokkeibon* is, as argued above, its heavy reliance on dialogue. The earliest example of a *sharebon* composed in this style is found in *Gekka yojō,* a work by Kenshōkaku Shujin published in Osaka in 1746.[24] The first half of this work is in Chinese, as were many of its predecessors in the genre, but the second half consists of conversational exchanges among the clients and employees of a brothel that are recorded in precisely the same *serifu* (play-script) format that soon became standard in the *sharebon.*[25]

Speculating on the origins of this style of presenting dialogue, Honda notes that the publisher of *Gekka yojō,* Kyūkodō Harimaya Sahei, seems to have specialized in publications closely related to the pleasure quarter and its entertainments. Among his products were a number of detailed "how-to" guides for the amateur that dealt with *jōruri* song, puns and other wordplay, and how to mount informal performances of *niwaka,* an amateur theatrical entertainment then popular in the Osaka pleasure quarters that was heavily dependent upon wordplay. All these arts were accomplishments required of the aspiring *tsū* in the gay quarter. These books were written as practical handbooks in an easy, colloquial style and, more important, provided actual examples of, for instance, wordplay as it might appear in actual conversation, and *niwaka* in its social setting (the *zashiki*—"parlors"— of the teahouses and brothels of the quarter), recorded according to the same conventions as the dialogues in *Gekka yojō* and subsequent *sharebon.* Unfortunately for Honda's argument, the examples he provides all date from after the publication of *Gekka yojō,* but the fact remains that in the publications of the Harimaya we see what are probably the origins of the dialogue-based *sharebon* in "scripts" written to show how certain of the social arts of the true connoisseur were incorporated into his conversations and entertainments in the pleasure quarter. (A further link between these guide books and the *sharebon* is found in the fact that *Gekka yojō* and the guide to puns and wordplay mentioned above seem likely to have been written by the same author.)[26]

It is thus apparent that the most common type of *kokkeibon,* made up for the most part of conversational exchanges and typified by works like *Ukiyoburo* and *Hizakurige,* was part of a larger tradition of dialogue-based literature that included the *sharebon,* the *dangibon,* and the *ninjōbon.* Once this tradition was begun and its conventions established—in works like *Gekka yojō*—it took on a life of its own, independent of its origins, as the techniques of dialogue representation were mastered and refined by successive generations of writers. But it is also evident that, throughout the century or more of its history prior to contact with the Western novel, the tradition of fiction built around dialogue was constantly refreshed by interaction with a parallel tradition of oral storytelling and caricature. This interaction came about in many ways: through the writing of fiction by men who were themselves practitioners of one or another of the oral arts, through personal interaction and collaboration between fiction writers and professional raconteurs, and through the much more general cross-influences that resulted from the fact that, from the mid-eighteenth century onward, the interrelated oral arts of *rakugo, ukiyomonomane, niwaka,* and *kōshaku* were all-pervasive in *chōnin* culture.

One senses, in fact, that the spoken word itself was an object of intense fascination throughout this period, whether in everyday conversation (itself highly textured by the profusion of regional and class dialects in the increasingly cosmopolitan city of Edo) or in the more elaborate and artificial utterances of the elegant punster, the actor, or the raconteur. Throughout Sanba's *kokkeibon,* the reader is aware of an extreme sensitivity to language on the part of both the author and the characters he portrays. If this awareness of the phonetic and semantic richness of both the spoken and the written language—revealed not only in wordplay but in direct conversation *about* language—can be taken to have been shared generally by the literate urban population, then it is little wonder that those who wrote in genres like the *kokkeibon* and the *sharebon* which concentrated on conveying in accurate detail the flavor of urban life found it necessary to include generous portions of realistic dialogue in their works in order to reflect properly the importance of linguistic matters in the lives of their characters.

The preoccupation of *sharebon* authors and, in the main, of *kokkeibon* authors with linguistic realism is but one manifestation of a more general characteristic of these kinds of late-Edo fiction: an almost scholarly fascination with the ephemera of everyday life, an interest not unlike that of an anthropologist in recording the quotidian trivia of the popular culture of Edo. One of Santō Kyōden's best-received works was a *sharebon* of 1791 entitled *Nishiki no ura* (The other side of the brocade).[27] It was, indeed, the tangled threads of the reverse side of the orderly, patterned brocade of daily life that interested Sanba and his contemporaries. To recreate all the meandering digressions, lapses in logic, pauses, and elisions of natural speech on the printed page was not an exercise in stenography, but a means to the general end of revealing a "true" vision of life in the licensed quarter, for instance, as in *Nishiki no ura,* or in a public bath, as in *Ukiyoburo.* Whether the vision turned out to be ironic or satiric was almost beside the point;

"probing" or "penetration" (*ugachi*), looking for contradictions ("holes," *ana*) between reality and the conventional view of things was the objective. Historical circumstance had made for an unusually large gap between Japanese as it was actually spoken and its literary counterpart. The simple act—artistically, no mean feat, of course—of bringing a conversation to life in print was in and of itself a kind of *ugachi:* fidelity to living speech permitted the creation of fictional worlds that revealed, rather than obscured or idealized, the complex subtleties of personality and social interaction that are conveyed in natural conversation.[28]

Most of Sanba's *kokkeibon*—sixteen of the twenty-three identified by Honda—belong to this new tradition of dialogue-based fiction. Some make *ugachi* an explicit objective: "Quick Changes of Heart" (*Hayagawari mune no karakuri*, 1810),[29] "In Human Affairs, Nothing But Lies" (*Ningen banji uso bakkari*, 1813),[30] "A Mechanism for Peering into the Human Heart" (*Hitogokoro nozoki karakuri*, 1814),[31] "Theater Chic This Side of the Curtain" (*Gejō suigen maku no soto*, 1806),[32] and others of more ambiguous title all assume the existence of a false front (*omote*) in human behavior and devote themselves to revealing—through conversation and monologue—the seamy backside (*ura*) of the human brocade. These are *kokkeibon*, "funny books," and so Sanba's presentations are humorous, but his basic point is serious: self-deception and pretense, hypocrisy and expedience are the rule in human affairs. There is less vitriol and more tolerance in others of his dialogue-based *kokkeibon; Ukiyoburo* is the most impressive of several works that only indirectly or occasionally treat of the conflict between the ideal and the real, appearance and actuality in human behavior. In all these works, however, exposition and argument are overwhelmed by dialogue. Sanba's characters, the hopelessly arrogant and boorish, the pathetically self-deceiving, and the happily normal alike, tell us about themselves. Sanba himself as narrator normally gives us as points of reference only a few basics: age, occupation, dress, perhaps a word or two about hair style or timbre of voice.

Seven of Sanba's *kokkeibon*, however—almost a third of the total—lie outside what has been called the "mainstream" of the medium, the dialogue-based variety of *kokkeibon*. These seven works are a miscellaneous lot, evidence enough in their variety of how difficult it is to accept *kokkeibon* as a "genre" designation:

some of them, indeed, should be called essays rather than fiction. They share, however, beyond their humorous intent and their physical similarity as *chūbon*, several points with their dialogue-based brethren. All but one (*Kyōgen kigyo*) take as their point of departure the concept of *ugachi*, here almost synonymous with "satire": parody and sophistry, rather than dialogue, are Sanba's tools in these works. And, without exception, the objects of their probing, their *ugachi*, are various aspects of the broadly shared popular culture of their day. Irrespective of the style in which they are written or the way they are structured or their ruling conceits, all of Sanba's *kokkeibon* address themselves to subjects of immediate concern to the general run of *chōnin*, to any Edoite of average education possessed of a sense of humor and an interest in the world around him.

The first two titles that appear in the canon of Sanba's *kokkeibon* are among this group of seven non-dialogue-based works. They date from shortly after 1800, the period in his life described in the previous chapter as one during which he was experimenting with new writing styles and at the same time attempting to establish for himself a claim to legitimate *gesakusha* status by studying and copying the styles of earlier writers. The comic works of Hiraga Gennai were the obvious inspiration for these earliest of Sanba's *kokkeibon, Mashin gigen* (A whimsical discourse on the measles, 1803),[33] and *Kyōgen kigyo* (1804). The degree to which the advertisements and *kyōbun* essays collected in *Kyōgen kigyo* were influenced by Gennai's models has already been treated in some detail in Chapter 3.

Mashin gigen, which is a satirical treatment of a grim subject, the disastrous measles epidemic that swept Edo in the spring of 1803, bears a striking stylistic and structural resemblance to one of Hiraga Gennai's most famous comic essays, *Hōhiron* (On flatulence, 1774).[34]

Hōhiron is divided into two parts. The first is an account in *kyōbun* style of an entertainer who has become a sensation in Edo for his ability to fart out on command imitations of frogs, birds, fireworks, *jōruri* music, and any number of other familiar sounds for hours on end; this description is followed by a rambling, mock-serious "learned" discourse on the history and physiology of flatulence, and the diet and training such performances require. The second part of this peculiar work consists of a similarly erudite defense of the performer for his enterprise and self-discipline, a tour-de-force of sophistry prompted by a long-winded attack by a priggish samurai who visits the narrator to complain about this affront to good taste and public morals.

Mashin gigen likewise consists of two parts. The first is a cynical description of how the people of Edo reacted to the epidemic—a sudden upsurge in piety, the appearance of charlatans claiming special knowledge of measles cures, a rush to market new patent medicines, and so on. The second part, prefaced by a playful, punning commentary on the tendency of Edoites to succumb to fads (the verb *hayaru* is used for both "to become popular" and "to spread," as a disease does), consists mainly of a pseudo-scholarly discourse on dialect linguistics, epidemiology, ichthyology, and folklore, delivered for the benefit of the neighbor's cook, who has come to the erudite narrator to settle a bet with his fellow servants about whether the proper name for the present disease is *hashika* (the common word for measles) or *ashika* (a dialect variant of *hashika*, but normally "sea lion").

Mashin gigen is not particularly amusing and fails utterly to reach the heights of elegant crudity achieved in *Hōhiron*, but there can be little doubt that Sanba was consciously copying this work of Gennai's or something very similar to it. He evidently realized that his talents lay elsewhere, however, for *Mashin gigen* was his only essay in this direction. Sanba continued to write *kyōbun* in the *Hiragaburi* style, but only in short introductions to works in other styles, as advertising texts, and in fan inscriptions and the like. Both this work and *Kyōgen kigyo* remain as evidence, however, of his abiding respect for Gennai and of his interest in trying to preserve the best of the old *gesaku* traditions.

Another of Sanba's non-dialogue-based *kokkeibon* was *Ono no Bakamura usojizukushi* (Ono no Bakamura's complete dictionary of lies, 1806),[35] all in all a slight work; as its title (based on puns on the name of Ono no Takamura, a semi-legendary ninth-century poet, and *utajizukushi*, "dictionary of poetic words") suggests, it is a parody of combination dictionary-poetry handbooks, and includes as well parodies of selected portions of standard *setsuyōshū*, which were all-purpose popular dictionaries and guides to seasonal festival observances, popular epistolary style, etiquette, and other miscellaneous social skills. It has a close parallel in an earlier work by Koikawa Harumachi entitled *Sato no Baka-mura mudajizukushi* (1783). Honda suggests that one of Sanba's objects in this work was to poke indirect fun at Takizawa Bakin and other *gesakusha* who occasionally wrote simple textbooks of similar format but serious intent for use in village schools.[36] In any case, this work is also one of a kind in Sanba's oeuvre.

Four theater-related works complete this group of "non-main-stream" *kokkeibon*. The earliest is *Shibai kinmō zui* (An illustrated encyclopedia of the theater, 1803), described briefly in Chapter 3. This was published as a *hanshibon*, a format slightly larger than the *chūbon*, but it is nevertheless classified as a *kokkeibon*, evi-dently because its nature as a parody of the form of conventional "encyclopedias" marks it as humorous in intent, and because it does not fall readily into any other category. The next work in this sub-group to be published was *Hatsumonogatari* (1808),[37] a reworking in *chūbon* format of a play written and performed in honor of the actor Nakamura Utaemon III's visit to Edo from Osaka; it is a tale of the adventures of a stage-struck country girl who wants to go to Edo to see her beloved Utaemon perform, but is deceived by a former cook in an actor's household who manages to pass himself off as Utaemon, setting in motion a series of comic complications. *Hatsumonogatari* was clearly little more than an attempt to cash in on the excitement of Utaemon's visit. It is a *chūbon* in format, and a *kokkeibon* because it is funny, but has far more in common with Sanba's theater-based *kibyōshi* and *gōkan*, and with his "advertising novels," than with his other *kok-keibon*.[38]

The third title in this sub-group is probably the best known and most interesting of Sanba's non-dialogue-based *kokkeibon, Chū-shingura henchikiron* ("The treasury of loyal retainers": A crack-pot view, 1812).[39] This work is a tongue-in-cheek criticism of the famous puppet play *Kanadehon chūshingura*, which by Sanba's day had become one of the central myths of Tokugawa Japan, having spawned numerous *kabuki* versions and countless novel-izations and parodies. Pretending to present the theories of a fictional moralist-critic named Henchiki-sensei, Sanba analyzes each major character in the play in a way precisely contrary to the received wisdom: the heroic Ōboshi Yuranosuke, the leader of the vendetta, is attacked as a besotted incompetent; the schem-ing, self-serving Sagisaka Bannai is hailed as a paragon of loyalty;

En'ya Hangan is a miserly hothead, and Kō no Moronao a man of charity and common sense. Nakamura Yukihiko identifies *henchi-kiron*, which might be translated loosely as "perverse sophistry," as one of the major subtypes of late Edo satire. The humor of the technique in this work of Sanba's arises from an intentional mis-reading of the motives for a character's actions, based on a selec-tive application of conventional ethical tenets or accepted theories of human motivation.[40] Commenting on *Chūshingura henchikiron*, Donald Keene has written:

Shikitei Samba could not have been entirely serious in his contradictions of all the accepted views, but his criticism seems to go beyond mere frivolity to something approaching a rejection of the ideals expressed in the play. At the same time, Samba's quibbling is proof of how avidly interested he and his readers were in every detail of the play. Yuranosuke, Moronao, Kampei, Ban-nai, and the other characters were a part of their lives, and their desire to learn more and more about them, as if they were real people whose secrets were not fully revealed in *Chūshingura*, occasioned the many revisions and ex-pansions of the original work.[41]

It would probably be a mistake, however, to grasp too eagerly at *Chūshingura henchikiron* as evidence that Sanba was at heart a cynic and a social critic. On the contrary, Nakamura regards the work as a distinctly unserious reworking, played almost entirely for laughs, of an earlier, similar work by Hatakenaka Kansai en-titled *Chūshingura jinbutsu hyōron* (A critique of the characters in *Chūshingura*, 1786)[42] that is far more clearly a genuine satirical attack on the received ethical wisdom about *Chūshingura.*

It is certainly true, however, that, even in Sanba's day, *Chūshin-gura* still exercised a remarkable hold over the popular imagination generations after the play was first performed; such, at least, is the implication of *Kanadehon kuraishō* (Gleanings from the copy-book storehouse, 1813),[43] the last *kokkeibon* Sanba produced that was not written predominantly in a dialogue format. The work is a pseudo-scholarly compilation of "historical" materials relating to the events and personages of *Chūshingura*, such as fac-similes—complete with wormholes, blots, and erasures—of docu-ments like the original oath signed by the forty-seven loyal *rōnin* (masterless samurai) and an advertising placard announcing the self-sacrificing Okaru's arrival in the brothel, a rubbing of a deco-rated end-tile from the roof of the Ashikaga palace where En'ya

Hangan drew his sword on Moronao, and drawings of a paper doll once owned by Yoshimatsu (the son of Amakawaya Gihei, the *chōnin* hero of Act 10 of the play), a clock once owned by Momonoi Wakasanosuke, and one of the lanterns carried by the *rōnin* on their daring night raid on Moronao's mansion. *Kuraishō* is not wholly Sanba's creation; the original inspiration and parts of the final work are from the hand of Manjutei Shōji, a *jōruri* playwright active in Kyoto and Osaka who had published a similar work in Kyoto in 1804 and evidently asked Sanba to revise and expand it for publication in Edo.[44] The point of the work is, on the one hand, to satirize the deadly, fussy style of contemporary antiquarian scholars and, on the other, to poke fun at the lengthening tradition of increasingly tedious and trivial critiques and exegeses of *Chūshingura*. Underlying the work and the source of its humor is the fact that the elaborately reproduced and annotated "relics" are of course wholly spurious; they are not souvenirs of the actual vendetta of 1703, but of the fictitious events of the play, which was set in the Ashikaga period. While the work is not entirely Sanba's, Yamaguchi Takeshi found it to be vastly superior to the original Kyoto version and attributed the improvement to Sanba's extensive emendations.[45]

With the possible exceptions of *Mashin gigen* and *Kyōgen kigyo*, products of a period in Sanba's life when he was trying on the persona of the old-style, unabashedly elitist *gesakusha*, all the works described above deal with one aspect or another of Edo popular culture. *Chūshingura henchikiron* and *Kanedehon kuraishō* take as their subject the one play that virtually every adult inhabitant of Edo could be expected to be familiar with. *Ono no Bakamura usojizukushi*, nominally based on a species of dictionary of interest only to poets, is actually for the most part a parody of the *setsuyōshū*, a kind of practical guide to the culture of the upper-middle classes that to all appearances was aimed at the greater mass of upward-aspiring and socially insecure townsmen. *Shibai kinmō zui* and *Hatsumonogatari* would have appealed to anyone with even a passing interest in the theater; to judge from the phenomenal popularity of *kabuki*-based *kibyōshi* and *gōkan*, their potential audience probably included a rather large proportion of the population. Even *Mashin gigen* and *Kyōgen kigyo* were not, in the final analysis, aimed at a small elite. The former dealt with an epidemic that must have touched just about everyone in

Edo. The latter was composed largely of advertisements, intended by definition for mass consumption, and the remaining *kyōbun* exercises, while written in a complex and allusive style, required little of the reader beyond a good general knowledge of the commonly shared popular culture.

Any attempt to define the term *kokkeibon* in its modern sense must take into account the fact that works in this medium not only are products of urban merchant-class culture, but take that culture itself as their subject matter and make it the object of their satire. The other main varieties of comic literature of the period—the *sharebon* and the *kibyōshi*—certainly appealed to the merchant class as a whole, but they did not make the generality of urban culture their subject. Prior to its metamorphosis into a species of romantic, melodramatic fiction, the *sharebon* was a comic genre, but its satire was elitist in tone and took as its object a stylized and expensive world and way of life that were inaccessible to the great majority of townsmen. As Sanba so often wistfully reminded his readers, the *kibyōshi*, too, developed originally as a comic genre; it was a form, however, that was a part of but not about popular culture. *Kibyōshi* satire was most often directed at historical subjects, the literary tradition, or other objects that stood at a remove from the daily life of the streets; the *kibyōshi* author tended to prefer fantasy to the real world, and filled his pages with dreams, reincarnations, magic, supernatural beings and interventions, and larger-than-life imaginary heroes. In contrast to the *kibyōshi*, Sanba's *kokkeibon* are down-to-earth and of the present; in contrast to the *sharebon*, their point of view is non-elitist, and they deal with the broadest conceivable spectrum of *chōnin* life.

Sanba published a total of sixteen *kokkeibon* composed principally of monologues and conversations. For the purpose of discussion, these works will be divided into four categories. These groupings are not proposed as any sort of formal typology; the categories tend to run into each other and some works fit as well in one as in another. The first group might be defined as works that are conceptually similar to the early-eighteenth-century *kata-gimono:* collections of verbal portraits or sketches of a series of "types" of people within a specific category. The second group consists of works that are constructed around a ruling conceit, theme, or particular conception of human psychology. The third contains works that focus on a single setting or subculture, rather than on unrelated individuals sharing certain attributes or traits (as in the first group above) or on some "truth" of human nature (as in the second group). The final group consists of only two works, *Ukiyoburo* and *Ukiyodoko,* which are here regarded as combining features of works in the three other groups.

The earliest work in the *katagimono* group to appear was *Yakusha hiiki katagi* (Portraits of actors' patrons), not a separate work but published as the second book of *Yakusha gakuya tsū* (A connoisseur's guide to the actors' green room, 1799), discussed briefly in Chapter 2. It is a series of sketches of the members of a family of theater fans, each character exhibiting a different aspect of *kabuki* mania. The portraits are executed mainly by means of their subjects' own words. Another book in this group is *Kyakusha hyōbanki* (Critiques of theater patrons, 1811),[46] a far more fully developed exploration of the same theme. This latter work, organized according to the general scheme of the actors' critiques (*yakusha hyōbanki*) published in the major cities at regular intervals throughout the latter half of the Edo period, consists of a series of verbal portraits of types of theater patrons, either singly or in conversational (or argumentative) groups: the typical Edo, Osaka, or Kyoto theatergoer, the adolescent girl, the foul-mannered little boy, the theater *tsū,* the know-it-all, the occupant of the cheap balcony seat (or the ground-floor private box), the amateur theater historian, and others. While, in one respect, *Kyakusha hyōbanki* is no more than a collection of disconnected images of different kinds of theatergoers, it is also a storehouse of contemporary theater lore; the monologues and conversations of the characters portrayed are as lifelike and lively as any in Sanba's oeuvre, but they serve also as a medium to convey a great deal of specific information about historical and contemporary theater practice, performance styles, and actors. As one of Sanba's relatively late *kokkeibon,* this work shows him at his most competent. By this time he had fully mastered the techniques of writing realistic dialogue; the speeches in *Kyakusha hyōbanki* still show the influence of *rakugo* and *ukiyomonomane* storytellers, but Sanba had domesticated their art to the point where he was free to elaborate the content of his characters' speeches as much as he wished, without sacrificing the startling realism he had achieved in earlier works more closely dependent on the oral artist's repertoire. The work has only limited appeal to modern readers, however. While it offers a fair share of immediately recognizable and amusing characters, they are part of a subculture that no longer occupies a central place in Japanese life. Part of the attraction of *Kyakusha hyōbanki* to its original audience no doubt lay in Sanba's clever diversion of the familiar format of the actors' critiques to his own uses, but, with the disappearance of its model as a popular-cultural institution, the work loses its universality and becomes in many of its parts a literary curiosity that is often difficult to decipher. Further to compound the modern reader's confusion, Sanba appends to the beginning of his work a seemingly irrelevant, rambling tale in Kamigata dialect about the misadventures of a hardware merchant given to wearing a fox skin. Sanba's penchant for parody and imitation seems to have run away with him here: since *Kyakusha hyōbanki* is to be modeled on actors' critiques, it opens with an introduction purportedly written by Hachimonjiya Jishō IV, whose famous publishing house in Kyoto and Osaka had, since the days of Ejima Kiseki (1667-1738),[47] been identified with *yakusha hyōbanki;* the fox-skin story is there, it seems, as a reference to an earlier *kokkeibon* by Utei Enba and the actor Ichikawa Danjūrō V that used a similar tale to introduce what was itself a parody of the *hyōbanki* form.[48]

A much simpler work that has proved to have much greater staying power than *Kyakusha hyōbanki* is the earlier *Namaei katagi* (Portraits of drinkers), which clearly marked the beginning of Sanba's exploitation of oral art forms. In spite of the homage Sanba paid to the Hachimonjiya in the former work, *Namaei katagi* is far closer in spirit to the classics of Ejima Kiseki, the Hachimonjiya's star writer. It does, however, show clearly the immense changes that had overtaken comic fiction since the days of Saikaku and Kiseki. Both *Namaei katagi* and the "character sketch" pieces of Ejima Kiseki are structurally uncomplicated works made up of portraits of anonymous representatives of certain types of people within a larger category. Kiseki reveals the essence of his "types" to the reader through third-person descriptions or brief stories illustrating their behavior. The characters never really come to life, since our knowledge of them comes only indirectly through appeals to our general knowledge of human nature or our special familiarity with the culture of the time and place that are based on implicit formulations like "He is the sort of man who wears this sort of clothing," or "She is the sort of girl who wears her hair that way."

Sanba's characters, on the other hand, reveal themselves directly, without the mediation of a narrator. The sketches that make up *Namaei katagi* are monologues, interrupted occasionally by brief notes describing the speaker's dress, particular quirks of speech or tone of voice, carriage, or movements. There are usually others present in the scene, but their comments and movements are revealed only indirectly in the reactions of the speaker: "Well yes, thank you, I will, but only a little . . ." "Why the hell don't you *say* something? . . . I am *not* drunk!" The character type under consideration ceases to be a type and becomes highly individualized as the reader becomes involved immediately and actively with the text. In being forced to imagine the absent parts of the exchange, the reader in effect becomes the drunk's absent conversation partner.

There are twelve sketches in *Namaei katagi,* including the Superstitious Drunk, the Loud Drunk, the Weeping Drunk, the Abusive Drunk, and others. Most of the sketches are accompanied by an illustration with a short caption describing the behavior of the subject, and many are prefaced with a brief note suggesting how the drunk's speech should sound when read aloud. Here is an excerpt from the third sketch in the series, the Unfunny Drunk (*omoshiro-kunai jōgo*):

The Unfunny Drunk

(How to read: should be read quietly and calmly, in a spirit of seriousness.)

(The sound of a throat being cleared): Ehen, eheh, ehen . . . gohori, gohori, uhha, uhha, goho, goho . . . (he spits out some phlegm): Pyoi . . . Excuse me. Hello? . . . It's very lively over here tonight, isn't it? . . . No, it's just that I could hear it all perfectly over at my place, and I thought it would be a lot more fun if I saw what was going on, so here I am. I certainly don't mean to bother you . . . No, no, don't trouble yourself . . . (He stands swaying in the entranceway.) . . . Anyway, anyway, it's too early to go to bed. Eh heh heh. Ah, Tora! are you helping out? I suppose Orin got tired. Ya. One, two, three, *up* we go. (Steadying himself on his wobbly legs, he heaves himself up out of the entranceway.) I suppose the old gentleman is in his rooms. Was that dancing I heard just now your daughter who's studying with Kineya? I could only hear the sounds of her feet, but even that was marvelous . . . Ah, excuse me. My goodness! So many guests. Well, here we go. Heave ho! (Bracing himself against the wall as he walks, he reaches the entrance to the guest parlor.) . . . Eh, hello, I'm Tazaemon . . . Eh, eh, eh, kind of you, by the way, to see me home last time. Eh, heh, heh, heh, hee hee hee, thank you. Eh, eh . . . (He has a habit of going "eh, eh," as if he were thinking and unable to find the right words.) Eh . . . No, no. Don't trouble yourself . . . Heave ho, down we go. (He seats himself in the lower part of the room, and begins fumbling at his sash and inside the lapels of his kimono.) Now, where in the world . . . Could I have left it somewhere? . . . Eh? Well, if you insist, thank you, I'll have just a puff of yours. (He picks up the host's tobacco pouch.) Isn't this a fine one! What would you say it's made of? Cloth? Leather? Hmm . . . No, leather is different . . . Eh? Oh, I see now. You know, I've heard they're getting so good now that uh, yes, they can make paper tobacco pouches so that they look just like leather or cloth . . . Pardon me? Yes, I think Takeya Seibei in Yokkaichi and Miyakoya Denzō [i.e., Santō Kyōden—trans.] in Kyōbashi are supposed to be good . . . Really? I didn't know that . . . Ah, this is very good tobacco. I have mine brought down from Gunma in the leaf and cut it myself. It's better than the tobacco you pay eighty a *kin* for in Edo . . . No, no. I insist. Do *not* go out of your way on my account. Besides, I just had some at home, and you saw what my legs were like when I came . . . Well, if you insist. Just one more . . .[49]

Translation destroys, of course, many of the fine points of the characterization that are dependent on the hems and haws and slurrings and garblings in the drunk's speech; but the general style and structure of the sketch should be clear, even if some of the humor of the original is lost. The proximity of this sort of writing to the kind of oral caricature that is the stock in trade of the stage comic, including the stand-up comedian of our day, should also be obvious. *Namaei katagi* was written, as we have seen, as a text for the raconteur Sakuragawa Jinkō, so it is not surprising that it is so close in feeling to an oral form of humor. This work appears to have been the first in which Sanba was consciously manipulating the techniques of the stage comic; it feels almost as if he were sticking intentionally close to his model in order to master its stylistic tricks in pure form before attempting to adapt them to more conventionally literary ends. The training he gave himself in writing *Namaei katagi* stood him in good stead in many later works. Drunks, of course, were common inhabitants of the worlds he created elsewhere, but the skill he developed here at reproducing quirky habits of thought and speech and slurred pronunciation turned out to be useful in portraying a wide variety of other, soberer types as well.

Namaei katagi was followed by two similar collections of sketches of drunks, *Tōsei nanakuse jōgo* (Seven habits of modern drunks, 1810)[50] and *Ippai kigen* (One cup and they're on their way, 1813),[51] which complete the roster of Sanba's *katagimono*-like pieces. These later works are technically no less competent than *Namaei katagi,* but their effect is somewhat different. Both concentrate in the main on unattractive drunks: the *kuse* of the first title suggests "habits" in a negative sense—bad habits, unpleasant tendencies. *Ippai kigen,* despite its cheery title, also presents a series of vignettes whose subjects are decidedly bad drinking partners. Among the drinkers of *Namaei katagi* were some who were less than attractive, but those in *Ippai kigen* are perilously close to being alcoholics, more to be pitied than laughed at: a priest who can say nothing good about anyone, "looking as though he has been pulled from a barrel of *sake*"; the near-bankrupt doing his accounts, gaining courage to face his creditors with each midday cup; the drunk who "goes on and on about the same thing," pressing plans for a expedition to Ōji on a reluctant friend, who shows little interest in planning another drinking bout with the disheveled, runny-nosed boor before him; the staggering inebriate who sticks his companion with a bar bill, then picks a fight with him in the street. Such portraits are a far cry from the stylized playboys of Kiseki, and more convincing than all but the best of Saikaku's finely drawn pictures of self-deceiving gadabouts.

The works in the second category of Sanba's dialogue-based *kokkeibon* are very similar to those of the first, except that the sketches contained in them are united not by their portrayal of a certain category of person—the drunk, the theatergoer—but by a particular theme: "Everyone lies sometimes"; "There are two sides to every personality"; "Unpleasant habits"; or "People think one way and act another." There is a vein of cynicism running through all these works that is more apparent than in most of Sanba's other writing, but it never produces much beyond a gentle mocking of human foibles. The personality types Sanba holds up to ridicule here are those that by general social agreement are acceptable objects of satire. "The husband who is afraid of his wife" and "the husband who plays around," for instance, are fair game, but "the wife who does her husband's bidding" or "the filial son" would not be: Sanba's ridicule is directed at aberrant types, not at the society that defines them as aberrant. Still, though his satire remains within such bounds as these, Sanba seems to be warning us that we are all capable of saying things and acting in ways that leave us open to mockery: not, perhaps, a very highly developed critique of human nature, but one that serves Sanba well as a basis for comic writing.

The first work of this group to appear was *Hayagawari mune no karakuri* (Quick changes of heart), which takes as its central metaphor the fast costume changes that were a staple bit of flashy *kabuki* performance practice at the time. In many plays, a single popular actor might display his virtuosity in as many as six or seven different roles; Sanba borrowed this idea as a metaphor for the way in which a single individual sometimes exhibits sudden changes of personality—the seemingly self-effacing wife who becomes a ranting harridan, the repentant, introspective hangover victim whose first "medicinal" morning-after cup of *sake* turns him into an abusive bully, the modest country girl who suddenly begins acting like the mistress of the household in which she serves. Most of the sketches in *Hayagawari mune no karakuri* are monologues similar to those of *Namaei katagi,* but a few are in dialogue form.

This work, like *Kyakusha hyōbanki,* suffers for being perhaps a little too clever. Its opening pages are designed and illustrated to be cut along a horizontal center line so that the top half of one illustration can be aligned with the bottom half of another, for comic effect (a shop assistant, for instance, fully dressed and standing behind a counter on which an account book is spread, when the cut page is turned, raises his skirts and reveals a pile of watermelon slices hidden between his legs). Included also are several pages of paper-doll cutouts with multiple costume changes. The purpose of such gimmickry is obscure. Clearly enough, it is modeled on children's toys and is consistent with the controlling metaphor of the work, the quick change. But *Hayagawari mune no karakuri* is not a children's book, and these visual puns on the quick-change theme seem a little obvious and heavy-handed. The same graphic device, however, was used the same year in a *gōkan* written by Kentei Bokusan and illustrated by Bokutei Tsukimaro,[52] and in his introduction to the first edition of *Hayagawari mune no karakuri* Sanba notes that such pictures, popular in his youth but long out of fashion, had recently been revived with great success by Utagawa Toyokuni (who illustrated this work of

Sanba's).[53] It seems likely that it was Toyokuni's success with "quick-change pictures" (*hayagawari-e*) that inspired Sanba's work, not the reverse; as we have seen, Sanba was extremely sensitive to fads and fashions in the *gesaku* marketplace. The work seems to have been a popular success. Sanba calls it a "big hit" (*ōatari*) in *Shikitei zakki,* and it was reprinted several times and ultimately reissued under a new title.[54] Sanba and Toyokuni had clearly assessed the market correctly.

Modern readers may be puzzled and indeed put off by the seemingly unnecessary and pointless interweavings of disparate literary and visual elements that characterize works like *Kyakusha hyōbanki* and *Hayagawari mune no karakuri;* yet, they were obviously not only tolerated but welcome in their day. The paper dolls and trick pictures of the latter work should be viewed in the light of a larger tradition in *gesaku* of serving up adult reading matter in forms outwardly reminiscent of children's books—the *kibyōshi* was, after all, in its origins a kind of adult fiction, usually satiric, presented in the format of the older *akahon* and *aobon,* at the time associated with juvenile fiction and fairy tales. Throughout their history, the *kibyōshi* and the *gōkan* had split personalities. Some works in these categories were clearly written with an adult audience in mind, but many others could only have been intended for juvenile or adolescent readers. With text visually subordinated to pictures and printed largely in *kana,* all *kusazōshi* looked like children's books. To present writing intended for sophisticated adults in such a format was to establish an intentional dissonance between the medium and its content—an act of parody. The elaborate machinery of the actors' critique and the intrusive and seemingly irrelevant presence of the fox-skin story in *Kyakusha hyōbanki* and the cut-outs of *Hayagawari mune no karakuri* are not simple mercenary, market-minded gimmickry. They are further evidence, if any is needed, of the omnipresence of the parodic impulse in *gesaku* fiction.

Shijūhachikuse (Forty-eight nasty habits)[55] was published in four parts between 1812 and 1818. This work is made up of wholly independent sketches of people with certain undesirable habits or idiosyncrasies. A total of only twenty sketches out of the promised forty-eight ever appeared, among them pieces like "Worrying about Every Little Thing," "Making Everything a Lot of Work," "The Wife Who Puts Down Her Husband," or "Making

Fun of Other People Behind Their Backs." Several of these sketches, Honda suggests, are among the best things Sanba ever wrote; they are vignettes of life in the *uranagaya*, "back-alley tenements," the long, low multi-family houses that filled the alley-laced interiors of city blocks in Edo.[56] "Cataloguing Other People's Faults" (*Shijūhachikuse* I:7) is a representative example; in the translation that follows, the speakers are distinguished by "bullets" of different shape, the modern printer's equivalent of the solid and open circles, triangles, and other marks used for the same purpose in Sanba's works:

● Okichi-san, are you home?

▲ Oh! Is that you, Otoku-san?

● I'm just back from the bath.

▲ Really, you're too much—wait a minute—you might have thought to go with me!

● I know, but I *can* manage on my own, you know.

▲ Never mind, never mind. How about some white?

● "White." What's that? I haven't ever drunk anything called "white."

▲ All right, I'll lower myself: "white *sake*."

● Oh, no! Now *dry* sake—*that* I can put away a *shō* at a time.

▲ Oh, ugh!

● "Oh, ugh" yourself! Listen—did you put out any dolls?

▲ Mm. Look at this. (She arranges a set of tiny dolls on a butterfly-leg serving tray).

● Oh, they're *darling!* They're so tiny they look like they'd fit in your eye. And look at that darling lantern. Oh! It has something scribbled on it, did you notice? Huh—"A childless woman," something, something, "doll show sad." What's that supposed to mean?

▲ No, no. "A childless woman playing with dolls, how sad." That's what it says. My dear husband wrote that when he was drunk.

● Really—what does he mean by that! Maybe he means somebody else.

▲ I didn't know what I was getting into, but here I am. I *would* like to be nicer to him, I guess, but—I *do* have a little girl, don't I? If the seed's not there, as they say. What can you do, you know?

● Well, it *is* a mutual thing, after all. You know, this really is a lot better than putting out a lot of traditional dolls—they're so old-fashioned-looking.

▲ That's what I think, but then again when I see them at the doll shop I want them, too!

● I just don't want a bunch of half-naked little boys and "miniatures" cluttering things up. I'd much rather have a Five-man Band—a Shūgetsu or a Gyokuzan.

▲ Oh yes, yes! And I'd want the accessories, too. If I could set out a

Shūgetsu Five-man Band and all the accessories, I wouldn't want anything else in the world. It's so much trouble having a whole clutter of dolls, isn't it?

● Oh, listen, listen! Did you see the dolls at Omatsu's place?

▲ I did, I did!

● Honestly, I could hardly believe it. Really shameless! Before the festival she was bragging so much I guess I expected something special, but really, what *could* she have been thinking? So I just played dumb, you know, and I said, "Omatsu, is this what you were talking about, that big Court group?" She was so surprised she couldn't come up with one of her usual lines—she just turned bright red and said, "No, this isn't it. I gave *those* dolls to somebody else." That's how she tried to get out of it.

▲ She brags about everything—you can't take her seriously. Well, that's neither here nor there. How's the little muck-up? Everything straightened out?

● What little muck-up?

▲ You know, Okama-san, over at Hachi-san's.

● Mm. I'm afraid they're still at it.

▲ You're not really surprised, are you?

● Listen. Why did you call her a muck-up?

▲ That was just for you. It's just that she's so much like that "Muck-up" in that "Dreams of Meeting" thing by Kyōden.

● Hm, hm, hm. You're right. Did you hear how awful Hachi-san was the other night?

▲ No-o, I don't know anything about it. But they've been fighting for so long I'm not surprised. I still act perfectly innocent, as if I didn't know a thing.

● Just as well. It really isn't funny. This time, nobody else went over, so I had to, and I broke it up. I swear I simply don't know what to say about either of them. Hachi-san has a quick temper, but I must say Okama-san has an awfully quick tongue. Hachi-san was saying, "Listen to me! Don't blabber on about money like that in front of other people. 'Oh, I just spent a few dribs and drabs,' you say, 'just five or ten *ryō*.' Don't be such a snotty show-off. It's still *money*, you know. There you are, your fat little face practically made of sweets, all puffed up like you swallowed the south wind. Here I've been behaving myself all year, and I'm about to be done in paying for all your 'medicines.' I've heard of lazy women, but *oh*, you're worthless—getting the laundry to do everything for just the two of us! I haven't figured it out, but they must take thirty-two or maybe even fifty *mon* just for a singlet. And the corridors and such, they don't even see a dust rag except for the big seasonal cleanings. The kitchen isn't any bigger than a cat's forehead, but you never clean it, you just let everything rot. The breakfast dishes pile up until it's time for lunch, and you don't clean out the kettle at night before you use it the next day, so stuff builds up in there all year long. I get to drink crust left over from the year before last every time you heat the pot. And there are still beans from the *setsubun* festival from the year *before* the year before last sitting in the oil pan of the lantern. They're so swollen up they look like broad beans, but we've been through two big cleanings since then and you didn't even touch them. You just plant yourself by the brazier and you don't even mind the soot all over the cupboard, you just scribble in it with your finger. What kind of attitude is that? You're just a housewife, so you don't have to be particularly sexy or romantic, but honestly—you let your eyebrows grow out, and your tooth black keeps coming off. You pat your hair into place once in a while, I guess, but look at you! With your kimono looking like you store it in an oil jug. . . . They say Japan is a big place, but even a pair of iron sandals wouldn't carry somebody far enough to find a slut the likes of you. No matter how nice a husband I was I'd be fed up with you by now." Isn't that awful? He was just vicious.

▲ My goodness! You remember it all—and such a long story.

● Well, I ought to! Hachi-san sort of specializes in being nasty. I hear it coming from next door all the time, so I don't have to try to remember it, I just do! Ah, well—oh, by the way, I notice the landlord's new wife isn't very nice, either.

▲ No—she certainly thinks a lot of herself, doesn't she! But you can't expect her to be like his last wife, can you?

● I wonder what she thinks a landlord is, anyway! Such a damned busybody.

▲ Every time she comes out into the street she walks along peeking into people's houses. What do you think she's up to?

● She's finding out how well off they are, that's what. You know, no matter what she looks like she's really old, that woman is. Somebody told me she has three kids, you know. They say she left them with an uncle and came here pretending she didn't have any. A landlord may have his tenants, but this one's really got his hands full now! It's enough to make you cry.

▲ I know, I know. We've had four here that we've sent out to other people, little ones, too, but what are you going to do?

● You know that girl they call "Onabe the heiress"? She really has a sharp tongue.

▲ I know, you have to watch yourself. She's terrible.

● You're telling me! I hear Otako-san from the Yorozu-ya out front is back for a visit, by the way. Why don't they send her around the *nagaya*? I'm sure she's made the rounds up front.

▲ They act like they can't stand to have anything to do with us, just because we live around back. I wish they'd cut it out. They always put us down because we're "the people in the back," but we're all tenants, aren't we? It's not as if they're making up the odd penny or so that we don't pay. That Otako-san, even when she was still at home she was stuck up and inconsiderate. I can just imagine what she's like now that she's been out serving in some big house.

• Oh, I know. It's awful. But you know, I ran into her yesterday when she was seeing off the *nagaya* watchman, and believe it or not she was a lot nicer. On the other hand, she's *really* gotten *fat!*

▲ She was *always* fat, you know.

• But she's such a *slug* now, or whatever. I don't know what to call her. When she walks along she looks like she's just about to roll over.

▲ I haven't heard anything about it for a while—has she given up the *samisen?*

• I hear she's all thumbs. Oh—didn't you tell somebody you got an earful of some of her awful *koto* playing?

▲ It's pretty twangy, I'll admit. Her parents are so silly. They just dote on her.

• Speaking of doting on people, whatever happened to that priest you liked so much that sang *saimon* ballads? He hasn't come by for while.

▲ I know. I like *saimon,* but *Shinnai-bushi* is so much better! *He*'ll be along any time now.

• You give him a hundred *mon,* too?

▲ "To each other a hundred we give—"

• And he's not a "Dōjōji priest!"

▲ No wonder my husband complains!

• They *always* complain, even though there are always expenses. Not that you waste money, mind you.

▲ Yes, but there's waste and then there's waste!

• Still, when you know *everybody*'s husband has his own little vices—they really should let us do what we want when they're away, once in a while. Listen—there's a new sea-eel place up off the main street. Oio-san went yesterday to take a look, and she says it's pretty good. Do you want to go?

▲ Let's go, let's go. I think I've four hundred or so tucked away in the drawer of my sewing box that I managed to put aside.

• And you say you need a bigger allowance! Change a couple of *shu* for me, won't you? It doesn't go very far, though, does it?

▲ You're telling me! Well, I should start getting lunch ready.

• Oh, it's still early. Take it easy for a while. If you rush around like that you'll need a cane by suppertime!

▲ Don't say that! When the sun gets around to there, it's lunchtime.

• Hmm—why hasn't that blabbermouth vegetable man been around yet—
(Wiping her lips with her right sleeve, she knocks the ash out of her long pipe).[57]

In the course of this seemingly aimless, unstructured series of conversational exchanges, two distinct personalities gradually take shape: Otoku-san, the visitor, reveals herself to be a sharp-tongued gossip; Okichi-san, her hostess, while not unopinionated, is more tolerant. Okichi-san is made uncomfortable by her friend's unremitting criticism of other people, and is at pains to deflect the conversation in a more serious direction. Thus we learn of her own domestic unhappiness, her resentment of the people living "out front" in the more fashionable tenements, her willingness to see her husband's point of view about her spending her household money as alms for the *Shinnai-bushi* balladeer. Otoku-san, for her part, refuses to let her friend take charge of the conversation. She unsympathetically changes the subject whenever Okichi-san makes a tentative effort to talk about herself or to head off another spurt of nastiness. (Otoku-san's long-winded imitation of Hachi-san berating his wife—which allows her to command center stage while skewering two victims at once—follows immediately on a futile effort by Okichi-san to suggest that Hachi-san's and Okama-san's squabbles are none of their business.) When Okichi-san ventures an attack of her own on Otako-san, the girl from "out front" who is back on a visit from the "big house" where she is now in service, Otoku-san rushes to contradict her: the girl is actually "a lot nicer" now, at least to Otoku-san.

In this piece, Sanba's ostensible purpose is to draw satiric aim on the habit some have of "cataloguing other people's faults"; that purpose he surely achieves, but in the process he gives us something more, a splendid picture of life in an anonymous corner of Edo. Sanba intrudes only twice as narrator, once to clarify physical movements ("She arranges a set of tiny dolls. . . .") and again at the end to put the piece in a frame, withdrawing us from the scene in a conversational pause with a description of Otoku-san, evidently settling in for a while longer, wiping her lips on her sleeve and emptying her pipe. Yet the time and place could not be clearer: we learn that it is a lazy day in early summer (the dolls suggest that it is not long before the doll festival on the 5th day of the 5th month), probably mid-morning, and the sun is out; the setting is Okichi-san's apartment, only too obviously in a "rear" tenement. We learn not only where the women live, but also their place in the social microcosm of the block: that is, at the bottom of the local hierarchy headed by the landlord and occupied above them by the people who live "out front."[58] Sanba gives us clues that suggest Okichi-san is, or wants to appear to be, a little higher in the local pecking order than Otoku-san—her self-conscious attempts at sophisticated wit, her attraction to traditional dolls, her distaste for her visitor's gossipy, slatternly ways. (In the original, Okichi-san's speech is more refined that Otoku-san's, which is markedly more slangy and colorful.) Sanba had at his command sensitivities and skills a novelist might envy, but the traditions of fiction in his day limited his notions of how they might be put to use—his portraits, however skillfully drawn, are self-contained and static, never subordinated to a larger plan or plot.

Ningen banji uso bakkari (In human affairs, nothing but lies), the third in this subgroup of Sanba's works, examines the white lies and minor deceptions that complicate human intercourse in six sketches consisting of monologues or dialogues depicting the original lie-filled transactions followed by after-the-fact comments by the participants on what was really on their minds at the time. The third sketch, for instance, "The Lies of the Man of Elegance" ("Gajin no uso"), begins with a dialogue between two connoisseurs of the finer things of life who have gone out on a snow-viewing excursion. Their conversation consists mainly of efforts to outdo each other in their appreciation of the beauties of the snowy landscape through references to classical poetry and popular songs and other evidences of their mastery of the arts and pastimes required of an elegant man of the world. They part, and we are next shown them in their respective homes, huddled under heavy quilts by the brazier. The first is muttering:

Oh, I'm cold . . . Hey! Hurry up and fix me my hot bean curd. Put some more charcoal in the brazier, too. . . . I'm still shivering. Oh, I feel terrible. Never again will I go out "snow viewing," for goodness' sake! I can't think of anything less elegant. What could be more elegant, after all, than sitting by the brazier at home with some hot bean curd and warm *sake?* I thought I was going to burst out crying right there in the middle of Mukōjima, but I managed to hold out and not embarrass myself in front of Kottō. And then to rub it in, the damned snow started coming down harder than ever . . . Come on! Hurry up with the bean curd!

The second connoisseur, hunched over his own brazier, is shown complaining loudly:

I've never *seen* so damned much snow as I did today. That damned Gyūkotsu kept pestering me about "snow viewing," so I finally gave in in spite of myself, but it just kept coming down and we got soaked to the skin . . . Snow's snow, whether you look at it from a verandah or your back stoop . . . I must say I've learned my lesson about "elegance." Give me a boor any day. Even a boor can look at snow and tell it's white and cold. If being elegant meant you could look at it and think it was black and warm, that'd be one thing, but what the hell, it's still the same damned stuff, so you might as well be elegant staying home with a hot bowl of blowfish soup. Wow, I'm *still* shivering.[59]

In sketches like these and the others—"Lying About How Handsome He Is," "The Lies of the Young Man Who Hates Women," "The 'The-Past-Was-Better' Lie," and two others—Sanba's cynicism is in full view. The "changes of heart" of the characters in *Hayakawari mune no karakuri* take place sequentially, and are thus little more than illustrations of human predictability, but the characters in *Ningen banji uso bakkari* are treated simply (though sympathetically) as hypocrites who say one thing while thinking another. *Hitogokoro nozoki karakuri* (A mechanism for peering into the human heart), the fourth title in this subgroup, is written around the same simple notion, the contrast between what one says and what one thinks. This work borrows its title and its central conceit from one of Sanba's first *kibyōshi, Ningen isshin nozoki karakuri* (1794),[60] but is constructed of a series of five dialogue-based vignettes, each consisting of two scenes showing the "front" and "back" of a character's personality—the man who praises domesticity and his wife's cooking to her face, but damns them both behind her back when he is out carousing; the charlatan who flaunts his learning in front of his patients, but sweats in private over his ignorance of real medicine and his fear of being found out; the housewife who splurges on a treat of grilled potatoes for herself and a friend next door, only to offer them to the husband she has been bad-mouthing all afternoon when he unexpectedly returns. (Honda praises this last sketch as another example of Sanba's skill at depicting the lower-middle-class world of the *uranagaya*.)[61]

The last work in this group is *Kokon hyakubaka* (A hundred fools, ancient and modern, 1814),[62] composed, despite its title, of only four relatively lengthy sketches of types of fools, all "modern": the husband who lets his wife make a fool of him, the bad chess player who gets angry when he loses, the teahouse jester who scolds the customers for their improvident ways, and the man who prides himself on being able to eat inhumanly large quantities of food. The first sketch is particularly effective, perhaps because it has a certain universality that is lacking in the others, which are dependent for their humor on specifically Japanese situations and attitudes to an extent that makes them often either tedious or incomprehensible to a modern Western reader.

If *Namaei katagi* stands out among his *katagimono*-like works and if *Shijūhachikuse* is the best of his *kokkeibon* that concern themselves with quirks and twists of personality, then *Gejō suigen maku no soto* (Theater chic this side of the curtain) is the most interesting of the four works that make up the third group of Sanba's dialogue-based *kokkeibon,* those that take as their subject a specific subculture. This work attempts to recreate the rich atmosphere surrounding the great theaters of Edo, principally the Nakamuraza. Its primary focus is on the members of the typical theater audience as they reveal themselves in conversation, but its field of vision extends far beyond that of works like *Kyakusha hyōbanki* to include not only the people in the audience but also the vendors and hawkers inside and outside the theater itself and life in the streets surrounding the theater. There is a far greater proportion of narrative description in this work than in *Namaei katagi,* which appeared the same year; it is the first of Sanba's *kokkeibon* to attempt a strong sense of "place." In this it foreshadows strongly *Ukiyoburo* and *Ukiyodoko,* both of which devote much attention to evocations of the atmosphere of their fictional neighborhood and to the physical arrangements of the bathhouse and the barbershop in ways reminiscent of those seen in *Gejō suigen maku no soto.*

Namaei katagi shows clearly how the *kokkeibon* benefited from contact with the arts of the stage storyteller, but this work shows that the influence of the *sharebon* remained equally strong in the development of the "mainstream" *kokkeibon,* for in a sense *Gejō suigen maku no soto* is basically a *sharebon* that has shifted its focus away from the pleasure quarters to the world of the theater. Honda traces in it the clear influence of several specific *sharebon,* although a more immediate model was probably *Kyūkanchō* (discussed previously), which itself also shows the strong influence of the *sharebon.* (Both works pay much attention to the figure of the rustic theatergoer as a device for satiric commentary on the theater world.)[63]

The world of the theater is the setting for the other three works in this group, *Kyōgen inaka ayatsuri* (A puppet troupe in the countryside, 1811),[64] *Inaka shibai chūshingura* ("The treasury of loyal retainers" on tour in the countryside, 1813-1814),[65] and *Shirōto kyōgen monkirigata* (The archetypal amateur theatrical, 1814).[66] The first two are set in the provinces and the last in Edo, but all three, like *Gejō suigen maku no soto*, pay close attention to "local color," the physical and human surroundings of the events that are their principal focus. These works differ, however, from the rest of Sanba's *kokkeibon* in that they are structured around "plots." All consist mainly of dialogue, but in principle, at least, the conversations are intended to advance the action, not merely to evoke atmosphere and to portray amusing character types. *Inaka shibai chūshingura* and *Kyōgen inaka ayatsuri* have essentially the same plot: the arrival of a touring troupe in a small town, the preparations for the performance, the performance itself and the reactions of the audience; *Shirōto kyōgen monkirigata* describes the preparations leading up to an amateur theatrical performance sponsored by a wealthy Edo merchant.[67] Despite their reliance on rudimentary plots, however, these works do not differ radically from Sanba's other *kokkeibon;* one senses that most of Sanba's energy went not into their simple story lines but, as usual, into the conversational interludes that were his real forte. His principal interest here, as in *Gejō suigen maku no soto*, was in recreating the unique atmosphere of a particular subculture through verbal self-portraits of its members.[68]

CHAPTER FIVE

Ukiyoburo and
Ukiyodoko

The first book of *Ukiyoburo* (The bathhouse of the floating world), the work that would earn Shikitei Sanba his lasting reputation, appeared during the spring publishing season of the 6th year of Bunka—that is to say, either late in 1808 or early in 1809, since, as the competition in commercial publishing became more intense, works that were nominally spring publications had tended increasingly to appear well before the lunar New Year, the traditional beginning of spring in Japan. (Given the amount of time necessary to carve the printing blocks, this means that Sanba finished his manuscript probably no later than the spring or early summer of 1808.) *Ukiyoburo* and its sister work *Ukiyodoko* (The barbershop of the floating world, 1813-1814) are by far the best known and most often reprinted of Sanba's works.[1] Along with Jippensha Ikku's *Tōkaidōchū hizakurige* (1802-1814, translated by Thomas Satchell as *Shanks' Mare*),[2] and Takizawa Bakin's *Nansō Satomi hakkenden* (Tale of the eight "dogs" of the Satomi clan, 1814-1841), these books are probably the best remembered of all the vast number of works of fiction published in the late Edo period. Although, without a doubt, *Hizakurige* eclipses the others in enduring popularity in modern Japan, *Ukiyoburo* and *Ukiyodoko* continue to be read and enjoyed. (A reading of extended portions of *Ukiyoburo* was broadcast not long ago on radio on the cultural channel of NHK, the Japanese national broadcasting service; and the popularity of *Ukiyodoko* is evidently such that a major publisher has seen potential profit in bringing out a modern Japanese translation of the work.)[3]

This chapter will treat both *Ukiyoburo* and *Ukiyodoko*, but will deal with the latter work primarily in relation to *Ukiyoburo,* which is the better known of the two; much of what can be said about *Ukiyoburo* applies equally to *Ukiyodoko,* which may be regarded almost as a sequel to the earlier work, allowing for certain important differences between the two.

Of the textual development and publishing history of both *Ukiyoburo* and *Ukiyodoko* little need be said beyond a recitation of the bare facts of publication, since no manuscript drafts are known, and the variations among pre-Meiji editions are minor and attributable simply to the idiosyncrasies of the woodblock carvers rather than to the revising hand of the author. Because the original blocks from which Book I of *Ukiyoburo* was printed were destroyed in a fire in spring 1809, a second edition of that part of the work, printed from newly carved blocks, was published in 1820,[4] but this single instance of an entirely new edition of one of his works issued during his lifetime shows no evidence of revision or emendation by Sanba himself. A brief publisher's afterword present in the first edition was dropped from the second, but otherwise the two versions are virtually identical: Sanba seems to have been content to ignore this opportunity to improve upon his original effort. The versions of Book I in the modern texts of *Ukiyoburo* edited by Nakamura Michio and Jinbō Kazuya cited in the Translator's Note immediately following the translation are based respectively on the edition of 1820 and the now exceedingly rare 1809 edition; but the differences between the two texts are so minor that only scholarly protocol dictates calling Jinbō's edition the definitive text of this portion of the work.

In format as well as in content, *Ukiyoburo* and *Ukiyodoko* are very similar, although *Ukiyodoko,* in two books, is considerably shorter than *Ukiyoburo* in four. Each book opens with one or more introductory sections by Sanba or other writers, usually in *kyōbun* style, and some close with afterwords of one kind or another; all were published originally in two or more individual volumes (the second and succeeding volumes of a book, called "parts" in this discussion, are simply continuations and contain no prefatory material), and all conclude with advertisements for Sanba's medicine shop and publishers' notices of forthcoming works. Compared to Sanba's *kibyōshi* and *gōkan,* *Ukiyoburo* and *Ukiyodoko* are not heavily illustrated: each book contains only a few full-page illustrations, uncaptioned and tied only loosely to events described in the text.

In its final form, *Ukiyoburo* consisted of nine fascicles or volumes (*satsu;* here, "parts") in four books (*hen*). The only organizational principle evident in the work overall is its basic division into sections treating separately the men's bath (Books I and IV) and the women's bath (Books II and III). In Book I, Sanba arranges his materials according to the time of day, a scheme that appeared occasionally in Kyōden's *sharebon.*[5] The rudiments of a similar structure are visible in Book II. But thereafter structural unity is provided only by the unchanging setting itself and by occasional author's interjections on the order of "Meanwhile, back in the dressing room . . ." or "Next to appear was a man in his early twenties . . ." which establish the simplest sort of transition between unrelated scenes and serve to reinforce the reader's awareness of the physical location of the various conversations. A character from an early scene in a book will sometimes reappear in a later scene, and once in a while conversational groups will overlap; but, generally speaking, the scenes of which each book is composed are discrete, unrelated units. (In the translation, independent scenes have been separated by a pair of asterisks; in the original, a short description written in a typographically distinctive double line of smaller characters and introducing the next scene often serves the same purpose.)

Ukiyoburo has sometimes been described as a kind of inside-out *Hizakurige:*

In *Hizakurige* the two main characters remain the same, but their constant travels provide them with a great variety of new situations; in *Ukiyoburo* the place, a public bath, remains the same, but the customers are constantly changing, producing a similar result.[6]

The unifying presence of the characters of Kitahachi and Yajirōbei throughout *Hizakurige* and the unity provided by setting *Ukiyoburo* in a public bath (or *Ukiyodoko* in a barbershop) are drastically different things, however. *Hizakurige* has no real plot, but it does tell a "story," that of its principal characters' progress up the Tōkaidō; *Ukiyoburo* has neither plot nor story. *Hizakurige*'s story is, to be sure, made up of a series of unrelated adventures experienced by Yaji and Kita, and *Ukiyoburo*'s scenes are likewise unrelated to each other; both works succeed in describing, largely through dialogue, an impressive array of different kinds of people; both are funny; but there their similarities end. The absence of a hero or set of heroes and Sanba's own brand of humor, so unlike Ikku's, make *Ukiyoburo* distinctly different from *Hizakurige.* The fact that *Ukiyoburo* is set in a single location does make for a certain kind of conceptual or atmospheric unity, but in the end it is a fragmented work, best approached as a succession of unrelated scenes—verbal genre paintings of town life—rather than in the expectation of finding anything resembling a novel in the usual sense of the word.

The scenes of which *Ukiyoburo* is composed may be broadly broken down into three general groups: those that evoke the atmosphere and surroundings of the bathhouse itself, those that portray inherently comic situations or people, and those that portray ordinary people in ordinary situations. All three types of scene are heavily dependent on dialogue and fit Bakin's description of the later *kokkeibon* as being "very like *ukiyomonomane*,"[7] his general term for entertainments based on oral mimicry; the techniques Sanba uses, however, vary according to the type of scene and seemingly derive from several different genres of oral storytelling as well as from literary sources. The discussion of these scene types that follows will be based on the portions of *Ukiyoburo* that are translated in the Appendix below. These translated portions (Book I, Part 1, and Book II, Part 1) are not fully representative of the whole of *Ukiyoburo,* but they do contain examples of all three scene types, even if certain types are more prevalent in these early sections of the work than in later books.

The first scene type is represented in the translation mainly by brief interludes that mark the passage of time: the description of the bathhouse sign and the early-morning sounds that open Part 1 of "The Men's Bath"; the hawkers' cries and the bathhouse manager's banter with the mendicants that are symbolic of the increasing bustle in the neighborhood; the brief interchange between the pot-mender and the anonymous local wag that closes the "morning" section and introduces the "noon" section; and the babble of mendicants that opens "The Women's Bath." Other examples are scenes or parts of scenes that focus on people and activities specific to a bathhouse: interchanges involving the bathhouse manager and the bath attendants and, of course, the lengthy description of the bustling interior of the bathhouse in a mixture

of *kyōbun* prose and quoted speech that appears in the introductory sections of "The Men's Bath."

These passages are the means by which Sanba establishes the
vital sense of place that unifies the otherwise disconnected scenes
of *Ukiyoburo*. Except for the passages in the introductions, all of
them are indeed constructed around the representation of voices
and sounds on paper, but their primary purpose is to establish an
atmosphere or a sense of the time of day rather than to portray
or to caricature the people who appear in them. While certainly
such passages as these are as indebted as any of the others to the
techniques of the stage mimic (particularly those that include
highly distinctive and easily imitated "types" such as the mendicants or the street vendors), they are more immediately derived
from the *sharebon* tradition, particularly the works of Santō
Kyōden, who perfected the *sharebon* as a genre dedicated in large
part to evoking the atmosphere and flavor of the pleasure quarter
rather than simply to portraying the behavior of its patrons and
denizens. Sanba was thoroughly familiar, of course, with this characteristic of Kyōden's work, which he imitated and developed
himself, first in *sharebon* like *Tatsumi fugen* and later in *kokkeibon* like *Gejō suigen maku no soto*. Sanba's methods are the same
in *Ukiyoburo*, but the effect is different, for his voices and sound
effects here summon into being not the exciting, exotic atmosphere
of the entertainment quarters but the utterly familiar world of a
middle-class Edo neighborhood.

Scenes of the second type, those that portray innately comic
characters or situations, are especially in evidence in Book One of
Ukiyoburo. Examples include the several scenes of which the
spastic Butashichi is a part, the scenes with the retired gentleman
and the doctor, the bath attendant Sansuke's story of the yam
that turned into an eel, and the final scene in which the man from
the western provinces washes his face with a soiled loincloth.

These scenes are the closest of any in the entire work to the
stock routines of the storytellers. Sansuke's story and the loincloth routine both close with readily identifiable punch lines
(*ochi*) based on puns, and seem very close to standard *rakugo*
stories. The other scenes are not so obviously related to stage
comedy, but it is easy, nevertheless, to imagine them as oral performances. They all center on characters whose unusual personalities and speech habits would make them prime objects for oral

caricature. In this respect they may be seen as being of a type with the portraits of drunks in Sanba's *Namaei katagi,* which likewise derive their humor from atypical speech and abnormal behavior. The figures of Butashichi (very similar to a drunk, in terms of his erratic speech and behavior), the retired gentleman, and the doctor (as well as Sansuke and the man from the western provinces) are all very much like the stock figures that might appear in story-tellers' routines because of the ease with which such characters can be imitated and because they are innately funny. The kind of humor that all these scenes contain is readily understandable: it depends on wordplay, exaggerated quirks of character or speech, or ludicrous situations. It is in such scenes that *Ukiyoburo* is most like *Hizakurige,* whose humor comes in the main from similar sources—the puns and other linguistic games played by Yaji and Kita and subsidiary characters, the silly predicaments the heroes find themselves in, and a general atmosphere of slapstick mayhem. Neither Sanba nor Ikku betrays any extraordinary viciousness in his portrayals of defective or abnormal characters, but the author's stance both in *Hizakurige* and in these scenes from *Ukiyoburo* is that of a comedian whose job necessarily requires on occasion an uncharitable bit of mockery or condescension.

Such scenes are bound to provoke laughter, and Sanba's intent throughout *Ukiyoburo* was certainly to amuse his readers; but, unlike *Hizakurige,* Sanba's work is not on the whole dependent on this sort of obvious comedy for its humor. Book I, inspired by Sanshōtei Karaku's *rakugo* stories and perhaps conceived in part as Sanba's answer to the great popularity of *Hizakurige,* contains a rather high proportion of such insistently comic scenes, but the succeeding books consist almost entirely of scenes that belong in the third category established above, those that involve ordinary people in ordinary situations. The laughter these scenes provoke is gentle and slow in coming; one smiles at recognizing familiar types who reveal their inconsistencies and weaknesses gradually and unconsciously, instead of laughing at ridiculous people doing foolish things. In much of Book I and in most of the rest of *Ukiyoburo,* Sanba eschewed the cheap shot in favor of a subtler and more difficult kind of humor that created its own universal "types" instead of relying on the preexisting stock of comic stereotypes. Sanba's characters may remain types rather than fully developed individuals, but it does his art a disservice to say that he dealt merely in stereotypes. The difference is a subtle one, as minor but as vital as the distinction in English prose between definite and indefinite articles or lower- and upper-case letters: a representative character from "The Women's Bath," for instance, begins as an old woman complaining about her daughter-in-law's slovenly housekeeping but gradually becomes, in Sanba's portrayal, The Old Woman Who Thinks Her Daughter-in-Law a Slut.

Much of the appeal of Sanba's *kokkeibon* must have come from this ability of his to recognize universal types in unremarkable, ordinary people; his sketches are funny, not because they are about funny people doing funny things, but rather because they show us that the normal behavior of people in general, when put in a frame and hung on a wall, can be funny. We laugh when Jippensha Ikku points a finger at Yajirōbei and Kitahachi because he makes us think, Aren't they silly? When Sanba shows us a father speaking baby talk as he patiently guides his children through the rituals of the bath, we smile and exclaim, Isn't that the truth! *Hizakurige* and *Ukiyoburo* both remain popular because their humor is universal, but it is universal in very different ways. Donald Keene is right to distinguish the comic fiction of Ikku and Sanba from that of earlier writers:

The kibyōshi and sharebon of Santō Kyōden are read today only by specialists in the literature of the period, but the works of later gesaku authors like Jippensha Ikku and Shikitei Samba are still popular because their humor is derived not from the peculiar (and now vanished) atmosphere of the licensed quarters but from the lives of the common people.

He obscures an essential difference between Sanba's work and Ikku's, however:

When somebody in a novel has a bucket of excrement dropped over his head the effect is neither subtle nor literary, but the situation remains impervious to time. [8]

The humor of Book I certainly inclines to the sort of effects Keene describes: excrement is one of Butashichi's torments in his opening scene, and buckets appear, naturally enough for a bathhouse, in various scenes; more generally speaking, subtler humor, less dependent on comic mayhem but still recognizably similar to that of *Hizakurige,* is much in evidence in this part of *Ukiyoburo.* But, beginning with Book II, slapstick, puns, and mockery give way to sympathetic caricature and irony, qualities that not only set *Ukiyoburo* apart from *Hizakurige* but allow us to rank Sanba with Ihara Saikaku as one of the most accomplished of Japanese comic writers.

The later books of *Ukiyoburo* and much of *Ukiyodoko* consist in large part of scenes of a type represented in the translation by, as one example, the conversation in Book I between Hachibei and Matsuemon about the fallen playboy and his miserly father: scenes that both reveal the personalities and concerns of the speakers (here, the "types" of the young father trying to make his way in the world and the experienced, advice-filled elder) and at the same time relate, through the content of the conversations, to the larger world outside the bath. Such conversations—*seken-banashi*, "talking about the world," that is, gossiping—were surely the most common sort to be heard in bathhouses and barbershops, natural centers for collecting and passing on local news; in this sense, *Ukiyodoko* and the later books of *Ukiyoburo* may be said to re-create more realistically the atmosphere of their settings than either *Hizakurige* or Book I of *Ukiyoburo*. But Sanba here has done far more than simply to "record aimless gossip about incidents of daily life, the theater, and the brothels";[9] he has instead given us a collective portrait of a highly verbal society of storytellers whose stories, *hanashi*, whether merely gossipy or more calculated in effect, provided both entertainment and an opportunity for self-exposition.

These scenes do indeed seem more realistic than those built around structured comic routines, but they ring true because of their generally commonplace content, not because they seem recorded verbatim by a stenographer. Rarely in the real world, for example, even in a world that values a good story, can a speaker succeed in monopolozing a conversation to the extent that Sanba's purveyors of *seken banashi* usually do; these characters are simultaneously patrons of the bathhouse or barbershop and storytellers in their own right, narrating mini-tales that have nothing to do with the locale in which they are told and often requiring nothing of their fictional audience other than their presence, signified only by an occasional grunt of agreement or a brief request for clarification. Here again we can see the influence of the storytellers and comics of the *yose* theaters: *Ukiyodoko* in particular often reads like a montage of discrete *rakugo* or *rakugo*-like stories connected by more realistic bits of dialogue.[10] It is a measure of Sanba's artistry that even the most highly structured of these embedded stories do not obtrude unnaturally in the meandering flow of cónversation, whether they are comic yarns like Sansuke's tale of the yam that turned into an eel or cautionary retailings of urban gossip. Their presence in any case gives Sanba's masterpieces an erratic but pleasing texture as we are carried back and forth between aimless (if amusing and revealing) chitchat and the more organized and purposeful *hanashi* of his storytelling characters.

Because both works consist so overwhelmingly of dialogue, the language of *Ukiyoburo* and *Ukiyodoko* is necessarily a highly naturalistic vernacular quite beyond what Bakin and other writers of the nineteenth century referred to as *zokubun*, "vulgar language," in its proximity to the actual spoken language of Edo. There being at the time no impetus, institutional or otherwise, toward the standardization of a written vernacular Japanese, Sanba was able unself-consciously to follow his ear in dialogue, unencumbered by the kinds of conventions and strictures that make, for instance, the natural and successful rendering of dialect in the mainstream of modern English and American fiction so very difficult. The result is prose that is uncommonly alive and varied in its accents, rhythms, and colorings, since it lies so close to the equally variable language of the people of Edo, a complex gathering of speakers with a broad range of regional and class dialects, accents, and argots.

The linguistic complexity of *Ukiyoburo* (largely obscured in translation) is heightened by the contrast between dialogue and descriptive or narrative passages. The latter are written in what must by default be called literary Japanese, but they are stylistically far removed from the consciously archaized *gabun* (elegant language) cultivated by Akinari and Bakin and less fastidiously by Sanba and his fellow *gōkan* authors. Such passages in *Ukiyoburo,* almost always set apart typographically from the dialogue in double columns of smaller characters (giving them almost the appearance of interlinear commentaries on a classical text), are most certainly archaic in their grammar. For the contemporary vernacular copular verbs *da* or *ja* (or respect-language *de gozaru* and its kin) we see nearly universally the old, status-neutral *nari;* for existential *aru,* the old conjugation *ari;* for *kara* expressing causality, locutions with *-eba* or *yue,* and for directional *kara,* "from," *yori;* for agentive or locative *de,* the historic *ni te;* for past tense *-da/-ta,* the unambiguously and emphatically classical *-ki.*

Such classical forms, however, are not elements of a full-blown classical narrative style. They appear, rather, in hybrid locutions like:

Kakā-tabane, nijū ni, san no otoko, sarashi no tenugui, tokorodokoro kuchibeni no tsukitaru o kata ni kake, hamigaki no fukuro o yōji ni te tsuranukishi o, hake no aida e hasami . . . neoki no mama ni te ku.[11]

(A man of twenty-two or -three, with a "Mama-done" hairdo, bleached-cotton towel slung over a shoulder and marked here and there with lip-rouge, tooth-powder bag skewered to his topknot with a toothpick . . . and just out of bed, arrives.)

Here, *tsukitaru o, yōji ni te, tsuranukishi o, ni te ku,* intermediate and final verb endings, and syntax are in the classical mode, but everything else is thoroughly contemporary, even slangy (*kakā-tabane,* "hairdo by Mama"). Such juxtapositions of eleventh-century grammar and nineteenth-century vocabulary should be jarring, but they are not. They are sanctioned, for one thing, by a long conservative tradition in prose style; more important, they serve, by virtue of their non-vernacular style, to make absolute the separation between the narrative voice and the self-expressive voices of the wholly autonomous characters who people *Ukiyoburo.* Even when the conversational flow demands only brief authorial interjections, Sanba usually keeps to neutral classical forms, in part because of their telegraphic brevity: *to iedomo kikoezu* (she says, but [the other] does not hear her).[12]

Not all of Sanba's interjections are purely classical (*to kiite, Saikokumono kimo o yabushite;* "so hearing, the man from the western provinces grows angry"),[13] but, even when they slide toward the vernacular (Edo *kiite* versus historical *kikite*), their terse simplicity and marked avoidance of status-marking inflections set them off absolutely from the dialogue. Passages like

Matsuemon to iu otoko, kofū ni fundoshi no sagari o ago e hasande shimete iru[14]

(A man called Matsuemon, tying his loincloth by tucking one end under his chin in the old manner)

foreshadow strongly what would become a standard narrative mode in the modern novel in which neutral verb endings like *-te* *iru* wholly obliterate any sense of status difference, real or putative, between author and characters or author and reader.

In spite of such surprisingly modern-sounding bits of description, however, Sanba's narrative style in *Ukiyoburo* and similar works could not in its entirety serve as an adequate model for modern novelists. Its mixtures of classical and vernacular locutions, and of straightforward, barebones description with irony-laden caricature, are stylistic chaos from the point of view of modern fiction, which demands above all consistency in narrative point of view. In a comic work like *Ukiyoburo,* however, such inconsistency need not be a vice. It is amusing in itself and highly apposite in a work that celebrates the variety and inconsistency of human behavior. It is also a manifestation of the irrepressible playfulness of the classic *gesaku* author, here as always defiantly refusing to let the reader ignore him.

One of the commonplaces of literary scholarship is that *Ukiyoburo,* published in 1809, was in part inspired by the success of *Hizakurige,* which began to appear in 1802; but there is a far clearer and more direct descent to be traced from Sanba's own experiments with *kokkeibon* very unlike Ikku's work. As we have seen, the direct inspiration for *Ukiyoburo* was, on Sanba's own testimony, the *rakugoka* Sanshōtei Karaku's stories of the public bath, but the work is also a natural next step out into middle-class Edo at large from the more specialized fictional worlds of drunks and theatergoers treated in *Namaei katagi* and *Gejō suigen maku no soto,* both published in 1806, and the pleasure-quarter subculture of Sanba's *sharebon. Ukiyoburo* is peopled by characters from all of these worlds and others; this diversity sets it apart from all his other works, including *Ukiyodoko* with its predominantly male cast.

Sanba's practiced skill at rendering the speech of this extraordinary range of different kinds of people makes *Ukiyoburo* a masterpiece of its kind. No amount of technical virtuosity, of course, could have made *Ukiyoburo* a successful work if Sanba's perception of human nature had been less acute, but the painstaking verisimilitude of his dialogue is one of its most striking qualities. In this, as in so many other things, Santō Kyōden was there before him: Kyōden remains by far the more important writer historically for having established authentic dialogue as an integral part of fiction. Sanba went beyond the master, however, in both the range of types of speech he attempted and the purposes to which he put his dialogue. Both writers reveled in virtuoso re-creations of class and regional dialect and subculture argot, but for Sanba the end of such performances was believable, self-revealing characterization, while Kyōden often seems to have been less inter-ested in his characters than simply in the way they spoke—a reflec-tion, perhaps, of the origin of the *sharebon* in works designed mostly to be read as handbooks of pleasure-quarter repartee.

Still, Sanba lavished extreme care on his technique—necessary care, in the event, because the realistic representation of dialogue was still very new. There existed at the time no real standard for spoken Japanese, let alone anything like the conventions that have crept into English-language fiction as a standard for dialogue, against which accurate representations of the most commonplace elisions and vagaries of even educated real speech look like con-trived and awkward excursions into dialect-writing. In Sanba's day, all dialogue-writing was in effect dialect-writing, since all forms of natural speech were equally distant from the norms of even the most "vulgar" written idiom. Sanba's challenge, then, was the one facing any author who has chosen to write in dialect: how to use the resources of the standard orthography, inevitably limited by custom and linguistic history, to represent sounds that have no conventional "spelling."

Writers like Sanba and Kyōden could build, of course, on ex-amples from the extensive dramatic tradition, which had long since used in its scripts a stock of conventions for representing natural speech. The terminal ejaculation normally pronounced and accurately transcribed as *na*, for instance, often appears as *nō* (*nou* in *kana* orthography) in *jōruri* and *nō* texts, a spelling in-tended to represent the lengthened and rounded *na* of female and ceremonious male speech heard by theatergoers as something like the English *gnaw*. Likewise *he, he, he, ho, ho, ho, ha, ha, ha,* for laughter, *ufu, ufu,* for weeping: such transcriptions are far from truly accurate phonetically (although within the limits of the writ-ing system they are comprehensible approximations), but by com-mon consent they were accepted and readily understood in the same tolerant spirit as *tsk, tsk, ahem, uh . . .* (British *er . . .*), or *hee-hee,* their kindred in English dialogue.

The language of *jōruri* and *kabuki,* however, was stylized and restricted in its variety and range by theatrical tradition, and it was not in any case necessary that a play-script supply more than a minimum of guidance to actor or *jōruri* chanter, on whom the responsibility for full characterization ultimately fell. Realistic dialogue in fiction, therefore, required further attention to phonetic accuracy in spelling, the establishment of consistent new renderings of speech sounds previously unrecorded or poorly represented. It was by no means the case, of course, that writers before Sanba, whether of fiction or of drama, had wholly neglected living speech or been unconscious of its evocative power; but Sanba stands out among his contemporaries—Kyōden, Ikku, Shunsui, and the *kabuki* dramatist Tsuruya Nanboku chief among them—in elevating linguistic realism to a conscious principle. Sanba often, for instance, substituted phonetic spellings for historical *kana* orthography, ostensibly because they were "easier for women and children to read," but also certainly because such "uncorrected" spellings reinforced visually the authentic immediacy of his dialogue.[15] He was far from consistent, however, in supplying modernized spellings, as often as not leaving untouched such traditional forms as *kaharu* for *kawaru*, *mahe* for *mae*, *yafu* for *yō*, and the like; still, by his more consistent avoidance of extreme traditional spellings like *mawosu* for *mōsu*, Sanba was arguing quietly for a rationalization of the increasingly archaic writing system.

If for Sanba any dialect was "standard" Japanese, it was that of educated, middle-class, native-born Edo, shaped both by the general phonology of eastern Japanese and by a thousand-year-old "reading tradition" that had established a general consensus with regard to the proper pronunciation of the most basic elements of the language as differentiated by the writing system. Still, even from this history-conscious and generally tolerant perspective, the writing system had certain built-in defects. To the Edo ear, for instance, an intervocalic *g* was properly nasalized, a sound like the medial *g* of standard English "ringing," the "ŋ" of the International Phonetic Alphabet; to convey properly the "non-standard" feeling of the "hard," non-nasalized -*g*- in non-Edo dialects, Sanba had recourse to a special diacritical mark evidently of his own devising, an outline version of the double dots used to convert *k*-syllables to *g*- syllables in the *kana* system. In certain places in Edo speech (and in other dialects), what was in the historically dominant system -*sa*- was pronounced *tsa*, a sound that could be rendered in *kana* only awkwardly by a combination of the graphs *tsu-a;* Sanba marked such *-sa-* syllables with the small circle or open dot otherwise used to convert *h/f-* syllables to *p-*.[16] Sanba's use of these new diacritical marks has left no traces in modern orthography, but they stand as testimony to his thoroughgoing commitment to phonetic accuracy. He did not use his *-tsa-* or *-g-* diacritics consistently, although even an occasional *-tse-* or *-tso-*, formed from *-se-* or *-so-* with the *p-* syllable circle, is also to be found in *Ukiyoburo.* One can only assume that he felt that *-tsua-*, *tsue-*, *-tsuo-*, with the second vowel usually written subscript, the alternative spellings, were sufficiently intelligible versions of *-tsa-*, *-tse-*, and *-tso-*. Likewise *she,* a non-Edo syllable that Sanba usually wrote with the *kana* for *shi* plus the archaic *we,* universally read *e:* he could count on his audience to divine a pronunciation by analogy with the standard *shiu* for *shū, chiu* for *chū,* and the like; that Sanba flirted at all with special ways of writing *-ts-* and non-nasalized *-g-* but was indifferent to *she* is not evidence of inconsistency, but rather of his special awareness of Edo language as a standard, for *-ts-* and the nasal *-ŋ-* were common in Edo dialects but rare in the Kamigata dialects, their chief rival, while *she* was provincial from both points of view. (The same can be said of *fuha/fuwa* and *fuwo* for *fa* and *fo,* as seen in the northern provincial speech of Sansuke in Book I of *Ukiyoburo* and elsewhere.)[17]

Given this desire to people *Ukiyoburo* with characters speaking a broad variety of dialects, Sanba had not only to find ways to represent their ways of speech accurately, but also to guarantee that what he had them saying would be intelligible to his readers. The Japanese writing system, in some ways a handicap, was for the latter purpose possessed of one very useful feature, the long tradition of using *kana* glosses written alongside Chinese characters to show their pronunciation. Sanba had merely to subvert the process, using such *furigana* to indicate not the standard but the dialect pronunciation of words written with Chinese characters. Or, in a further variation, he could supply "translations" for otherwise hard-to-understand passages in non-standard language written wholly in *kana,* as in his virtuoso (if rather cruel) portrayal of the spastic Butashichi that opens *Ukiyoburo* so memorably, where to the left of a virtually unintelligible utterance of Butashichi's like *namohonegyo totte, odemoku sabape, sabape toneta* he supplies a parallel gloss in a combination of *kana* and ideographs, *namu myōhō rengekyō totte, o-daimoku sanbyakuhen, sanbyakuhen tonaeta* ("'Hail the Lotus Sutra of the Wonderful Law'—I chanted the prayer three hundred times, three hundred times").[18] Such glosses would be wholly out of place in the modern Western narrative tradition, where they would represent a bizarre and intrusive confounding of narrative and editorial voices, but they are consistent with Japanese practice and therefore surprisingly unobtrusive. Takizawa Bakin has never, for instance, been taken to task for his even more complicated orthographic ornamentations: not infrequently in his *yomihon* one encounters a not necessarily uncommon string of ideographs glossed to the right—the usual position—with one reading, often idiosyncratic and chosen for atmospheric effect but still reasonably related to the meaning of the Chinese original, and to the left as well with a second reading, usually the dictionary standard but sometimes a second "translation" rather than simply a guide to pronunciation. It would seem that such glosses, which would in a more familiar tradition appear as footnotes or intrusive parenthetical asides, were an accepted convention of Japanese prose, even if to the modern eye they bespeak a philological obsessiveness out of place in fiction.

It was not as a philologist or linguist, however, but as a writer that Sanba devoted so much attention to these seemingly mundane matters of spelling and dialectology. Living in Edo, a city that was a magnet for immigrants and transients from all over Japan, entranced by the pungency of *rakugo* storytelling, and necessarily attuned like everyone else to the important social signals imbedded in the *keigo* respect-language system, Sanba could hardly fail to see speech as uniquely revealing of character—how you spoke said nearly as much about where you came from, what you did, what you thought of yourself, in short, who you were, as what you spoke about. It might just as well be said of any culture, not just nineteenth-century Japanese, that style and content are virtually inseparable aspects of conversation; what is special about *Ukiyoburo* and its author is Sanba's keen ear and the historical circumstances that gave him both a written language flexible enough to record the significant details of speech naturally and an audience free of preconceived notions of what written dialogue must look like.

If we can believe Sanba's preface, it was happy circumstance—sitting with his publisher as Sanshōtei Karaku told his stories of the public bath—that gave him the opportunity and inspiration to write *Ukiyoburo*. But happier still was the bathhouse setting itself. The public bath (*sentō, yuya, furoya*) in Sanba's day was an Edo institution. Other cities had such baths, of course, but not on such a scale. In Edo they numbered some 550 on the eve of the Meiji Restoration, and many boasted tubs large enough to accommodate twenty and more bathers at a time. Such figures were largely the result of economics, for land, firewood, and water in a city the size of Edo were commodities sufficiently scarce to make private baths out of the question for most householders; yet immigrants from less urban places (and Edo was a city of immigrants) found daily bathing a hard habit to part with, and so, by collecting a few coppers a day from each bather and exploiting the economies of scale, the *sentō* owner could both turn a profit and provide a welcome service.

The bathhouse quickly became not just a hygienic facility but a vital social institution, a natural daily (or for many a twice-daily) gathering-place where the full range of neighborhood social business could be transacted. In addition, the second floor of the bathhouse normally offered tea and light refreshments for a few coppers more, and a place to relax with conversation or a game of *go* or *shōgi*. Some bathhouses, most especially those near the entertainment districts and the post stations on the outskirts of Edo— Shinjuku, Shinagawa, Senjū—doubled as brothels, but that seems to have been the exception to the general rule. Most *sentō* were no doubt like Sanba's, upright neighborhood service institutions that observed the sorts of rules laid down by the Edo *machibugyō* city magistrates to govern their conduct that Sanba parodies in his introduction to Book One of *Ukiyoburo*, including the injunctions against mixed bathing. (Given how often the authorities reiterated that rule, it would appear that it was routinely violated, no doubt mainly because segregated facilities were simply uneconomical. Many *sentō* avoided legal sanctions by establishing men's hours and women's hours, the women usually being allotted time in the early forenoon and late at night, others by hanging a largely symbolic curtain across the middle of the tub. Dressing rooms were usually segregated at least to the same extent, although sometimes the appearance of modesty was maintained simply by having men and women enter a communal dressing room from opposite sides of the partition that separated the bathhouse manager from the facilities proper. It is by no means true that mixed bathing was

abolished only because of Western missionary protests after the
1860s; in a sense its final abolition in 1885 was simply the culmi-
nation of a very long campaign dating from as far back as the early
eighteenth century.)[19]

The title *Ukiyoburo* suggests that Sanba is writing about a public bath serving an idealized neighborhood as diverse as the "floating world" at large. Here *ukiyo* is being used in its broadest sense
to mean "urban life," the real world of the book-buying literate
classes as opposed to the world of romance and fantasy or the un-
imaginable private worlds of the highest social orders. *Ukiyo* most
certainly has also been used and understood as referring more nar-
rowly to the life of the entertainment quarters, and so takes on ad-
jectival meanings of "chic," "fashionable," "decadent," and even
"erotic," but there is little in *Ukiyoburo* or *Ukiyodoko* to hint
that Sanba had such meanings in mind. Although neither he nor
his publishers were likely to have been upset if some readers were
mistakenly attracted by the suggestive ring of the titles, the preface
to *Ukiyoburo* makes very clear that the publisher himself, from
the very beginning, ruled out a pleasure-quarter setting and even
stories about the pleasure quarters.

Sanba's *ukiyo* was therefore to be a more or less representative
Edo neighborhood. It could not have been physically far distant
from, say, the Asakusa entertainment district, to judge from the
occasional appearance of *geisha* and theater hangers-on, but it was
otherwise peopled generally by the straight middle class. The
lower classes are represented only occasionally and by characters—
street hawkers, bath attendants, mendicants, servants—who would
normally be present in such a neighborhood, not by the laborers,
bearers, or even thieves that inhabit the squalid corners of Edo
depicted by dramatists like Tsuruya Nanboku. The upper classes
do not patronize Sanba's bathhouse, probably as in life, for they
have their private baths or, if they are samurai, they bathe at communal facilities provided for them in their residential compounds;
they are offstage presences, however, as names to drop, people to
emulate, envy, fear, or just gossip about.

Ukiyoburo thus presents a somewhat truncated and sanitized
slice of life, but its world is surprisingly varied. Every age from
infancy to the very old, every region from Tōhoku to Kyūshū has
its representative. And, remarkably for a work of its time, the
sexes have equal time, two books for the men, two for the women;

Sanba's women are incisively and sympathetically treated in a collective portrait more detailed and lifelike than anything that had yet appeared in the fiction of the period. Sanba no doubt strove to include a wide variety of characters in *Ukiyoburo* partly because he was interested in giving himself an excuse to display his gift for dialogue; one wonders whether such a babble of dialogue and sometimes bizarre speechways was ever heard in a single place. But *Ukiyoburo* is also a celebration of Edo itself as metropolis, the premier city of Japan, predicated on the Edokko's not altogether unfounded but still in its way provincial pride in his city as national symbol of all the best that Japan could offer. What was more natural than that the idealized neighborhood served by Sanba's bathhouse should show in its very population how cosmopolitan Edo had become, how pleasantly exciting and varied life was in the city that shone with the luster of the Tokugawa house that had brought about peace and prosperity?

Sanba's vision of Edo in *Ukiyoburo* is a sentimental one. There are no suggestions here of the violence and grinding poverty that other sources tell us were facts of contemporary life. (There were no less than eight large-scale rural riots or rebellions recorded in 1809, when *Ukiyoburo* made its debut, an unusually quiet year in that respect.)[20] Nor have we any hint here of the frustration and discontent that common sense and instinct tell us the rigid and authoritarian style of *bakufu* rule must have engendered. But neither Sanba nor his readers thought of fiction as a medium for social protest; far from it. Even now fiction remains, except for a distinct minority of its readers and practitioners, a reassuring entertainment, a medium that confirms, if sometimes in roundabout ways, the conventional pieties, which do not include a vision of life as bleak and unsusceptible to improvement. And so on the human level, too, *Ukiyoburo* is a sentimental work, benign in its humor and inclined not to explore too deeply the real poignancy of the human situations that underlie the bathhouse chitchat.

Yet such a denial of the deeper emotions and of the darker side of urban life does not make *Ukiyoburo* an unrealistic work, for its chosen subject is not private but public conversation in a society that not only did not rebel against conformity and convention but embraced and affirmed them as positive cultural values. The public bath is, to be sure, a leveling institution, for the superficial distinctions of social rank come off with one's clothes, and a shared humanity is evident enough in the irregularities of the flesh; but that does not mean that everything is laid bare, in spite of Sanba's pronouncements in his introduction, "On the Greater Meaning of the Bathhouse of the Floating World," to the effect that no secrets can be maintained, no fraud concealed, in such surroundings. The "greater meaning" of the kind of relaxed social intercourse described in *Ukiyoburo* is precisely the way in which it softens the hard edges of life to allow both the individual and society at large to live with painful realities by submerging one's doubts and anxieties in a warm bath of mutual sympathy and reassurance.

What saves *Ukiyoburo* from being nothing but a sentimental display is Sanba's keen irony, deftly muted but omnipresent, underlying the entire conception of the work. The format of *Ukiyoburo* gave Sanba no opportunity to display the little hypocrisies and white lies of daily life in the clear but mechanical manner of later works like *Ningen banji uso bakkari* or *Hayagawari mune no karakuri;* but, by presenting his vignettes of bathhouse life virtually without commentary, as if they were snapshots in an album, Sanba was consciously adopting what was effectively an ironic stance. Few of his scenes are demonstrably satiric, save for set pieces like his portrait of the physician in Book I, but the cumulative effect of the unconnected scenes of *Ukiyoburo* is a satiric group portrait of the Edo citizenry as, one by one, two by two, they confirm the vision that underlay all Sanba's best work, his perception that no one is immune from the temptations of self-deception, rationalization, and self-aggrandizement at the expense of others. *Ukiyoburo* is finally a call for tolerance: if we are all equally unable to hide from the camera eye of the narrator, which has captured bits and pieces of all of us in the archetypes that people the bathhouse, we are not much entitled to exalt ourselves over others. Such is not the stuff of biting social criticism, since its final command is not "Repent!" but simply "Be nice."

But, in spite of the gentle, sentimental urging toward simple self-awareness and tolerance that shapes it, *Ukiyoburo* is a literary achievement of rare energy and sparkle, largely because of the extraordinary vividness of its portraiture. A work whose essential quality is seemingly so dependent on the very color and texture of the language in which it is written, whose characters seem to live only because of their lifelike speech, would appear to be a poor candidate for translation into English. The difficulties are certainly there. Assuming one has fully understood the original—not a hopeless task, thanks to unstinting Japanese scholarly annotation—how then to deal with the fine distinctions of class, sex, age, occupation, and regional dialect built into the text? Inevitably such niceties are overwhelmed by the utter foreignness of English and the exigencies of its conventions regarding dialogue. What makes an effort at translation neither quixotic nor arrogant is what makes *Ukiyoburo* a major work of art in the first place—its clarity of vision and the sharply drawn quality of its characterization, which even the grosser distortions of translation need not obscure.

Assuming, therefore, that what mattered to Sanba finally was not how his characters spoke but what their speech revealed about the kind of people they were, I have made little effort in the translations from *Ukiyoburo* that conclude this volume even to approximate the range of dialects and argots that give the work its superficial color, even though the author himself tended to favor intelligibility over stenographic accuracy in reproducing dialect speech. To do otherwise is simply impossible, since Japanese and English dialects or accents are inevitably incommensurable, although one can only admire the remarkable congruency that Thomas Satchell managed to create between a modified Cockney and the unregenerate Edokko speech of Yaji and Kita in his translation of Jippensha Ikku's *Hizakurige.* I have aimed instead at what is intended to be a generalized, contemporary, colloquial American English idiom, with minor adjustments for age, temperament, and sophistication, on the principle that the inevitable artificiality of my attempts at an English not my own would misrepresent the authenticity and incisiveness of Sanba's Japanese. At the risk of obscuring the genetic relationship between the *kokkeibon* and the *sharebon* and their joint debt to theatrical tradition, I have also converted the play-script-like format of *Ukiyoburo* to something more like that of traditional English narrative, presuming that one convention may safely be traded for another.

Notes to the Text

Abbreviations Used in the Notes

Honda, *SSB*	Honda Yasuo, *Shikitei Sanba no bungei* (Kasama Shobō, 1973).
KBZ	*Kokkei bungaku zenshū* series (Bungei Shoin)
Iwademo no ki	Takizawa Bakin, *Iwademo no ki,* in *Shin enseki jisshu,* ed. Kokusho Kankōkai, 5 vols. (Kokusho Kankōkai, 1913).
NKBT	*Nihon koten bungaku taikei* series (Iwanami Shoten)
NKBZ	*Nihon koten bungaku zenshū* series (Shōgakkan)
NMZ	*Nihon meicho zenshū: Edo bungei no bu* series, 30 vols. (Nihon Meicho Zenshū Kankōkai, 1926–1929)
Sakusha burui	Takizawa Bakin, *Kinsei mono no hon Edo sakusha burui* (preface dated 1834), in *Onchi sōsho* Vol. V, part 2, ed. Kishigami Misao (Hakubunkan, 1891).

Chapter One. Introduction

1. Nakamura Yukihiko, *Gesakuron,* pp. 17–80, offers a comprehensive discussion of the development of the concept of *gesaku* in China and Japan. Nakamura is one of the most incisive modern interpreters of the literature of the Edo period (1600–1868), and this study of the fiction of the latter half of the period has strongly influenced my interpretations of Sanba's milieu and works.

2. Ozaki Kyūya, *Kinsei shomin bungaku ronkō,* ed. Nakamura Yukihiko, pp. 87–90.

3. Yamazaki Fumoto, *Kaitei Nihon shōsetsu shomoku nenpyō,* ed. Shoshi Kenkyūkai, lists nearly 7,000 titles in all categories of *gesaku* fiction published between 1775 and 1868, counting as separate titles annual installments of serial works and new editions of earlier works. Since the listings in this pioneering bibliographical work, first published in 1929, are known to be somewhat incomplete (Introduction, pp. 2–3), this figure is open to challenge, but there is little doubt that it is of the right order of magnitude as an indication of the volume of publishing activity in this period. Between 1806 and 1815, Sanba's own most productive decade, Yamazaki lists an average annual output of some 119 fiction titles.

4. I have followed the example of most art and literary historians in the West in using the designation Edo period, after the seat of shogunal power, to refer to the years 1600 (or 1603) to 1867, known to scholars in other disciplines as the Tokugawa period after the ruling house. Donald Keene, in *World Within Walls,* pp. xi–xii, argues for "pre-modern era" because the literature of the first half of the period was written almost entirely in places other than Edo. Keene's term recognizes the fact that literary developments do not necessarily have much to do with geography or power, a virtue it shares with the common and happily vague Japanese designation *kinsei,* "recent times," but it may cause confusion for the many to whom "pre-modern" has come to mean the whole of Japanese history prior to 1868.

5. Takizawa Bakin, *Kinsei mono no hon Edo sakusha burui* (hereafter Bakin, *Sakusha burui*), pp. 58–59.

6. Nakamura Yukihiko and Nishiyama Matsunosuke, *Bunka ryōran,* Nihon bungaku no rekishi series, no. 8 (hereafter Nakamura and Nishiyama, *Nihon bungaku no rekishi* 8), p. 47, says there were 656 such libraries in 1808, but 655 is more likely the correct figure. See Suwa Haruo, *Shuppan kotohajime,* pp. 217–218, citing a manuscript in the Keiō University Library entitled *Eiri yomihon gedai sakusha gakō shoshi meimokushū.* Suwa cites an estimate of about 300 lending libraries in Osaka at about the same time, and cites Terakado Seiken, *Edo hanjōki,* to the effect that there were some 800 lending libraries in Edo by the early 1830s. See Asakura Haruhiko and Andō Kikuji, eds., *Edo hanjōki,* II, 209. I am indebted for much of the above to P. F. Kornicki, "The Publisher's Go-Between: *Kashihonya* in the Meiji Period," *Modern Asian Studies* 14.2:331–344 (April 1980).

On *yomihon* sales and the lending libraries, see Maeda Ai, "Shuppansha to dokusha: kashihon'ya no yakuwari o chūshin to shite," *Kokubungaku kaishaku to kanshō* 26.1:124–125 (January 1961).

7. For discussions of publishing volume and distribution practices in England in this period, see Kathleen Tillotson, *Novels of the Eighteen-Forties,* pp. 23–28; Louis James, *Fiction for the Working Man, 1830–1850,* pp. 12–44; Victor E. Neuburg, *Popular Literature: A History and Guide from the Be-*

ginning of Printing to the Year 1897, pp. 183-234. Eighteenth-century English statistics, while difficult to come by, may be more strictly comparable to those of early nineteenth-century Japan, since advances in printing and paper-making technology after about 1820 produced dramatic changes in the economics of publishing in England that doubtless account in part for the burgeoning market for reading material. See James, pp. 12-13, and Ian Watt, *The Rise of the Novel*, pp. 36-37. Watt cites scholarship estimating that "the average annual publication of new books, excluding pamphlets" between 1666 and 1756 amounted to less than 100 titles and, from 1792 to 1802, still only 372. The significance of such statistics in comparison with the Japanese case is questionable. When demand was strong enough, for instance, the technological deficiencies of wood-block printing did not inhibit production: the first wood-block-printed volume of Fukuzawa Yukichi's *Seiyō jijō* (1866) is said to have run to an edition of 150,000 copies or more. See Carmen Blacker, *The Japanese Enlightenment*, pp. 7-8.

8. Bakin asserts (*Sakusha burui*, pp. 11-12) that the term was originally written with characters meaning "smelly book," since early examples were bound in covers printed with a particularly foul-smelling, cheap ink, a thesis now generally discounted.

9. Mizuno Minoru, *Kibyōshi, sharebon no sekai*, is an intelligent, highly readable critical history of the origin and development of the *kibyōshi* and its sister medium, the *sharebon*. For a summary account in English, see Keene, *World Within Walls*, pp. 399-409.

10. Honda Yasuo, *Shikitei Sanba no bungei* (hereafter Honda, *SSB*).

11. See the introduction by Ueda Kazutoshi to this Chikamatsu concordance, finally published in 1930, for an interesting personal reminiscence about this period in Japanese literary scholarship; Ueda Mannen and Higuchi Yasuchiyo, comps., *Chikamatsu goi*.

12. Honda, *SSB*, pp. 24-27.

13. Futabatei Shimei, "Yo ga genbun itchi no yurai," *Futabatei Shimei zenshū* V, 170-172. Futabatei's indebtedness to Sanba's work is assessed inconclusively in Shimizu Shigeru, "Shikitei Sanba to Futabatei Shimei: ketsuron no nai nōto," pp. 180-186.

14. Honda, *SSB*, pp. 30-31. The most valuable contributions of Yamaguchi Takeshi to the study of late-Edo-period fiction are found in his carefully researched introductions to the late-Edo volumes of the most reliable comprehensive collection of the literature of the period, the *Nihon meicho zenshū: Edo bungei no bu* series, 30 vols. (Nihon Meicho Zenshū Kankōkai, 1926-1929; hereafter cited as *NMZ*). Mitamura Engyo is best represented by his comprehensive historical essay, "Kokkeibon gaisetsu," in *Kokkeibon meisakushū, Hyōshaku Edo bungaku sōsho* series no. X, 1-244, which virtually all more recent scholarship takes as its starting point.

15. Ebara Taizō, *Edo bungei ronkō*, Chapter 8: "Sanba no geijutsu."

16. A selection of articles that were particularly helpful in the early stages of preparing this study may be found in the Bibliography.

Mention should also be made here of Margarete Donath-Wiegand's *Zur literarhistorische Stellung des Ukiyoburo von Shikitei Samba*, a pioneering, if by now slightly dated, study.

Chapter Two

1. Also known as Seiundō. The full range of Mohei's activity is difficult to ascertain, since carvers only occasionally signed their work, but his name appears in a number of works published by major firms (Honda, *SSB*, pp. 38, 73). His name appears (as Kikuji Mohei) in Frank A. Turk, *The Prints of Japan*, p. 71.

2. Sanba's childhood name was Kyūtoku.

3. Shikitei Sanba, *Shikitei zakki*, reprinted in Kokusho Kankōkai, ed., *Zoku enseki jisshu*, I, 47. Sanba's brother, who was some 5 years younger than he, was known in his childhood as Sanojirō and later Sasuke; he served an apprenticeship with the book dealer Ishiwata Risuke, and at some time began calling himself Ishiwata Heihachi, under which name he acted as a junior partner, with Nishimura Genroku and Ishiwata Risuke, in the publication of the first two books of *Ukiyoburo*. (*Shikitei zakki*, p. 47; Honda, *SSB*, p. 41.)

4. See Chapter 1, note 5. This extended essay, written under the pseudonym Kaikō Sanjin but unarguably by Bakin, provides a wealth of biographical information on a total of 126 individual *gesaku* authors from the mid-1700s forward and much incidental and anecdotal information about contemporary popular fiction and publishing practices.

5. Iwamoto Sashichi (Darumaya Kattōshi), ed., *Gesaku rokkasen* (preface dated 1857), reprinted in Iwamoto Sashichi, ed., *Enseki jisshu*, 3 vols., I, 371–407. Based on a somewhat earlier manuscript of debatable authorship but associated with both Bokusentei Yukimaro and Kimura Mokurō.

6. See note 3 above.

7. Koikawa Harumachi, *Sono henpō bakemonobanashi*. The title page of the copy of this work bearing Sanba's autobiographical note is reproduced in Mizuno Minoru, ed., *Kibyōshi-shū I, Koten bunko* series, no. 264 (Koten Bunko, 1969), p. xxv.

Gesaku rokkasen (p. 381), otherwise seemingly reliable, says Sanba was born in An'ei 4 (1775), but Bakin (*Sakusha burui*, p. 34) gives his age at death in Bunsei 5 (1822) as 47 by Japanese reckoning, which would put his birth in 1776. In at least four places in dated introductions to his own works, Sanba gives his age. Honda (*SSB*, p. 73) cites the introductions to the following three works as supporting the 1776 date: *Katakiuchi Adatarayama*, illus. Utagawa Toyokuni (Nishimiya Shinroku, 1806), 10 vols; *Gejō suigen maku no soto,* illus. by Utagawa Kuninao (1806), 2 vols; and *Tōsei orimagai Hachi-jō,* illus. by Utagawa Kuninao (Nishimiya Shinroku, 1814), 6 vols. (The last-named work is a *gōkan* version of a *jōruri* play set on Hachijōjima, Kikuchi Mohei's birthplace, and in his introduction Sanba refers explicitly to his father's parentage and connections with Hachijōjima. Honda, *SSB,* p. 40.) A fourth work, however, yields 1777 (Honda, ibid.): *Nihon-ichi ahō no kagami,* illus. by Utagawa Toyokuni (Izumiya Ichibei, 1801), 3 vols. In the opening lines of *Shikitei zakki* (p. 44), Sanba calls himself 35 in 1810 (Bunka 7), yielding a birth date of 1776.

8. This shrine was dedicated to the legendary Minamoto Tametomo, a hero of the first round of the Minamoto-Taira rivalry in the mid-1100s. The shrine was actually located on Oshima, a small island off the coast of the main island of Hachijōjima. See: *Gesaku rokkasen,* p. 381; afterword by Sanba's disciple Shuntei Sangyō in Shikitei Sanba, *Kokon hyakubaka* (see Chapter 4, note 62), *NMZ* XIV, 744; Sanba's introduction to his *Tōsei orimagai Hachijō* (see note 7 above). Honda, *SSB,* p. 39, also cites several contemporary histories of Hachijōjima for further information about Mohei; one identifies him as the eldest son of Kikuchi Takehisa, the hereditary head priest of the Tametomo Daimyōjin Shrine. These local Hachijōjima records, however, confuse Sanba and Mohei, and one identifies Sanba as the author of Jippensha Ikku's *Hiza-kurige.* No evidence exists that Mohei himself ever pursued his family's priestly calling; to identify Sanba as "the son of a Shinto priest" (Keene, *World Within Walls,* p. 414) is to give a misleading impression of Sanba's childhood environment.

9. *Gesaku rokkasen,* p. 383.

10. See Sanba's portrayal of the proud *chōnin* mother of such a girl in service to a wealthy household in *Ukiyoburo* II:1 (translation, pp. 183–185 below); another such girl is discussed in his *Shijūhachikuse* I:7 (translation, pp. 85–86 above).

11. *Gesaku rokkasen,* p. 383.

12. Cited in Honda, *SSB,* p. 42. Bakin asserts in *Sakusha burui* (p. 32) that Sanba was apprenticed to "the wholesale book dealer Nishimiya Shinroku of Kayabachō," and makes a similar statement in *Iwademo no ki* (1819), reprinted in Hayakawa Junzaburō, ed., *Shin enseki jisshu,* 5 vols. (Kokusho Kankōkai, 1914), IV, 195 (hereafter *Iwademo no ki*). *Gesaku rokkasen* (p. 381), however, paraphrases a conversation with a book dealer named Hoku-rindō of Nakahashi, otherwise unidentified, who asserted that "Sanba, from his early childhood, had served in Hokurindō's house, and his surpassing talent was evident even as he was growing up." But the editor of *Gesaku rokkasen* remarks (accurately, if Sanba himself is to be believed) that "what I heard from one person is that Sanba was an apprentice to the book dealer Gangetsudō (Horinoya Nihei) of Honkokuchō 4-chōme. Hokurindō must have been mistaken."

13. *Gesaku rokkasen,* p. 381. The name Nishimiya Taisuke first appears in

print as co-publisher, with Yorozuya Tajiemon, of Sanba's *Shibai kinmō zui,*
illus. by Katsukawa Shuntei and Utagawa Toyokuni (1803), 5 vols. (Honda,
SSB, pp. 76, 399.)

14. *Gesaku rokkasen,* pp. 383-384. On the origins of the name Shikitei
Sanba, see Shikitei Sanba, *Kyōgen kigyo* (1804), reprinted in Hakubunkan,
ed., *Sanba kessakushū, Teikoku bunko* series, no. 13 (Hakubunkan, 1893), p.
805, where Sanba explains that, in order to express his admiration for the
gesakusha Tōrai Sanna and Utei Enba, he took one character from each of
their names. *Sakusha burui,* p. 33, tells substantially the same story. Honda
(*SSB,* p. 51) suggests further a punning connection with *shikisanbasō,* a ceremonial dance piece performed at the beginning of the *kabuki* season deriving
ultimately from the *nō* play *Okina;* the accompanying song to this dance includes a phrase reminiscent of another of Sanba's pen names, Tararirō. (Sasakawa Shurō, ed., *Sharebon kusazōshishū, Hyōshaku Edo bungaku sōsho* series,
no. 8 [Kōdansha, 1936], note to p. 611.) Other pen names and sobriquets
used by Sanba at one time or another, sometimes in conjunction with each
other, include Yūgidō, Sharakusai, Shikisanjin, Yūgidōjin, Gesakusha, and
Kokkeidō (*Gesaku rokkasen,* p. 381).

15. *Sakusha burui,* p. 34.

16. *Gesaku rokkasen,* p. 381; *Sakusha burui,* p. 32. *Iwademo no ki* (p.
195) places Sanba's marriage only vaguely "in the Kansei period," i.e., prior
to 1801. It is possible that Sanba moved directly from his apprenticeship to
employment under Tajiemon, which led, after a few years, to his adoption
and marriage. Honda (*SSB,* pp. 42-44, 398-399) finds evidence placing Sanba
in the Yorozuya household in 1802 and 1803, but not before (or after). In
this connection, it may be significant that descriptions (*Sakusha burui,* p.
33; *Iwademo no ki,* p. 195) of the *Kyan taiheiki* incident of 1799 refer to
"Sanba's house," suggesting that at that time Sanba had quarters of his own
apart from those either of his father or of Rankōdō Yorozuya Tajiemon; on
the other hand, Sanba laments (*Gesaku rokkasen,* p. 384) that this incident
caused pain and trouble not only to his publisher, Nishimiya Shinroku, whose
house was ransacked, but also to his father. Perhaps in 1799 Sanba was, after
all, living in his father's house.

In any case, Sanba's connection with the Yorozuya house was presumably
severed after the early death of his wife (who apparently bore him no children) some time in 1803 or 1804 (*Gesaku rokkasen,* p. 381; *Sakusha burui,* p.
32; *Iwademo no ki,* p. 195).

17. Illus. by Utagawa Toyokuni (Nishimiya Shinroku, 1794), 3 vols. Reprinted in Kōdō Tokuji, ed., *Kibyōshi hyakushu, Zoku teikoku bunko* series,
no. 16 (Hakubunkan, 1901), pp. 845-859.

18. Illus. by Utagawa Toyokuni (Nishimiya Shinroku, 1794), 2 vols.

19. *Sakusha burui,* p. 32.

20. In my discussion of this work, I have relied heavily on Honda (*SSB,*
pp. 45-49).

21. Illus. by Kitao Masayoshi (Owada Yasuhei, 1790), 3 vols. Reprinted in Mizuno Minoru, ed., *Kibyōshi sharebonshū, Nihon koten bungaku taikei* series (hereafter *NKBT*) LIX, 197-216.

22. For a detailed English treatment of Shingaku, see Robert N. Bellah, *Tokugawa Religion*, pp. 133-177.

23. This identification seems to have first been made by Yamaguchi Takeshi in his introduction to *NMZ* XI, xli.

24. The verse appears on p. 846 of *Tentō ukiyo no dezukai* and p. 199 of *Shingaku hayasomegusa* in the editions cited above.

25. Hōseidō Kisanji, *Tentō daifukuchō*, cited in Honda, *SSB*, p. 46.

26. Shiba Zenkō, *Ukiyo ayatsuri kumen jūmen*, cited in Honda, *SSB*, p. 46.

27. See Howard S. Hibbett, *The Floating World in Japanese Fiction*, for a detailed treatment of Ejima Kiseki and his *katagimono*.

28. See Honda, *SSB*, pp. 397-398, for a comprehensive list, and ibid., pp. 47-73, for descriptions and analyses of Sanba's works during this period.

29. Hiraga Gennai was perhaps the archetypal *gesakusha;* he was not only a fiction writer of considerable repute but an early experimenter in European painting techniques and an influential student of Western science. See Jōfuku Isamu, *Hiraga Gennai no kenkyū.* For a brief, near-contemporary account, see *Sakusha burui*, pp. 110-120.

30. Illus. by Utagawa Toyokuni (Nishimiya Shinroku, 1795), 3 vols.

31. Illus. by Utagawa Toyokuni (Nishimiya Shinroku, 1796), 2 vols.

32. *Go taiheiki Shiraishibanashi*, a play in 11 acts by Utei Enba and several collaborators, was given its first performance at the Edo Gekiza theater on the 2nd day of the 1st month of An'ei 9 (1780). Honda, *SSB*, p. 51.

33. Jinbō Kazuya, "Kaseido Tenpōki no Edo shōsetsu no sakusha to dokusha," *Bungaku* 26.5:98 (May 1958).

34. Honda, *SSB*, p. 51.

35. See note 41 below.

36. Honda, *SSB*, pp. 58-59.

37. ?-1815; writing here under the pen name Kantōbei.

38. Also known as Rakutei Bashō; the *jōruri* chanter Takemoto Sōdayū IV. Iwamoto Sashichi, *Gesakusha shōden* (1857?), reprinted in his *Enseki jisshu* I, 361.

39. Umebori Kokuga, *Keiseikai futasujimichi*, reprinted in Mizuno, ed., *Kibyōshi sharebonshū*, pp. 441-465. (Sanba's introduction, p. 442.)

40. Yamaguchi Takeshi, *NMZ* XII, xcvii.

41. *Tatsumi fugen*, illus. by Kitagawa Utamaro, 1798. Reprinted in, for example, *NMZ* XII, 567-602, and Sasakawa, ed., *Sharebon kusazōshishū*, pp. 659-696.

42. In, for instance, *Shikake bunko* (1791), reprinted in *NMZ* XII, 541-565.

43. Most prominently, in *Shunshoku umegoyomi.*

44. Hōraisanjin Kikyō, *Fukagawa haiken*, cited in Honda, *SSB*, pp. 61-62.

45. Especially, according to Honda, *SSB*, p. 62, *Keiseikai shijūhatte* (1790), reprinted in Mizuno, ed., *Kibyōshi sharebonshū*, pp. 387-416. Yamaguchi Takeshi (*NMZ* XII, xcviii) cites also *Shikake bunko* and *Nishiki no ura* (1791), reprinted in Mizuno, ed., *Kibyōshi sharebonshū*, pp. 417-440, as other works by Kyōden that Sanba seems to have borrowed from in *Tatsumi fugen*.

46. See, for instance, the opinion of Yamaguchi Takeshi, *NMZ* XII, xcviii.

47. By Muchūsanjin Negotosensei. Reprinted in Mizuno, ed., *Kibyōshi sharebonshū*, pp. 295-318.

48. While most *sharebon* had on their covers only a narrow pasted-on strip of paper with the title printed on it, *Tatsumi fugen* bore a large rectangle that had, in addition to the title, a brief snatch of dialogue:

An itinerant booklender [*kashihon'ya*], carrying a cloth-wrapped bundle slung on his back:

"*Hai!* A new *sharebon*'s out! Still in its wrapper . . ."

He leaves a book, and departs.

"Hmm. What's this? This is a new kind of story—might be good . . ."

And when he turned the page . . .

Honda, *SSB*, p. 66, notes that a "teaser" of similar format appeared on the cover of Kyōden's *Nishiki no ura*, but Sanba's version gives evidence that he was conscious of the novelty of his setting, and, further, saw either this work, or *sharebon* in general, as aimed not at a small audience of connoisseurs but at the much broader readership who patronized the *kashihon'ya*. (The cover of *Tatsumi fugen* appears in facsimile, and its text is reproduced, in *NMZ* XII, 567 and xcvii respectively.) Sanba himself hints strongly in his introduction to *Sendō shinwa* (see note 52 below) that one reason he chose to write about the Furuishiba quarter in *Tatsumi fugen* was simply because it had previously gone untreated.

49. *NMZ* XII, xcviii.

50. Reprinted in Sasakawa, ed., *Sharebon kusazōshishū*, pp. 585-612.

51. Reprinted in Hakubunkan, ed., *Sanba kessakushū*, pp. 535-598.

52. Reprinted in Hakubunkan, ed., *Sanba kessakushū*, pp. 599-625.

53. See, for instance, Teruoka Yasutaka and Gunji Masakatsu, *Edo shimin bungaku no kaika*, *Nihon no bungaku* series V, pp. 293-296. Teruoka includes the *Tatsumi fugen* trilogy among other late works in the genre by Kokuga, Ikku, and Shinrotei as an example of the transitional *sharebon* type.

54. *Haratsutsumi heso no shitakata* (The fox-gut drum and the navel bandsmen), illus. by Utagawa Toyokuni (Izumiya Ichibei, 1798), 3 vols. Discussed in Honda, *SSB*, p. 57.

55. *Sono atomaku baba Dōjōji* (After the final curtain: The Dōjōji Temple crone), illus. by Utagawa Toyokuni (Nishimiya Shinroku, 1798), 3 vols. Discussed in Honda, *SSB*, p. 56.

56. Translated in James R. Brandon, *Kabuki: Five Classic Plays*, pp. 239-349.

57. *Sakusha burui,* p. 33, quoting Sanba; *Gesaku rokkasen,* p. 386, quoting Rakutei Bashō, *Kuruwa setsuyō* (1799), to the effect that it was "Shiba Zenkō's final wish that Sanba become Zenkō II."

58. Iwamoto, *Gesakusha shōden,* p. 345.

59. *Sakusha burui,* p. 33, quoting Sanba, says only that "events conspired to prevent" him from assuming Zenkō's name, but *Gesaku rokkasen,* p. 386, again quoting *Kuruwa setsuyō,* says he held back for fear of "sullying the name of the deceased," since "he still thinks of himself, as always, as 'Zenkō's pupil.'" Since Zenkō died when Sanba was only 17, it seems strange both that he would have bequeathed his name to the as yet unpublished youth, and that Sanba regarded Zenkō as his teacher. Possibly Sanba (then Taisuke) had had personal contact with Zenkō through his father or his master during his apprenticeship, but, if such was the case, it would seem likely that Sanba's reminiscences, in *Gesaku rokkasen* or elsewhere, would mention the fact, given Sanba's obvious reverence for the older man.

60. Sanba's notoriety after the *Kyan taiheiki* incident caused him finally to discard the idea of taking Zenkō's name: "Thanks to my involvement with the incident of the fire brigade's battle, the name Sanba was suddenly being noised about, and so I gave up my original intention." (*Sakusha burui,* p. 33.)

61. Illus. by Utagawa Toyokuni and Utagawa Kunimasa (Kazusaya Chūsuke, 1799), cited in Honda, *SSB,* pp. 72, 398.

62. Introduction to *Yakusha gakuya tsū,* quoted in Honda, *SSB,* p. 72.

63. Illus. by Kitao Shigemasa (Nishimiya Shinroku, 1799), 3 vols. The first character of the title, usually pronounced *kyō* and meaning "chivalry," was often given in the late Edo period the pronunciation *kyan,* possibly an attempt to reproduce a vernacular Chinese pronunciation, particularly in the compound *kyankaku,* often glossed, and identical in meaning to *otokodate,* "chivalrous commoner," "champion of the underdog," a term conjuring up an image of flashy, street-wise toughs who, in the course of sometimes disreputable private business, acted as guardians of defenseless "little people." The image is reinforced in this title by *mukō hachimaki,* a headband tied in front, seen as a symbol of a certain class of *otokodate,* or at least of a certain sort of hot-tempered swaggerer.

64. The curtain in question was the *mukō hikimaku,* hung at the far end of the *hanamichi* (the runway stretching between the rear of a *kabuki* theater and the main stage); the *mukō hachimaki* of the title may be a punning reference to this element of the story.

65. *Sakusha burui,* p. 33; *Iwademo no ki,* p. 195.

66. *Ikazuchitarō gōaku monogatari* (The story of the villainous Ikazuchitarō), illus. by Utagawa Toyokuni (Nishimiya Shinroku, 1806), 10 vols. in two parts. Sanba's first and highly popular *gōkan.* Modern edition: *Ikazuchitarō gōaku monogatari,* ed. Suzuki Jūzō and Honda Yasuo.

67. *Gesaku rokkasen,* p. 384.

Chapter Three

1. Dating Sanba's moves in this period is difficult. Various sources place him in the Yorozuya in 1802 and 1803 (see Chapter 2, note 17), but in *Shibai kinmō zui,* which he wrote and co-published with Yorozuya Tajiemon in 1803, Sanba's name appears in the colophon as "Nishimiya Taisuke, of Honkokuchō 4-chōme," the location of the Gangetsudō bookstore (see Chapter 2, note 14). This seems to show that Sanba severed his Yorozuya connections and moved in with the Horinoya family in 1803. But another of his works published in 1805 lists as publishers Yorozuya Tajiemon and "Yorozuya Taisuke," which argues rather that, even at this later date, he was still regarded as heir by Tajiemon (colophon to Book II of *Kyōkakei* [see note 8 below], cited in Honda, *SSB,* p. 399).

Bakin (*Sakusha burui,* p. 32) says Sanba moved to Kokuchō (probably Honkokuchō) after his first wife's death; *Gesaku rokkasen* (p. 381), however, has him at that time opening his used-book store in Yokkaichi, the location of the Kazusaya-Ishiwata establishment where his brother was employed (*Shikitei zakki,* p. 47). On the fire and Sanba's subsequent move to Honkokuchō 4-chōme, see *Shikitei zakki,* p. 44.

2. Sanba's note in his copy of *Ta ga sode nikki* (Honda, *SSB,* p. 42) says that the Horinoya house went bankrupt in 1804.

3. *Iwademo no ki,* p. 195.

4. In his introduction to *Oya no kataki uchimatakōyaku* (see note 30 below), Sanba himself says that, "having had much private business to attend to, I have not had time to write very much." Quoted in Honda, *SSB,* p. 92.

5. Reprinted and annotated in Sasakawa, ed., *Sharebon kusazōshishū,* pp. 223-240.

6. See Chapter 2, note 13.

7. Or Hachikazukihime. See Chigusa Steven, "*Hachikazuki:* A Muromachi Short Story," *Monumenta Nipponica* 32.3:303-331 (Autumn 1977), for an analysis and translation. Sanba's choice of this story as a parodic vehicle suggests that, even as late as the early 1800s, this and perhaps other *otogizōshi* tales were still a familiar part of popular culture.

8. Discussed in Honda, *SSB,* pp. 85-86.

9. See Chapter 2, note 14. This work is not, as its title might suggest, "a theater-related work" (Ozaki, *Kinsei shomin bungaku ronkō,* p. 101).

10. Honda, *SSB,* pp. 85, 399.

11. Sanba is not mentioned in the standard summary treatment of late Edo *kyōka* contained in Hisamatsu Sen'ichi, ed., *Shinpan Nihon bungakushi* V, 638-657.

12. *Sakusha burui,* p. 35. The Kyōkadō mentioned in the passage was Shikatsube no Magao's residence, located not far from Sanba's in Sukiyabashi Yamashitachō.

13. *Gesaku rokkasen*, p. 383.

14. While, by Sanba's time, the term *gesaku* itself seems to have been restricted to prose fiction, comic verse in Japanese and Chinese had long been part of the repertoire of the *gesakusha*, although not all *kyōka* poets called themselves or were called *gesakusha*. See the discussion in Nakamura, *Gesakuron*, pp. 17ff., of historical and modern definitions of *gesaku* and *gesakusha*.

15. Also known as Yomo no Utagaki.

16. For contemporary biographies of Ōta Nanpo, see *Sakusha burui*, pp. 19-20, 75-76, and *Gesakusha shōden*, p. 347. The classic modern study is Tamabayashi Haruo, *Shokusanjin no kenkyū;* Hamada Giichirō's *Ōta Nanpo* is concise, authoritative, and readable.

17. According to Nanpo's diary, cited in Honda, *SSB*, p. 77, Sanba was among those present at a party to mark Shikatsube no Magao's departure on a trip to Suruga.

18. Honda, *SSB*, pp. 90-91.

19. Also known as Manzōtei.

20. *Kyōgen kigyo*, p. 785.

21. "Jūdaijin o kotobuku ji," *Kyōgen kigyo*, pp. 803-805.

22. W. G. Aston, *A History of Japanese Literature*, p. 222. Elsewhere (pp. 298-299), Aston offers this appreciation of the language characteristic of *kyōbun* prose:

> Our old enemy the pivot-word is here, also the pillow-word, and several varieties of the ordinary pun, with various fearfully complicated contortions of speech which I shall not attempt to describe. Even the reader who has a competent knowledge of the language requires a special study to understand and appreciate them. He follows these far-eastern waggeries with a halting step. . . . It may be doubted whether such an excessive fondness for mere verbal wit does not amount to a disease, and whether it has not constituted a serious obstacle to the development of higher qualities in their literature.

23. *Shikitei zakki*, pp. 58, 69-70, 78. In only one instance (*Shikitei zakki*, p. 70) does Sanba seem to make reference to a payment received for his calligraphic services; this does not necessarily mean, of course, that the many orders he filled for poems and inscriptions were done free of charge.

24. Illus. by Utagawa Toyohiro (Izumiya Ichibei, 1802), 3 vols. Discussed in Honda, *SSB*, pp. 43, 84.

25. Illus. by Utagawa Toyohiro (publisher unknown, 1804), 1 vol. Discussed in Honda, *SSB*, p. 90. On "advertising novels," see Hisamatsu, *Shinpan Nihon bungakushi* V, 780-781.

26. For a general introduction to *kyōka*, see Hamada Giichiro, "Kyōka," in *Kōza Nihon bungaku* VIII, 17-33, which contains a selected bibliography. See also Keene, *World Within Walls*, pp. 513-525.

27. Imaizumi Genkichi, *Katsuragawake no hitobito* II, 1–66, is the most detailed recent biography of Morishima Chūryō.

28. Nobuhiro Shinji, "Utei Enba," in *Rakugo no subete*, pp. 93–99, and the same author's ongoing research on Enba's career as represented by his "Tenmei kansei ki no Utei Enba," in *Inoura Yoshinobu-hakase kakō kinen ronbunshū: geinō to bungaku*, pp. 117–140.

29. I am indebted to Konta Yōzō, *Edo no hon'ya-san*, pp. 95–123, for his detailed and suggestive discussion of overlapping intellectual and literary coteries revolving around the Edo publishers Suwaraya Ichibei and Tsutaya Jūzaburō.

30. Illus. by Utagawa Toyohiro (Nishimiya Shinroku, 1805), 3 vols. Discussed in Honda, *SSB*, pp. 95–98. The title puns on *oya no katakiuchi* (smiting one's parent's enemy) and *uchimatakōyaku* (a plaster on the inside of a thigh), a common metaphor for someone who vacillates.

31. Introduction to *Naburu mo yomi to utajizukushi*, illus. by Utagawa Toyohiro (Izumiya Ichibei, 1805). Quoted in Honda, *SSB*, p. 95.

32. Nansenshō Somabito, *Katakiuchi gijo no hanabusa*. Cited as the work that inspired the fad for *katakiuchimono* in, for instance, Yamaguchi Takeshi, introduction to *NMZ* XI, x, and Hisamatsu, *Shinpan Nihon bungakushi* V, 776.

33. Honda, *SSB*, p. 93, summarizing Suzuki Jūzō, "Gōkanmono no daizai tenki to Tanehiko," *Kokugo to kokubungaku* 38.4:62–63 (April 1961).

34. *Azuma kaidō onna katakiuchi*, illus. by Utagawa Toyokuni (Nishimiya Shinroku, 1798), 3 vols. Discussed in Honda, *SSB*, pp. 54–56.

35. *NMZ* XI, x–xi.

36. This work is summarized and analyzed in detail in Honda, *SSB*, pp. 95–98.

37. About two-thirds of those of Sanba's works identifiable by title as vendetta pieces were published by Nishimiya Shinroku. Data from Honda, *SSB*, pp. 399–400.

38. Ibid.

39. Introduction to *Oya no kataki uchimatakōyaku*. Quoted in Honda, *SSB*, p. 97.

40. See the summary of arguments in Suzuki, "Gōkanmono no daizai tenki," and Mizuno Minoru's comments in his *Edo shōsetsu ronsō*, p. 174.

41. *Shikitei zakki*, p. 45.

42. Honda lists 67 *gōkan* titles out of Sanba's lifetime total of 127 works (data from *SSB*, pp. 397–406); Ozaki, *Kinsei shomin bungaku ronkō*, p. 101, lists 79 *gōkan* out of a total of 136 titles.

43. Honda, *SSB*, pp. 386–389.

44. See, for instance, Takizawa Bakin's letter to Suzuki Bokushi dated the 28th of the 10th month, Bunsei 1 (1818), contained in Takizawa Bakin, *Kyokutei ikō*, ed. Hayakawa Junzaburō, pp. 394–395:

I am told my great-grandfather, my grandfather, and my father were all upright in their behavior . . . and did not even once in their lives sit cross-legged; nor did they ever lie down unless they were ill. I, on the other hand . . . never pass a day without crossing my legs or reclining. And I eke out a living in the marketplace. How dare I speak of my ancestors to even the closest of my friends?

45. *Shikitei zakki*, pp. 45-47.

46. Bakin wrote extensively about such theoretical issues as, for instance, the relative proportions of elegant (*ga*) and vulgar (*zoku*) language appropriate to fiction, as in the following passage from a letter to Suzuki Bokushi, dated the last day of the 7th month, Bunsei 1 (1818), in *Kyokutei ikō*, p. 375:

A work will always sell that is seven-tenths vulgar and three-tenths elegant; one that is seven-tenths elegant and three vulgar will not sell very well . . . and a work that is all elegance and not even a tenth vulgar will not sell at all.

There is no hint of irony or cynicism here. A question of critical theoretical and practical importance to later writers, the language of the novel is reduced by Bakin to the simple matter of what constituted a marketable style.

Bakin seems to have been no more eager than Sanba (or any other writer of the time) to sacrifice sales to a fastidious concern for artistic purity, but he drew the line at sacrificing his moral integrity, as in the following passage from *Sakusha burui* (p. 83):

Only Bakin never wrote *sharebon*. At the time, there were many who, driven by greed, came to him to solicit such manuscripts, but Bakin did not accede, telling them: "I am fond of *gesaku*, but, if I were to be led by greed to write a *sharebon*, and if later I had children, what would I tell them? Do not ask me a second time."

47. Yamazaki Yoshinari, *Kairoku*, ed. Hayakawa Junzaburō, p. 86.

48. Takayanagi Mitsuhisa et al., eds., *Nihonshi jiten*, pp. 1154, 1157. Hamada Keisuke, writing in Nakamura and Nishiyama, p. 56, says the going rate for a standard 6-volume *gōkan* in Bakin's day was 5 *ryō*, but does not cite sources. If Hamada's figure is correct, Sanba's 10 *gōkan* in 1810 would have earned him perhaps 50 *ryō*, probably a comfortable income.

49. *Sakusha burui*, p. 35. Kyōden's and Sanba's incomes could not have been vastly greater than Bakin's or Ikku's; either Bakin is being modest, or (more likely) what set Kyōden and Sanba apart in his mind was their success in establishing family businesses. Bakin's samurai pride prevented him from capitalizing on his success as they did. Ikku's notorious profligacy and the fact that he was often on the road no doubt kept him from investing his writing income, which must have been impressive.

50. *Shikitei zakki*, p. 46.

51. Ibid., p. 47; *Sakusha burui*, p. 32.

52. Introduction to *Ukiyoburo* III, 1.

53. *Sakusha burui*, p. 22.

54. Yamaguchi Takeshi, *NMZ* XII, lxxxix.

55. Nakamura and Nishiyama, pp. 33-34.

56. *Gesaku rokkasen*, pp. 385-386.

57. Ibid.

58. Keene, *World Within Walls*, p. 410, quoting Nakamura, *Gesakuron*, p. 120.

59. *Gesaku rokkasen*, pp. 383-384, regarding Sanba's break and reconciliation with Toyokuni; *Shikitei zakki*, pp. 67-68, regarding the same with Katsukawa Shuntei.

60. *Sakusha burui*, p. 35.

61. *Iwademo no ki*, p. 190.

62. *Gesakusha shōden*, p. 366; *Sakusha burui*, p. 56.

63. Nakamura Yukihiko, "Yomihon no dokusha," *Bungaku* 26.5:74-75 (May 1958).

64. A survey of the authors treated in *Sakusha burui* and *Gesakusha shōden* shows that, of the total of 93 whose family occupations can be determined, 51, or 55%, may be classified as *chōnin*, as opposed to 31 (33%) clearly of samurai origins (the remaining 12% are of other or uncertain class background); this 5-to-3 preponderance of *chōnin* over samurai would be even more disparate did not these collections include a sizable number of prominent *gesakusha* of the earlier generation, who were virtually without exception of samurai origin.

65. *Gesakusha shōden*, p. 366.

66. In 1816, Sanba published only 2 titles (4 volumes in total), followed by 6 in 1817 (23 volumes), 2 (2 volumes) in 1818, and none in 1819. Tamenaga Shunsui, writing as Nansenshō Somabito II in an introduction to the third book of *Ukiyodoko* (by Ryūtei Rijō) in 1823, describes Sanba's last years as having been beset by many illnesses. Cited in Honda, *SSB*, p. 296.

67. *Shikitei zakki*, p. 49.

68. San'yū's real name is unknown, but he seems to have had connections with a well-known patent-medicine business in Nihonbashi. (*Gesakusha shōden*, p. 361.)

69. Izumiya Kan'emon, a rice dealer who lived in Koishikawa on the north side of Edo, and studied *kyōka* under Shikatsube no Magao. (Honda, *SSB*, p. 200; *Gesakusha shōden*, p. 36; *Shikitei zakki*, pp. 50, 52.)

70. Mikawaya Kichibei, a drug wholesaler from Asakusa; with Rakutei Bashō and Ittei Sanshō, one of Sanba's three "old disciples." (*Gesakusha shōden*, p. 361.) From about 1808, he lived with Sanba's father, Kikuchi Mohei. (*Shikitei zakki*, p. 80; Honda, *SSB*, p. 201.)

71. Originally a purveyor of decorative goods to the shogunal house, Isaburō lost his position through profligacy, and became an entertainer; he later placed himself under the patronage of Sanba's brother-in-law Gangetsudō and became a book dealer. (*Shikitei zakki*, p. 58.)

72. A painting- and calligraphy-viewing party organized by Sanba in the 3rd month of Bunka 8 (1811) included Kyōden among its pre-opening patrons (zenjitsu yori no sewayaku). (Shikitei zakki, p. 50.)

73. Sakusha burui, p. 84.

74. Ibid.

75. Illus. by Utagawa Toyokuni and Utagawa Kunisada (Tsuruya Kiemon, Tsuruya Kinsuke, 1810), 5 vols. Discussed in Honda, SSB, pp. 119-120, 201-208.

76. Takizawa Bakin, Heiben, reprinted in Hayakawa, ed., Kyokutei ikō, pp. 275-296.

77. Shikitei zakki, p. 46.

78. Sakigakezōshi, illus. by Utagawa Kuniyasu (Tsuruya Kiemon, Kawachiya Taisuke, 1825), 5 vols. Discussed in Honda, SSB, pp. 380-381.

79. Data from Honda, SSB, pp. 400-404.

80. See, for instance, Sanba's introduction to his Hitogokoro nozoki karakuri, in Hakubunkan, ed., Sanba kessakushū, p. 663: "Written during the span of a 2-day stay at a brothel in Odawarachō." Also, his introduction to Namaei katagi (Sanba kessakushū, pp. 866-867): "Written the morning after, with a hangover, in a day and a night."

81. The following discussion is based on Shikitei zakki, pp. 51-78.

82. In the section of his diary summarized above, Sanba mentions (p. 56) that, on his visit to his brother's grave, he encountered by chance his stepmother and his brother (presumably half-brother or stepbrother) Kinzō. This brief notice is the only evidence that his father had at some time taken a second wife. The presence of a stepmother in his father's household may help to explain Sanba's evident unwillingness to share living quarters with him.

83. Gesaku rokkasen, p. 385. In Hara no uchi gesaku shubon (An author's internal musings: A rough draft), illus. by Kogawa Yoshimaro, 3 vols. (Tsuruya Kiemon, 1811), one of his last kibyōshi, Sanba describes vividly the hectic life of a popular writer. Summarized and excerpted in Honda, SSB, pp. 273-275.

84. Gesaku rokkasen, p. 385; Shikitei zakki, p. 67.

85. Afterword to Kyakusha hyōbanki, in Sanba kessakushū, p. 503.

86. Sakusha burui, p. 34.

87. The most extensive existing list of Sanba's disciples is given in Gesakusha shōden, p. 361:

Rakutei Bashō	Tokutei Sankō
Kokontei Sanchō	Settei Santō
Ittei Sanshō	Shōtei Sansei
Fukutei Sanshō I	Shuntei Sangyō I
Fukutei Sanshō II	Shuntei Sangyō II
Ekitei San'yū	Ittei Sanraku
Ittei Sanshi	Sanro (Tamenaga Shunsui)

To this list might be added two names from Sakusha burui, p. 51, Gakutei

Sanshi and Shōtei Sanshichi, although Bakin was not certain whether these men were indeed pupils of Sanba's or had simply adopted names similar to those of his legitimate disciples.

Donath-Wiegand, p. 45, citing Yamazaki Fumoto, "Shikitei Sanba no deshi," *Edo jidai bunka* (1927), p. 38, adds the following names:

Oka Sanchō (Described in *Gesakusha shōden*, p. 373, as a disciple of Bakin but so close a friend of Sanba's as to be almost a disciple.)

Santei Shunba (Described in *Gesakusha shōden*, p. 365, as a disciple of Jippensha Ikku.)

Santei Goran

Rakutei Seiba (Sanba's publisher and friend Nishimiya Shinroku.)

Very few of these men seem to have actively pursued writing careers; Sanba may have bestowed pen names on some simply as signs of affection (Nishimiya Shinroku would certainly be one of these), and others seem to have been only briefly his students or to have acted more as scribes, general assistants, and drinking partners than as serious students of literary art. One or two, principally Rakutei Bashō, were Sanba's collaborators in writing enterprises.

88. Jinbō Kazuya, "Shinrotei to Tamenaga Shunsui," *Kinsei bungei* 7:49 (March 1962); Nakamura Yukihiko, introduction to Tamenaga Shunsui, *Shunshoku umegoyomi*, pp. 4-7.

89. Keene, *World Within Walls*, p. 410, quoting Nakamura, *Gesakuron*, p. 132.

90. *Gesaku rokkasen*, p. 385.

91. *Sakusha burui*, p. 34, gives the date of Sanba's death as the 16th day of the intercalary 1st month of Bunsei 5, but both *Gesaku rokkasen* (p. 381) and contemporary records in the possession of the Shōzenji, the temple in Meguro-ku in Tokyo to which Sanba's remains and grave marker were removed after the earthquake of 1923, give the date as the 6th of that month. See Nakamura Michio, "Sanba arekore," *Nihon koten bungaku taikei geppō* 5:6-7 (September 1957).

Sanba seems to have left no "parting verse" (*jisei no uta*) written in anticipation of death, despite the persistent attribution of one such verse to him. See *Gesaku rokkasen*, p. 381, for an early and seemingly trustworthy refutation of the attribution.

92. Honda, *SSB*, p. 405.

93. *Sakusha burui*, pp. 34, 56.

Chapter Four

1. The best comprehensive survey of the *kokkeibon* remains Mitamura Engyo's "Kokkeibon gaisetsu" (see Chapter 1, note 14). Yamaguchi Takeshi's introduction to *Kokkeibonshū* (NMZ XIV, i-lxxv) is a shorter but no less insightful study tied to the works reprinted in that volume.

A sound, popular survey is Teruoka and Gunji, pp. 320–344. See also the comprehensive outline in Hisamatsu, ed., *Shinpan Nihon bungakushi* V, 913–945, a tedious but fact-filled presentation of the mainstream of current scholarly opinion on the *kokkeibon*. Donald Keene's treatment is found in *World Within Walls*, pp. 411–416.

2. Keene, pp. 411–412, says that the terms *kokkeibon* and *ninjōbon* came into use to distinguish the two varieties of *chūbon* "about 1820," but Mitamura ("Kokkeibon gaisetsu," pp. 93–94) shows that it was probably only in the late 1820s that *ninjōbon* became a generally current genre designation.

3. *Sakusha burui*, pp. 83–84, describes the disproportionate profits publishers and *kashihon'ya* were accustomed to earn on *sharebon* as opposed to other forms of fiction.

4. Ibid., p. 72. Honda Yasuo, "Ukiyomonomanemekitaru esemonogatari no koto," *Kinsei bungei* 8:61–67 (1962), discusses Bakin's perception of the connections between the *chubōn* and *ukiyomonomane*.

5. Okitsu Kaname, *Rakugo to Edokko*, p. 169. See Mitamura, "Kokkeibon gaisetsu," pp. 169–173, on the professionalization of *rakugo*.

6. "Author's Note" prefacing Book I, *Ukiyoburo*, ed. Nakamura Michio, pp. 34–35.

7. Illus. Utagawa Toyokuni, 2 vols. (Kazusaya Sasuke, 1806), reprinted in Nakano Mitsutoshi et al., eds., *Sharebon, kokkeibon, ninjōbon, Nihon koten bungaku zenshū* series (hereafter *NKBZ*) XLVII, 201–254; also Hakubunkan, ed., *Sanba kessakushū, Teikoku bunko* series, XIII, pp. 865–921, and Furuya Chishin, ed., *Kokkei bungaku zenshū* series (hereafter *KBZ*), VI, 313–350.

8. *NKBZ* XLVII, 207.

9. See Okitsu, *Rakugo to Edokko*, p. 171.

10. Book I: publisher unknown, 1813, 2 vols.; Book II: publisher unknown, 1814, 2 vols. Discussed in Honda, *SSB*, pp. 301–303.

11. Honda, *SSB*, p. 302.

12. Discussed in Honda, *SSB*, pp. 196 (note 34), 302, citing the manuscript in the National Diet Library, Tokyo. On the roles played by Utei Enba and Sanshōtei Karaku in the development of Edo *rakugo*, see Mitamura, "Kokkeibon gaisetsu," pp. 161–164, 170–171, and Nakamura and Nishiyama, pp. 438–439, 442–446. A *hanashibon* by Utei Enba entitled *Kotoba no hana* (1797) appears in *NMZ* XIV, 1157–1174.

13. Reprinted in Mitamura, *Kokkeibon meisakushū*, pp. 628–704. Discussed in Honda Yasuo, "Kokkeibon to wagei," Zenkoku Daigaku Kokugo Kokubungakkai, ed., *Kōza Nihon bungaku* VIII, 124–125. It has often been pointed out that Ikku's *Hizakurige* was strongly influenced by *niwaka*, another late-Edo comic storytelling art (Honda, "Kokkeibon to wagei," p. 126; Mitamura, *Kokkeibon meisakushū*, pp. 114, 125).

14. A short, contemporary biography of Onitake may be found in *Sakusha burui*, pp. 38–39.

15. Ryūtei Rijō, *Hanagoyomi hasshōjin*. Reprinted in *NMZ* XIV, 749–930.

16. See Okitsu Kaname, *Nihon bungaku to rakugo*, p. 40.

17. The name puns on *kyōkun*, "instruction," and refers to Kinryūsan, "Mt. Golden Dragon," a hill close by the Yoshiwara.

18. Okitsu, *Nihon bungaku to rakugo*, p. 41.

19. The following discussion follows closely Honda's analysis in "Kokkeibon to wagei," which seems in turn to be heavily indebted to Mitamura's discussion in "Kokkeibon gaisetsu."

20. Honda, "Kokkeibon to wagei," pp. 115-117, citing also the *dangibon* author Ken'a Midabutsu.

21. Reprinted in *NMZ* XIV, 1-53.

22. See Honda, "Kokkeibon to wagei," pp. 119-121, on the relationship between Gennai and Shidōken.

23. At least one contemporary reader took *Shidōkenden* to be a genuine biography. See Jinbō Kazuya's edition of Fujusanjin Suiōken, "Shidōkenden hyōron nantōshi" (1766), in Hamada Giichirō, ed., *Tenmei bungaku: shiryō to kenkyū*, pp. 301-328.

24. Reprinted in *NMZ* XII, 25-38.

25. Hisamatsu, *Shinpan Nihon bungakushi* V, 887, 889-890.

26. Honda, "Kokkeibon to wagei," p. 122.

27. Full title, *Seirō hiru no sekai nishiki no ura* (The world of the brothel by day: The other side of the brocade). Reprinted in Mizuno Minoru, ed., *Kibyōshi sharebonshū*, *NKBT* LIX, 417-440 (1958). For an enlightening study of this work and probably the best English-language summary to date of the Kansei Reforms as they pertained to literary activity and publishing, see Peter F. Kornicki, "*Nishiki no Ura*: An Instance of Censorship and the Structure of a *Sharebon*," *Monumenta Nipponica* 32.2:153-188 (Summer 1977), which includes also a full translation.

28. See Nakamura Yukihiko, *Gesakuron*, pp. 135-152, for a discussion of *ugachi*.

29. Illus. Utagawa Toyokuni (Nishimura Genroku, Ishiwata Risuke, Ishiwata Heihachi, 1810), reprinted in *NMZ* XIV, 393-422; *Sanba kessakushū*, pp. 627-659.

30. Illus. Utagawa Kuninao (Igaya Kan'emon, Sekiguchi Heieimon, 1813), reprinted in *NMZ* XIV, 599-622, and *KBZ* IV, 237-284. A sequel by Ryūtei Rijō was published in 1833.

31. Illus. Utagawa Kuninao (Chōjiya Heibei, 1814), 2 vols., reprinted in *KBZ* III, 509-592, and *Sanba kessakushū*, pp. 661-695.

32. Illus. Utagawa Kuninao (unknown publisher, 1806), 2 vols., reprinted in *KBZ* V, 65-108.

33. (Yorozuya Tajiemon, 1803), introduction in Chinese by Yomo no Utagaki (Shikatsube no Magao), 1 vol. in *kobon* format, reprinted in *Sanba kessakushū*, pp. 923-939, as *Hashika no kami o okuru hyō*.

34. Reprinted in Nakamura Yukihiko, ed., *Fūrai Sanjin shū*, *NKBT* LV, 228-255.

35. (Seiundō Eibun, private ed., 1806). No modern edition exists. Discussed in Honda, *SSB*, pp. 113–115.

36. Honda, *SSB*, p. 114.

37. (Surugaya Hanbei, 1808), 1 vol. Discussed in Honda, *SSB*, pp. 177–178. No modern edition.

38. Honda, *SSB*, pp. 177–178.

39. Illus. Utagawa Kuninao (Tsuruya Kinsuke, 1812), 2 vols., reprinted in Engei Chinsho Kankōkai, ed., *Engeki bunko*, Vol. III, book 5, part 5, pp. 1–20, 1–37.

40. Nakamura, *Gesakuron*, pp. 219–220.

41. Donald Keene, trans., *Chūshingura: The Treasury of Loyal Retainers*, pp. 21–22.

42. Cited in Nakamura, *Gesakuron*, pp. 221–222. For another critique of Sanba's work, see Matsushima Eiichi, *Chūshingura*, p. 207.

43. Illus. Utagawa Kunisada (Nishimura Genroku, 1813), reprinted in *NMZ* XIV, 637–686.

44. *NMZ* XIV, lviii–lix.

45. Ibid.

46. Illus. Utagawa Kunisada (Tsuruya Kinsuke, 1811), 3 vols., reprinted in *NMZ* XIV, 423–510. For a detailed summary and analysis of this work from the point of view of a theater historian, see Jacob Raz, "The Audience Evaluated: Shikitei Sanba's *Kyakusha Hyōbanki*," *Monumenta Nipponica* 35.2:199–221 (Summer 1980). Raz has located a more recent reprint in Geinōshi Kenkyūkai, ed., *Nihon shomin bunka shiryō shusei* VI, 481–529.

47. Traditionally called the originator of the *katagimono* form and author of *Yakusha kuchijamisen* (1699), generally regarded as the model for all subsequent *hyōbanki*.

48. Utei Enba and Ichikawa Danjūrō, *Iozaki mushi no hyōban* (1804), cited in *NMZ* XIV, 50–52.

49. *Namaei katagi*, in *NKBZ* XLVII, 214–216.

50. Illus. Utagawa Kunisada (Nishimura Genroku, Nishimiya Yohei, Nishimiya Heihachi, 1810), 3 vols., reprinted in *KBZ* IV, 1–42.

51. Illus. Utagawa Toyokuni (Ishiwata Risuke, 1813), reprinted in *KBZ* IV, 211–236.

52. Kentei Bokusan, *Hayagawari kufū no adauchi*, illus. Bokutei (Kitagawa) Tsukimaro, cited in Yamaguchi, *NMZ* XIV, xli.

53. Quoted in ibid., pp. xl–xli. The main text in *NMZ* XIV is based on the later edition (date unspecified) entitled *Kyōkun mune no karakuri*, whose introduction differs in many places from that of the first edition quoted here.

54. *Shikitei zakki*, p. 47.

55. Book I, illus. Utagawa Kuninao (Tsuruya Kinsuke, 1812); Book II, illus. Utagawa Kuninao (1813); Book III, illus. Yanagikawa Shigenobu (1817); Book IV, illus. Utagawa Yoshimaru (1818), reprinted in *KBZ* IV, 43–174. *Sanba Kessakushū*, pp. 427–495, reprints only Books I and II.

56. Honda, *SSB*, pp. 306-308; in addition to the translated passage, Honda singles out II:6, "The Philanderer and the Insincere Person" ("Uwaki naru hito no kuse narabi ni fujitsumono no kuse"), *Sanba kessakushū*, pp. 488-495.

57. "Hito no hi o kazouru hito no kuse," *Sanba kessakushū*, pp. 454-460. In the original, the disparaging term by which Okichi (called "Okittsan" by Otoku) refers to Okama-san and which I have translated as "muck-up" is *dabohaze*, a Chichibu dialect term for a generally inedible variety of goby or gudgeon that lives in brackish, stagnant waters; the nickname was used by Santō Kyōden in his *Harasuji ōmuseki*, (1809-1811). The ellipsis in Otoku's rendition of Hachi-san's tirade represents culinary failings. The exchange toward the end of the translated passage about the itinerant minstrel priests remains obscure—one senses that the modern reader misses something here.

58. On the economic and social relationships among property owners (*jinushi*), resident managers (*ōya* or *ienushi*), and tenants (*tanako*) in the microcosm of the Edo *nagaya*, see under those headings in Miyoshi Ikkō, *Edogo jiten.*

59. "Gajin no uso," *Ningen banji uso bakkari*, in NMZ XIV, 611-612.

60. See Chapter 2, note 18.

61. Honda, *SSB*, pp. 313-314.

62. Illus. Utagawa Kuninao (Tsutaya Jūzaburō, et al., 1814), 3 vols., reprinted in *KBZ* IV, 175-210; NMZ XIV, 717-748; *Sanba kessakushū*, pp. 389-426.

63. Honda, "Kokkeibon to wagei," pp. 127-128.

64. Co-authored with Rakutei Bashō, illus. Utagawa Kuninao and Kitagawa Utamaro (Mikiya Kizaemon, Nishimura Genroku, 1811), 4 vols. No modern edition available to writer; discussed in Honda, *SSB*, pp. 271-272.

65. (Unknown publisher, 1813-1814), 4 vols. No modern edition; discussed in Honda, *SSB*, pp. 301-303.

66. (Unknown publisher, 1814), 2 vols., reprinted in *KBZ* V, 109-172, and *Sanba kessakushū*, pp. 941-1005.

67. Honda, *SSB*, pp. 271-272, 301-302.

68. In addition to *Ukiyoburo, Ukiyodoko*, and the works discussed in this chapter, there are three others sometimes included in the canon of Sanba's *kokkeibon* that for various reasons have been excluded from this study:

Daisen sekai gakuya saguri, illus. Utagawa Toyokuni (Tsuruya Kinsuke, 1817), 3 vols., reprinted in *Sanba kessakushū*, pp. 807-863. This seems to be an experimental fragment, only roughly finished, of a much longer planned work.

Chaban kyōgen hayagatten. Book I, illus. Utagawa Kuninao (Nishimiya Shinroku, 1821), 2 vols.; Book II, illus. Utagawa Kuninao (Nishimiya Shinroku, 1824), 2 vols., reprinted in Hayakawa Junzaburō, ed., *Zatsugei sōsho*, II, 68-102. This work is best regarded not as a *kokkeibon* but as a practical handbook for amateur theater enthusiasts.

Keiko jamisen, revised and completed by Tamenaga Shunsui (Nansenshō Somabito II), illus. Utagawa Kuninao (Nishimura Yohachi, Osakaya Mokichi, 1826), 5 vols. No modern edition. Discussed in Honda, *SSB*, pp. 381–382. Very little of this work seems to have been Sanba's own.

Chapter Five

1. For a comprehensive list of modern editions of *Ukiyoburo* and *Ukiyodoko* published by the early 1960s, see *Kokusho sōmokuroku,* 8 vols. (Iwanami Shoten, 1963–1972), under their respective entries. *Ukiyoburo* has been reprinted in Nakamura Michio, ed., *Ukiyoburo, NKBT* LXIII; Jinbō Kazuya, ed., *Ukiyoburo,* Kadokawa bunko no. 2497; Mitamura, *Kokkeibon meisakushū,* pp. 716–903; *KBZ* III, 139–368; *NMZ* XIV, 221–392; *Sanba kessakushū,* pp. 1–22; and many other places. Only the first three editions are annotated.

For *Ukiyodoko,* see Nakanishi Zenzō, ed., *Ukiyodoko, Nihon koten zensho* series; Nakano et al., eds., *Sharebon, kokkeibon, ninjōbon,* pp. 255–369; *NMZ* XIV, 511–598; *KBZ* III, 369–488; *Sanba kessakushū,* pp. 223–388; and elsewhere. A translation into modern Japanese exists: Kubota Mantarō, trans., *Ukiyodoko,* in Hisamatsu Sen'ichi et al., eds., *Edo shōsetsushū* II, *Nihon no koten* series XXV, 271–309. Ono Takeo, *Edo no rakugo: Ukiyodoko, Edo fuzokū shiryō* series, Vol. V, contains the original text with parenthetical modern Japanese equivalents for difficult words and passages. Only the first two editions cited above are fully annotated.

The original publication data are as follows:

[*Odokebanashi*] *Ukiyoburo.* Book I: illustrations by Kitagawa Yoshimaro; Nishimura Genroku, Ishiwata Heihachi, 1809; 2 vols. Book II: illustrations by Yoshimaro; Nishimura Genroku, Ishiwata Risuke, Ishiwata Heihachi, 1810; 2 vols. Book III: illustrations by Utagawa Kuninao; Nishimura Genroku, Ishiwata Risuke, 1812; 2 vols. Book IV: illustations by Kuninao; Nishimura Genroku, Ishiwata Risuke, 1813; 3 vols.

[*Ryūhatsu shinwa*] *Ukiyodoko.* Book I: illustrations attributed to Utagawa Kuninao; Tsuruya Kinsuke, Kashiwaya Hanzō, 1813; 3 vols. Book II: illustrations by Kuninao; Tsuruya Kinsuke, Kashiwaya Hanzō, 1814; 2 vols.

2. Jippensha Ikku, *Tōkaidōchū hizakurige;* Thomas Satchell, trans., *Shanks' Mare: Being a Translation of the Tokaido Volumes of "Hizakurige," Japan's Great Comic Novel of Travel and Ribaldry.*

3. See the Kubota translation cited in note 1 above. The NHK broadcast was aired over a period of several weeks in spring 1975.

4. Nakamura, ed., *Ukiyoburo,* p. 106, reproduces the colophon of the 1820 edition of Book I. Jinbō, ed., *Ukiyoburo,* pp. 376–377, discusses the differences (or rather, lack of differences) between the two editions.

5. For instance, in *Nishiki no ura* (1790).

6. Keene, *World Within Walls*, p. 415, echoing a similar judgment by Mizu-tani Futō quoted in Nakamura, ed., *Ukiyoburo*, pp. 35-36.

7. *Sakusha burui*, p. 87.

8. Keene, *World Within Walls*, p. 410.

9. Ibid., p. 416.

10. Note that Ono Takeo's edition of *Ukiyodoko* (note 1 above) carries the subtitle *Edo no rakugo*.

11. Nakamura, ed., *Ukiyoburo*, p. 56.

12. Ibid., p. 113.

13. Ibid., p. 77.

14. Ibid., p. 67.

15. Sanba justifies his orthography in an explanatory note at the end of his introduction to Book III (Nakamura, ed., *Ukiyoburo*, p. 175.)

16. The first appearance of the special diacritical mark for non-nasalized *-g-* was in Sanba's *Itakobushi*, a *sharebon* treating the pleasure quarters of the Itako region of modern Ibaragi prefecture that was written in 1806 but not published until 1841 (Honda, *SSB*, pp. 78, 121-122); Sanba used the special mark for *-tsa-* earlier in *Sendōbeya* (1807), but, since it appears earlier still in works by other writers, it seems not to have been Sanba's own invention. (Nakamura, ed., *Ukiyoburo*, p. 37.)

17. Nakamura, ed., *Ukiyoburo*, pp. 37-38.

18. Ibid., p. 58.

19. Okitsu Kaname, *Edo shomin no fūzoku to ninjō*, pp. 137-139.

20. Takayanagi Mitsuhisa, ed., *Nihonshi jiten*, p. 1113.

An Annotated Translation
of Portions of *Ukiyoburo*

TRANSLATOR'S NOTE

This translation corresponds to Book I, Part 1 (zenpen, maki no jō), and Book II, Part 1 (nihen, maki no jō) of Ukiyoburo. *The introductory passage entitled "The Larger Meaning of the Bathhouse of the Floating World" appears at the beginning of Book I in the original, but was clearly meant as an introduction to the work as a whole, since both Books I and II have their own introductions.*

At several points in the translation, passages have been omitted that proved to be untranslatable, usually because they were too dependent on wordplay to be recreated in English without drastically distorting the meaning or the tone of the original. All such omissions are explained in the notes.

An Annotated Translation
of Portions of *Ukiyoburo*

THE LARGER MEANING OF THE BATHHOUSE
OF THE FLOATING WORLD

There is, one realizes on careful reflection, no shortcut to moral learning like the public bath. It is, after all, the way of Nature, and of Heaven and Earth, that all are naked when they bathe—the wise and the foolish, the crooked and the straight, the poor and the rich, the high and the low.[1] The nakedness of infancy purges them all of sorrow and desire, and renders them selfless, be they Sakya-muni or Confucius, Gonsuke or Osan.[2] Off with the wash water come the grime of greed and the passions of the flesh; a master and his servant are equally naked when they rinse themselves. As surely as an evening's red-faced drunkard is ashen and sober in the morning bath,[3] the only thing separating the new-born baby's first bath from the cleansing of the corpse is life, fragile as a paper screen.[4]

So it is that the old man who loathes Buddha enters the bath and at once recites a prayer in spite of himself. The rake takes off his clothes and, for once feeling shame, covers his private parts. The "fierce warrior" restrains his anger when someone pours water over his head, for the place is crowded. And the hotheaded bully, his arm tattooed with "invisible gods and demons,"[5] bows when he goes through the door, and says "Excuse me." Are these not signs of the power of the public bath?

While a man of feeling may have his private thoughts, the un-feeling bath affords no privacy. Should one, for instance, attempt to fart discreetly in the bath, the water will at once go *buku-buku,*

137

and bubbles will rise to the surface. In his thicket, Yajirō may do what he likes, but in the larger world of the bath, will not even he feel shame?[6]

At the bathhouse one sees demonstrated every one of the Five Virtues. Hot water warms the body, removes dirt, cures ills, and heals fatigue. This is Benevolence. A bather will not touch another's wash bucket without first asking if it is free; and far from being selfish with the rinse buckets, customers will hurry to finish and lend them to others. This is Integrity. Bathers denigrate themselves—"I'm just a bumpkin," "Oh, I'm cold-blooded, I guess"—and politely say to others, "Excuse me," "Good to see you," and "After you!" Or perhaps they will say, "Come, let's be a little quieter," or "Go ahead, please take your time." This is Propriety. The proper use of cleansing powder, pumice stone, or gourd skin to remove soil, or of cutting stones to trim the hair—this is Wisdom. Adding cold water when someone finds the bath too hot, or hot if it is cold, and scrubbing one another's backs—these things are Trust.

The public bath being this auspicious sort of place, its patrons come to understand, through using the square dipping-bucket and the round wash-pail, that water does, indeed, conform to the shape of the vessel, as the Lotus Sutra teaches. Like the floor boards of the bath, their hearts are constantly polished, and the filth of the world cannot long adhere. . . .[7]

The bathhouse rules[8] require watchfulness against fire, and, indeed, one must guard against the fires of human passion. The rules say, "In times of strong wind, the bath may close at any time;"[9] so it is that, when the winds of profligacy blow in the heart, a fortune may be lost in a moment. The Five Elements and the Five Bodily Parts have been placed in our safekeeping by Heaven, and so we carry with us naturally the "valuables" otherwise prohibited by the rules. Through wine and lust we are apt to leave behind consciousness and good sense, cautioned though we are about "leaving articles behind." And is it not true that we "are strictly forbidden" to blame on others the ills that we bring upon ourselves? Just as "There shall be no quarrels or arguments," neither should we pursue worldly fame and gain. "There shall be no raising of voices," whether in joy, in anger, in sorrow, or in pleasure. Ignoring these injunctions is as sure to result in loss as going to the bathhouse just before closing time, when one risks wasting the entry fee should the drain plug be pulled too soon. Chew as you will on your washcloth, there is no profit in regret![10]

As a general rule, the human heart is as apt to jump from good to evil as are the bathhouse fleas from Gombei's quilted coat to Hachibei's silk jacket, or from the country girl's simple robe to the stolid matron's kimono. The underwear that yesterday was dropped on the floor may today be placed high on a shelf: the high and the mighty, the lowly and the poor, are alike creatures of Heaven's will. But good and evil, rectitude and deviance are matters of individual choice. Once one comes to a full understanding of these truths, they will suffuse one's being like the warmth of a morning bath.

The body should be put safely away as if in a bathhouse locker, a lock placed upon the spirit, and care taken not to don mistakenly the wrong one of the Six Emotions.

"The above rules shall be faithfully observed." So saying, the chief of the guild of the gods, Buddhas, and Confucius placed his seal, as large as a "peony cake," on the regulations to be followed in caring properly for one's single life on earth.

In response to the publisher's request, urgent as usual, that I produce a book for the coming spring publishing season of the Year of the Dragon, the 6th of the Bunka era,[11] I took up the brush on the 9th day of the 9th month of the previous autumn, and, after partaking of the sweet potato that is *de rigueur* at moon-viewing parties in that month, I farted forth this little volume.

> By Shikitei Sanba (seal)
> At his humble abode in Kokuchō

One evening in Utagawa Toyokuni's lodgings,[12] we listened to Sanshōtei Karaku[13] telling *rakugo* stories, and, as always, his gifted tongue went right to the heart of human emotions. There is surely no one as funny as he; how hard it is to be even a tenth as effective on paper! Beside me that evening, laughing as hard as I was, sat a publisher. Greedy as ever, he suddenly asked me if I would put something together based on these stories of the public bath, leaving out the parts about the licensed quarter and emphasizing the humor in commonplace people and events. I agreed to try, and set myself to work on the first two books, a treatment of the men's bath.

The Bathhouse of the Floating World: A Burlesque
Book I, Part 1
The Men's Bath

COMPILED FOR THE SAKE OF AMUSEMENT, IN EDO
BY SHIKITEI SANBA

When the wind is calm (and in any case, they say, in a peaceful realm it blows only one day out of five),[14] the "Closing Early" sign is not hung up by the entrance to the bathhouse; when the rain is gentle (and it is said to fall on only one day out of ten), there is no need to put out the umbrella barrel. And, on the day the bathhouse closes each month, all is truly tranquil and quiet.

Wise or foolish, exalted or lowly, the human heart is bathed in blessings. If a bath on the day of the New Year's housecleaning washes away the dust of the Five Impurities,[15] the Six Passions will be scrubbed from the flesh in the Gift Day Bath.[16] And how splendid, how welcome a bath in the morning: it is as if every one were the first bath of the year!

Over here a priest mutters, "Buddha be praised," and over there a layman babbles drunkenly. For every man showing off by using the theatrical slang word for bath water, there is a woman drawling

about the "bawth." While the herbalist's apprentice may make a
simple-minded pun on the characters in the "Cash Only" sign, the
fledgling Confucian scholar misreads the characters for "Honeysuckle Bath" as "Bath of Escape from Winter."[17] Sometimes the
easiest things to read are the hardest to understand!

Should someone in the women's bath lose her comb in the tub,
the bath boy will plunge in and retrieve it, as if he were diving into
the Nameri River. "Adults, 10 *mon*," reads the sign—even Aoto
Fujitsuna, we may assume, would not begrudge a square-holed
coin for a bath![18] "Children, 8 *mon;* with nursemaid, 16"—ah, the
sixteen saintly *rakan!*[19]

Though there be a comely Kaoyo emerging from the bath, her
robe, like a monk's, revealing a naked right shoulder, no latter-day
Moronao would dare peek into the women's bath.[20] The men's
bath "will not be alone, but always have a neighbor"[21] in the
women's!

The bathhouse master, presiding like an image of the chief
rakan Binzuru,[22] stops lending out scrubbing bags[23] for a moment
and sneaks a sidelong glance into the women's bath, on the pretext
of summoning a bucket-boy for a customer with a rap of his
wooden clappers. Binzuru may not be conscious of the salve his
worshipers rub on his images, but surely even he must know that
the men's and women's baths "shall not be together," and the distinction between husband and wife.[24]

The master's wife manages the women's bath. This modern
Empress Kōmyō[25] heats soap powder over the brazier to extract
an oil to use as a salve for athlete's foot, and wrings out the towels
that people have rented, but the bathhouse still will not admit the
seriously ill, or the aged and infirm: while no disease-ridden incarnation of the Buddha Ashuku is likely to appear, not so the common louse, that crawling insect version of the thousand-armed
bodhisattva Kannon!

The pungent smell of soap powder wafts over to prick the nose
of the bath attendant, and someone raps the side of the wooden
tub to wake the bucket-boy. Wailing voices, excited babble: "Too
hot!" "Too cold!" "Add a little cold water!" "No, don't!" Through
the din and bustle cuts a voice singing *Makura tanzen,*[26] and suddenly a naked figure appears, striking exaggerated theatrical poses
in *roppō* style. Someone chants a *sumō* scene, and a bather makes

his exit imitating a wrestler entering the ring. A quavering rendition of "Here has misery lodged . . ."[27] comes from someone standing shivering by the door. Someone else begins to chant the lines, "And whereupon a voice was heard again, 'A horse, a horse,'"[28] but "horse" is hardly the word for a man so unimpressively equipped!

The old men who drone out *Edo-bushi*[29] tunes in the bath are convinced that the children who squeeze through the crowd shouting "Getting out! Getting out!" take remarkably long baths. But then again, to the real Edoite fond of *meriyasu*[30] songs, the rustic politely excusing his way toward the door seems to have barely wet his towel during his brief stay in the water. Long baths, short baths—"in front of the greengrocer's, every shape and size," sings the shop boy newly arrived from the capital, in a reedy-voiced rendition of a Matsuzaka[31] tune. A shrill voice adds a kind of counterpoint, in a pleasure-quarter ditty: "Long or short, it's not for us to choose . . . *Sai! Ne-e! Moshi!*"

For every old man gumming "Amida be praised," there is another coughing out, "Hail Amida of the Lotus of the Law." The voices are by turn gravelly and nasal, and here someone announces in a loud, coarse voice that he resides "in the foothills of the Golden Mountains of Cathay."[32] One person holds his head and groans, while another slaps his buttocks as he talks. One man sings with a foot in the air, and another shouts with his feet planted wide apart on the floor. Some sit, some stand; and a bad imitation of a *samisen*, in a voice as artless as a monkey's, comes from a figure crouched in a corner of the bath: *ne-te-te-ten tsuru.*[33]

This is the Bath of the Floating World, overflowing with gods and Buddhas, moral lessons, love, and evanescence: the place could be anywhere, but the time is the middle of the month. Dawn has just come to the bathhouse, which is not yet open for business.

THE MEN'S BATH: MORNING SCENES

In former days, the entrance to the bathhouse was marked by a carved wooden arrow, a play on the words for "Shoot an Arrow" and "Enter the Bath."[34] *Such signs appear in old illustrated books and may still be found, even now, in out-of-the-way places.*

It was dawn, and crows were crying, "Caw, caw, caw." An early
morning vendor hawking fermented soybeans called out, "*Nattō,
nat-to-o-o.*" From nearby houses came the sound—*kachi, kachi,
kachi*—of people striking flints to light their fires.

A man of thirty or so approached the bathhouse. He was still
dressed in his nightclothes, which were tied with a narrow sash.
The inner flap of his kimono hung low, its dangling hem nearly
hiding his high clogs. His towel, which looked as if it had been
boiled in grease, hung limply over one shoulder as he polished his
teeth with the fingers of his right hand. The man, who was called
Butashichi,[35] slouched along like some sort of crawling bug; he
was a victim of a kind of palsy popularly known as the *yoi-yoi*
disease.[36]

"Hunh! S-Still no' open, hunh? S-Still aslee', th-the slobs!"[37]

Talking to himself, Butashichi went up to the entrance of the
bathhouse and shouted harshly, "M-Manager! G-Ge' u'! Ge' u',
you s-slob! The s-s-sun's u', an' i''s alrea'y ho' enough to b-burn
your ass! He-e-y M-M-Manager!" Butashichi looked down. "Ah,
ah, ah! Shi', shi'!" he cried. "I s-s-st'd inh some sh'! Ugh! Ugh!
F-Filthy!" He turned to a dog sleeping nearby. "Wa' i' y-you, you
li'l b-bastar'? Ah, i' doesn' m-ma'er. D-Danh i' anyway, why'h I
h-ha' to g-go an' ste' inh a p-pile of sh-shi'?" Still muttering, he
finished cleaning his teeth, and spat at the dog.

As Butashichi stumbled around waiting for the bath to open, a
man of perhaps twenty-one or twenty-two appeared. He had a
plucked forehead, square cut forelocks, and a sloppy, home-
dressed topknot. He looked as if he had just risen; over his shoulder
lay a bleached cotton towel spotted here and there with lip rouge.
He had attached his tooth powder bag to his topknot with a
toothpick and was carrying a pair of baggy work pants rolled up
under one arm.

From the alley opposite came a second man in his twenties. He
appeared to have plucked his forehead recently, but apart from his
sash and his clogs, he was totally unremarkable. He tilted his head
slightly as he polished his molars with a toothpick. When he bent
over to spit, his towel slipped from his shoulder and fell to the
ground.

The other newcomer had been watching him, and laughed,
"Hey, stupid! You dropped your towel. Wake up!"

The second man turned on the tips of his clogs and picked up the towel. Still looking back over his shoulder, seemingly at the knot in his sash, he started forward again and stumbled over the sleeping dog, which let out a yelp.

"Sonuvabitch. What a dumb place to be," he swore.

"Who's dumb? Serves you right!" said the onlooker.

"Who are you to talk? Get a load of this guy—you get those clothes from a 'phoenix?'[38] Bath isn't open yet, huh? Sure sleep late, the lazy bastards. We've got our rights, too. What time do they think it is, anyway? The *nattō* guy has already packed up, and it's time for the sweet beans. Hey! Let me see that towel. Lip rouge? Powder? Shameless! Got it from *her,* I'll bet!"

"Come on! Don't piss me off. Get one yourself, if you're man enough. Some men just have it, and some don't."

"I'd rather *not* have it, thank you, if it meant I had to have a face like yours. If you didn't have a nose, it would look like a grater. With a face like that, you could be collecting royalties from pigs!"

"Ah, fuck off!" said the man with the spotted towel as he gave the other a playful push toward the covered gutter.

"Who-o-a! Look out for the shit," he cried, catching his balance and stepping aside just in time. "Looks like somebody else stepped in it before."

"Y-Yeah, I s-s-ste'd inh i' j-jus' n-now," volunteered Butashichi.

"Oh, it was you that stepped in it! You didn't have to, you know. Really. That's too much."

"M-Maybe, bu' I ste'd inh i'! C-C-Coul'nh hel' i'. M-M-My c-c-clog, m-my clogs g-go', 'gs g-g-go', g-g-g . . ."

"What? What? Can't understand a word you're saying. Boy! You're still really a mess. Aren't you any better?"

"Hunh? Oh, s-sure, I'm a l-l-lo' be'er. J-J-Jus' f-fine. L-Loo'!" Butashichi planted his feet firmly on the ground. Swaying back and forth, and shuffling to keep his balance, he said, "S-S-See? M-My legs are f-fine. T-There wa' a f-fire a' m-m-my a' my aunt's p-place in H-Honjo las' w-wee', an', an', I r-ran over an' h-h-help' ou'. Really kn-n-nock' mysel' ou'. She wa' v-very please'."

"What exactly did she tell you?" one of the men asked.

"She sai', 'T-Tha' f-fine. N-Now wh-why don' you g-go on a n-n-nice p-p-pil, p-pilgrimage to the K-K-Konpira S-Shrine in S-S-Sanuki?'[39] T-Tha' wha' she sai'."

"Listen. Why don't you try praying at Hori-no-uchi?[40] You're really not any better at all. You ought to take care of yourself.

"I alrea'y go' a c-charm f-from Ho-Horun, Hori-no-uchi. I s-sai'
than' you, an' I g-g-g, unh, I g-g-g, I sai' 'Hail t-the Lo'us Sutra'
three hun're' t-times, an' . . . ."

"Three hundred times isn't that many."

"B-Before b-b-breakfas'? You h-hafta do i' on an empty s-stoma',
or i' won' w-wor'. Anyway, t-the ol' lady really take' g-goo' c-care
of m-me. S-She's g-grea', b-bu' my unh-unh-uncle in A-Asakusa
hate' me. H-He wan' me to b-b-be a p-p-pries'!"

"You know, you might be better off being a priest. Maybe you
should listen to him."

"Are you k-k-kidding? T-The ol' l-lady woul'n' le' me. I-I-I'm
g-gonna ge', gonna g-ge' m-m-marrie', you know, any d-day now.
Whee-ooo! T-Take tha'! An' t-tha'! S-swish, swish. Unh. An' tha'!"

"What are you supposed to be, a samurai?"

"Y-You b-be'! W-With t-two s-sword'. Whoo-ee! S-See? L-L-Loo'
a' these legs. They're j-jus' f-fine, s-see?"

Butashichi jumped up and down on the gutter cover, his legs
jerking around wildly. Then, just as he began to totter and lose his
balance, the big shutters of the bathhouse started to open. Butashichi made a grab for one of the shutters as it swung inward, but
lost his footing and sprawled flat on his back with a *thud* on the
pounded earth floor of the entrance.

"Look out!" cried the others simultaneously.

Aghast, the manager leapt down from the raised floor of the
bathhouse into the entryway, and he and the other two men
grabbed Butashichi and helped him to his feet. He had been lying
on his back where he fell, simply gaping wide-eyed at everyone
around him.

"Are you hurt?" the manager asked.

"Guess he tripped on his tongue! Ah ha ha ha ha," laughed one
of the men.

"Hunh? I-I'm all righ', I'm all righ'. Hee hee hee." Giggling to
cover his embarrassment, Butashichi stepped up into the bathhouse.

"Well. Good morning, everybody," the manager greeted them
cheerfully.

"Yeah. You certainly do sleep late."

"Yes, I had a very late night."

"That sounds suspicious!"

"I'll bet he went to see the *niwaka*."[41]

"Ha ha ha. I wish I *had*," said the manager as he dusted off his cash box with the corner of a quilt and seated himself.

In the dressing room, the two men began to take off their clothes, and one of them turned to Butashichi.

"Now mind you don't slip again," he warned. "Oh, it's cold. Damn, it's cold this morning!"

"Well, in we go!" said the other. "Let's wash away those sins!"

They headed for the bath.

"Here we go!"

They went through the low "pomegranate door,"[42] and immediately began singing a bantering pleasure-quarter song. Butashichi, meanwhile, had finished undressing, and holding his towel hesitantly in front of him and scowling to cover his embarrassment, he wobbled uncertainly toward the door.

"H-Here I go-go!" He stooped and went through the door to the bath. "Loo' ou', here I c-come. Ooh, ooh, i' really h-ho'! Jus' like I-Ishikawa G-Goemon!"[43] he said as he clambered into the tub. With a defiant look on his face, he began to croon, "'Tonigh' I slee' in Yoshida-chō,[44] ro'-a-bye, ro'-a-bye . . .'"

"Well! Listen to the dashing youth! Hey-ho, hey-ho," the other men in the bath hooted.

Mistaking their scorn for praise, Butashichi went on proudly, "An' then i' g-g-goes, 'Ro'-a-bye, ro'-a-bye . . .'"

*　　　　*

In the meantime, a retired gentleman of about seventy had appeared at the entrance to the bathhouse, wearing a floppy cap and a sleeveless paper jacket. He gave his bathrobe to his boy, who was eleven or twelve, and leaned mumbling on his cane.

"Ah, good morning, sir," said the manager. "You're early today."

"Hullo, Manager. Gotten a lot colder, hasn't it?" the retired gentleman replied.

"Yes, indeed. It feels like the weather's gradually changing."

"'Gradually' is hardly the word for it. Tsurukichi! Watch my sandals." As the old man stepped up out of the dirt-floored entrance, he took a string of prayer beads from behind his ear and clasped it to his forehead. "Oh, I had a terrible time getting to sleep last night," he said. "Damned dogs just wouldn't stop barking. Never in all my days do I remember them barking so much! Finally, I just got up and got dressed. I sat at the head of the bed for a while and puffed on my pipe and thought, but I still wasn't sleepy, so I thought I might as well check over the house again. I took a lamp and looked all around, front and back, but everything seemed normal, so I went back to bed. I must say, young people certainly don't seem to have any trouble sleeping, do they? There I was, tiptoeing all over the house, and not one of them woke up. That's why you always have to keep an eye on things yourself." The old man spotted a friend who had just arrived. "Ah, Pinsuke! You're early today!"

"Ah! Good morning, sir," Pinsuke answered. "What time was the earthquake last night?"

"Well, I heard the clock strike three some time later, so it must have been a little after two. 'Sickness if twelve o'clock,' you know, 'rain if eight or four, dry spell if ten o'clock . . .'"[45]

Pinsuke continued, "'Seven, gold; five, water.'"[46]

"No, no, no," said the retired gentleman. "This one goes, 'Cold if six or two.'"[47]

"Oh, is that what it is? I guess I was getting the earthquake one mixed up with the one about souls. Yours makes more sense—I do feel as if I have a cold coming on."

"No, no, Pinsuke. They mean *temperature* cold."

"Well, what do you know. Mixed up again! I figured that, since it was 'sickness if twelve o'clock,' then the 'six or two' part meant 'catch a cold.' Ho! Watch you step there, sir!"

The retired gentleman and his friend entered the bath one after the other.

*   *

The neighborhood around the bathhouse was gradually becoming more and more crowded and lively as the morning wore on.

A tooth-powder vendor cried, "Get your Red Plum Tooth Polish, cure-all for the mouth! Red Plum here . . ."

And there were others hawking their wares:

"Shucked mussels, shu-u-u-cked clams . . ."

"Bean paste here, bean paste—Hishio, Kinsanji. Unfiltered soy sauce . . ."

"Get your pickles here! Pickled greens, Naras, Southern Barbarians . . . Pickled greens? Can't beat 'em anywhere . . ."

"The Ise-ya at your service . . ."

"Bring your empty bottles here. Empties? Empties?"

*   *

Hammering on a wooden gong, a mendicant priest appeared at the entrance to the bathhouse. "Hail Amida, hail Amida," he chanted. *Bonk, bonk, bonk, bonk* went the gong.

"Here you are," said the bathhouse manager as he handed him some money.

"Hail Amida, hail Amida. Your generosity today assures salvation to the souls of your ancestors to the earliest generation. Hail Amida, hail Amida," the priest cried again. *Bonk, bonk, bonk, bonk.*

*   *

The approach of two old nuns, bent with age, was signaled by the tinkle of bells, *chiririn, chiririn.*

The manager gave them alms, too. "Here you are."

"Thank you," said one of the nuns. "Hail Amida, hail Amida. Oh, Seikō! It looks like you have a new hood—or is it just that my eyes are bad?"

"What, this? This is the one," the other nun explained, "that showed up next to where I was kneeling during the all-night prayers at Tokuganji last year, during the Ten Nights.[48] I couldn't find out whose it was, so I just kept it, and I've had it ever since. It was getting a little ratty, though, and, just when I was thinking about maybe fixing it up somehow, I found this nice little piece of cloth. 'The faithful heart is rewarded,' wouldn't you say, Myōsei?"

"Really, Seikō, a gift from Nyorai[49] himself, isn't it? My goodness! Hail Amida! Hail Amida! Let's see—isn't it today that the Yorozu-ya usually gives alms?"

"Mm. Let's go by the Kanō-ya on the way, too."

"Oh my, does my back hurt!" complained Myōsei. She planted her staff firmly on the street, and the bells attached to it jingled, *chiririn, chiririn.* Bracing herself with the staff, she arched her back and stretched.

*   *

"May Inari and the Seven Gods of Wealth always be with you!" Two more priests had come to beg at the bathhouse. "Now, tell me—you haven't had a Buddhist worthy by here for a while, have you? 'Priest in the morning, handsome profits,'[50] they say."

"Nothing today, nothing today," said the manager.

The priest ignored the manager and said to his companion, "If you don't tell them something like that, they won't give." He turned back to the manager. "'Handsome profits,' you know. Come on—just a copper? One copper for two priests?"

"No, no. Not today, not today."

"'Not today, not today,'" the priest imitated the manager. He and his friend moved on down the street, bowls in hand.

*   *

A man in his forties arrived, holding by the hand a boy of five or so and carrying on his back, like a monkey trainer carrying his pet, a little girl of about two, who in turn was clutching a toy bucket made of bamboo and a ceramic baby turtle.

"Ho, ho, ho. Here we are," said the father, whose name was Kinbei, in a tired voice. "Where's the bath? Brother, don't fall over. Watch where you're going! Oh ho! *Here's* the bath! Oops. Look out for the dog dirt! Let's jump over it. Let's jump! Ooh, dirty. Brother almost stepped in the dog dirt, didn't he? Bō's on Daddy's back, so she's safe."

"Bō. Back," said the little girl, whose real name was Tsuru.[51]

"Ho ho ho. Bō's on my back, and Brother's walking. All right, down you go. Wait, wait! You're going to fall! You're going to fall! All right, Brother, you undress yourself, and Daddy'll take off Bō's clothes. There. The arm comes out here ..."

"I already got my clothes off," the little boy announced. "'Senjirō's the last, Senjirō's the last,'"[52] he taunted. "You're slow, you're slow," he said, tickling his sister under the chin.

"Come on! No horsing around," Kinbei warned.

A man nearby joked, "Hey! Brother's got a weenie, but where's Tsuru's?"

"Tsuru lost hers somewhere, I guess!" answered a man named Gen, laughing. "Looks like the good weather's going to last, don't you think, Fukusuke?"

"Seems so. If it does, it'll be a good harvest."

"All right, now let's go inside," the father said. "Look out, Brother. Don't slip. Don't drop your toys, Tsuru. There we go." He turned to the other men and said, "You know, Fukusuke, I'm still not doing as well as I'd like. But once the kids come along, I guess you're stuck."

"But they *are* a lot of fun, don't you think?" said Gen.

"Fun? A lot of trouble, if you ask me! They can really wear you down. Ah! Watch your head! Watch your head!" He led the little boy and girl through the "pomegranate door," with a warning call of "Children coming through!" and began to scrub them. "Now Brother, get yourself wet all over," he said. "There's a good boy. Sploosh, sploosh. Ah, good, good. The water's nice and hot."

"Better be careful it's not too hot for the kids, Kinbei," warned a man named Tokuzō.

"Yeah, thanks, Tokuzō. Say, where was it that you went yesterday? I hear you were in fine spirits."

"Oh, I went to Ōji,"[53] Tokuzō answered.

"Aha! The Ebi-ya? The Ōgi-ya?"[54]

"Yes, and I suppose I should have been satisfied with that, but I came home by way of the Paddies Road,[55] too."

"The Imaguchi Tomoe-ya,[56] I'll bet!" Kinbei laughed. "That's somehow the way it always turns out. Ha ha ha ha ha."

"Here, let's have it cooled down a little. If you try to force children to get used to hot water, they wind up not liking it." Tokuzō pounded the side of the tub—*thump, thump, thump*—to call the water boy to add some cold water. The boy signaled that he had heard with a *thump* in reply. "You really ought to chant the 'Sculling Scene'[57] while you're stirring the bath water. Come on. Let's everybody help swish it around. '*Yasshisshi, yasshisshi,*'" Tokuzō sang as he stirred the water.

"Thanks very much," said Kinbei. "All right, let's get in. Hurry up, Brother!"

"It's still too hot, Daddy," cried the little boy.

"Come on! How could it be too hot? After Uncle Tokuzō went to all that trouble cooling it off for you! Tsuru's a lot tougher than you are. Watch! There we go—she's in, see?"

"Even the hot water pipe is just lukewarm now," Tokuzō grumbled, but saying, "Oh, well," he thumped on the side of the tub again.

"Oh, Tsuru's tough, Tsuru's tough!" Kinbe was saying.

"Daddy," said Brother, "I'm tough, too. Watch! I'm in!"

"Oh, you *are* tough," Kinbei agreed. "Why don't you fill your bucket up, Tsuru? Slop, slop! There! Isn't that fun? Oh, look! The baby turtle's swimming! Blub, blub, blub. Good, good! Brother, be sure to sink way down and get good and warm."

"But, Daddy, if I sink way down in, a goldfish or a carp will swim up and get me!"

"Oh, don't be silly! If you cry, though, a *kappa*[58] will swim up and get you! Oh, scary! Stay away, *kappas*! Tsuru's a smart little girl, so she doesn't cry. Come on, Brother. Don't cry!"

"I'm not a sissy!" Brother said bravely.

"See? Brother's tough, too," said Kinbei as he scrubbed the little girl. "Okay, let's get behind your ears so there won't be any dirt there. Close your eyes. Now, let's do under your nose so the bugs won't bite you. There! What a good girl! Your Uncle over there thinks so, too, I'll bet. All right, now stick out your tongue. Good girl. Oops. Did I make you cough? Bad Daddy! He scrubbed your tongue too hard. Oh! You have a moxa burn[59] on your tummy, don't you! We'll stay away from that. Who gave you the moxa?"

"Mommy," answered Tsuru.

"Oh. Mommy did. Bad Mommy. I'll have to scold her—giving my little Bō a moxa burn!"

"Sco' Mommy?" Tsuru asked.

"Uh huh, I'm going to scold Mommy."

"I wanna get out, Daddy," Brother interrupted.

"Not yet, not yet. Get a little warmer."

"But I can't stand it anymore."

"Well. That's not very grown up. Look how grown up Tsuru is. Listen! I have an idea," Kinbei said. "Let's Brother and Tsuru sing songs!"

"'Oh Moo-oo-n, how old are you-ou?'" Brother began. "'Thirteen and seven.'"

Kinbei went on, "'Oh, how . . .'"

"'. . . Very young you are still,'" the little boy continued.

"'Though you've had that baby there . . .'"

"'And though you've had this baby here.'"

"All right, Tsuru, now you sing one," Kinbei suggested.

"'Gib' it Oma' cawwy it,'" Tsuru began.

"Oh, ho ho," laughed her father. "'Give it to Oman to carry.' What's next? Well? What's next, Tsuru?"

"'Pway the dwum.'"

"No, no. Not yet. Where does Oman go?"

Brother helped out with the next line: "'To buy the oil, to buy the tea she goes.'"

"Oh, Brother's good!" cried Kinbei.

"'But in front of the oil shop . . .'" Brother continued.

Tsuru sang out, "'A big batch of ice!'"

"Oh, ho ho," Kinbei laughed. "'A big patch of ice.'"

The boy went on, "'She slips and she tumbles . . .'"

"'. . . And spills a-a-all the oil!' Come on, Tsuru, you sing too. What happens to the oil? Come on—'Jirō's dog . . .'"

"Daddy, no-o-o!" Brother screeched. "It's Tarō's dog!"

"'. . . Licked it all up,'" Kinbei continued.

"A-A-Aww up!'" sang Tsuru.

"Daddy forgets the rest. Ha ha ha ha."

"What happens to the dog, Daddy?" Brother hinted.

"Ah, that's right! Now, Tsuru!"

"'Pway the dwum!'"

"'Facing over there, boom-boom-boom-boom,'"[60] sang Brother.

"'And now over here, boom-boom-boom-boom,'" Kinbei concluded the song.

"No, first I think it goes, 'Facing over *here,* boom-boom-boom-boom,'" Brother said.

"Really? Well, boom-boom-boom! What do you say we get out?" Kinbei said. "Getting out! Children coming through!" he announced. "Mommy's waiting for us, and she'll probably have something nice for you if you're good, like a sweet potato or a jam bun. You've both been good, haven't you? Oh, look! Hatsu came to meet us with some clean robes."

"Hatsu. Wobes," said Tsuru.

"Oh, ho ho. Here, Hatsu. They're all yours! They've been very good."

*   *

By the exit to the dressing room, the retired gentleman was talking to a physician named Takuan.

"How have you been, sir?" inquired Takuan. "Playing *go* as usual, I trust. You always play with the master of the Isejū and that Tarōbei fellow from Abuhachi's, do you not? One might say you *go* against those fellows, mightn't one! Ho ho ho."

Whenever the physician laughed, he seemed to be mocking someone. His speech sounded stilted and insincere, and he was given to saying things like "fellow."

"Well actually," the old man answered, "as a matter of fact, one of my relatives is ill, and the members of the household are taking turns with the nursing. So, what with one thing and another, I haven't been playing much *go* recently.

"Mm. That is unfortunate. Dear, dear. A thousand sympathies. How is the patient?"

"He can't keep a bit of food down. Anything he eats, he—pardon my language—just throws right back up. Seems worse lately, if anything."

"Whom have you called in?"

"Well, at first Dr. Chūkei was coming once every two weeks, but there was no improvement, so later we called in Dr. Sonhaku, too, and now we have Dr. Tankei as well,"[61] the retired gentleman said.

"And what, may I ask, is their diagnosis?"

"They all say it is a growth in the gullet."

"'A growth in the gullet,' indeed! What do they mean, 'a growth in the gullet'? Even a layman could make a guess and call it 'a growth in the gullet,' if someone is throwing up everything he eats. Now esophageal carcinoma, that's quite another matter. What do they think they're doing? Those men are such lightweights. What do they know? Hah! I know the type. They spout nothing but nonsense, like, 'The medical books from as far back as the *Wai-t'ai* and the *Ch'ien-chin-fang*[62] tell us that'—now let me see, what might that sort of fellow say? Ah yes, I have it: '. . . the books tell us that "The breath is like a flight of geese, flying and scattering; a man with a growth in the gullet is overfond of linked verse."[63] You see, a sick person's breathing is compared to geese flying in a straight line because he has as much trouble gasping for breath as he would if he had swallowed a long, straight staff, like the ones Kuan Yü and Chang Fei carried, you know, and so, of course, he wishes he could "fly and scatter." Now, it seems that poetry lovers often suffer from this growth-in-the-gullet fellow, and that is why the books say "a man with a growth in the gullet is overfond of linked verse." The disease arises in one who is so determined to write verse at any cost that people have to beg him to stop.'"

"That makes sense," commented the retired gentleman, interrupting the physician's parody. "Now that you mention it, he does like poetry!"

Takuan, continuing in the same vein, said, "And then he would say, 'Now, if it were simply a matter of, say, thirty-six link verse, that would be quite all right, but fifty or a hundred links? No, that would surely be too large a dose to digest at one sitting, and would likely aggravate his condition.' There, you see? You say he likes linked verse. I could tell you that without even seeing him! 'Feel the pulse, find the disease,' they say. But I found the disease simply by listening, did I not? Hah! Be careful to 'avoid repetition'[64] in his diet!"

"Seriously," the doctor went on, "there is something called 'cormorant disease' that looks like this esophageal carcinoma fellow, but isn't. The patient eats something, then immediately brings it up. Your patient probably has cormorant disease. It is not, I am sorry to say, an easy one to cure. I'm afraid doctors like yours are far better with their tongues than they are with their medicine spoons. But the patient's family are at their mercy, because the latest medical books imported from China are unpunctuated and hard to read. That sort of fellow will always tell you that the Chinese are slipshod in their methods, and then turn right around and spout his own brand of nonsense. Suppose you say, 'Dr. Tankei, I'd like to eat eggs. What shall I do?' He'll say something like, 'Er, well, the ovum of the *Gallus gallus*, the common domestic fowl, is of course, contraindicated, but if you must, then perhaps a few duckus ovums.'[65] My word, what these fellows don't know! Hah hah ha. Most lamentable. Hah hah hah!

"Listen. Come closer. I've taken up ball-playing recently, for my digestion—you know, that 'kickball' fellow. I am not in Lord Narimichi's[66] league, of course, but, even if all you manage to do is kick the thing to a pulp, it's marvelous for the digestion. Well, I must be off. What ho, Manager! The proconsul of the bath is a fellow of grave responsibilities, is he not? Hah hah hah!"

"Heh, heh, heh," laughed the manager. "And where are you going today?"

"Well," Takuan replied, "today I thought I would go to a picture-viewing party in honor of Li Li-weng, and then, after I stop by Ku Yen-wu's place, I believe I shall drop in at Huang T'ing-chien's poetry competition. Who knows? Perhaps Su Tung-p'o or Lu Yu[67] will ask me to ghostwrite a few lines! At any rate, I have plenty of things to keep me busy without listening to a lot of grumbling sick people. Unfortunately, that is how a doctor builds a good practice! Well. I'm off! Hah hah hah!" Carrying his robe under one arm, the physician made his exit.

*　　　　*

Two men were in the dressing room after their baths. One of them was Hachibei, from whose head steam was still rising in little puffs. He had wrapped a towel around his waist in place of a loincloth, and was shaking out his kimono. The other, Matsuemon, was holding one end of his loincloth under his chin, in the old manner,[68] while he tied it on. His towel, of course, perched in a little round bundle on top of his head.

"Hachibei. Look over there," said Matsuemon. "See that guy walking along with the big hat pulled down over his face? The one with the jacket that looks like it would fall apart if you touched it? He's a sad case. He's what's become of a big landowning family that had thirty-odd pieces of land."

"Your 'local playboy from the big house at the corner' sort of thing, huh?" Hachibei suggested.

"Yup. Pathetic. Absolutely pathetic. Could happen to anybody, though—you have to be careful."

"He looks just like one of those beggars that go around handing out charms to the kids and talking about the 'King of Heaven,'" Hachibei observed.

"His father came from Ise, you know, and built up a fortune all by himself," Matsuemon began to relate. "But he had to be a real penny-pincher to do it. You simply can't afford to treat anybody to anything, you know. Anybody else, for instance, when there's a lot of fish around, would decide to be nice and give the servants a special treat, but do you know what he'd do? He'd give them all of maybe five vinegar-dried anchovies on a big platter, all lined up like little soldiers at attention, with their heads and tails still on. Or if it happened to be those awful young thread herrings that the market was full of one day, he'd buy some and fry them up, then go out the next morning to the fish market in Nihonbashi. He'd take them all around the market, and if he couldn't get the price he wanted for them, he'd pick up some big pieces of white radish on the way home and put those fried fish inside. Then he'd have them boiled and sliced up and served for supper. Heaven knows he had enough servant girls that he could have given them to, but he'd pile the things up in front of everybody, even Grandma, when they sat down for supper. Even Grandpa had to force them down, too, head and all—he used to go on and on about how the head was the best part of a fish. And sure enough, all of his managers and shop boys, all forty or fifty of them, would wind up having to eat the rest of the things, every last scrap, especially the heads. That way nothing was wasted.

"All year round, he had gruel boiled in tea for breakfast, and just a little soup for lunch. At night all he had with his rice was pickled radish, but that takes a lot of salt to make, so he limited himself to just two slices for the whole meal, right up through his hot water at the end. Even if it was some relative's death anniversary, all he served was a big flat bowl of soup with a few pieces of noodle-cut bean curd swimming around in it. He let himself have soup made with real bonito stock only twice a year, on his own birthday and on the day of the Ebisu Festival.[69] The only thing he ever had for a snack between meals was a little salted fried rice, with maybe a few soybeans somebody had sent him from the country—but not so many, you understand, that you could find them without a search party![70] Besides the fried rice with the beans, once in a while he had a little home-brewed sweet *sake,* and, since Grandma was from Kazusa, sometimes he made her those little Satsuma tea cakes with the shredded sweet potato and rice. That was it! Those were his only luxuries! He honored his ancestors, and he kept a close watch on everybody's comings and goings, so it's no wonder he did so well for himself. Money makes money, and after a while he started cleaning up on foreclosures. His business got bigger and bigger, and before long he was a very rich man."

"You can say *that* again!" Hachibei exclaimed. "I remember my father telling me that the only time he had *sake* was for the Ebisu Festival, and, when guests came at other times, all he would set down in front of them would be two bowls of noodles. He'd say, 'Please go ahead, don't stand on ceremony' and all, but, since there were only two bowls, of course, the guests would eat only one, and then leave. Afterwards, he'd invite Grandma in to join the party, but then he'd say, 'Don't mind if I do' himself, and split the other bowl with her. No wonder he piled up so much money!"

"Well, first of all, it helps if you have the gods on your side," Matsuemon observed. "But still, it did take him only thirty years to put together thirty-two or thirty-three pieces of land, thirty earthen storehouses, and maybe twenty-five or twenty-six storage cellars. You could tell just from the number of people coming and going that he was a man to be reckoned with."

"And it didn't take his son more than two or three years to ruin it all, did it?" Hachibei commented.

"Nope. It always takes less time to spend it than to make it, and you can't make a copper, even, if all you ever do is fool around. You may still be young, Hachibei, but let me tell you, don't spend all your money. 'The spendthrift has his reward.' Isn't that so, Manager? The manager's keeping his mouth shut, but I'll bet he's bought himself a slice of the business!''

"Ha! The only slices I ever see," said the manager, "are the ones from the turnips I cut up for my soup. I somehow never can manage to put any of that good old copper and gold away."

"Oh, you really should try to save some money, you know," Matsuemon advised. "You're just not determined enough, that's all. That's why you can't manage to put anything aside. How can anybody *not* build up a little capital in this bountiful city of Edo? It's such a wonderful place—money just seems to accumulate naturally here. Isn't that why so many people can come here from all over the country and make successes of themselves? Even you, Manager, if having money really didn't interest you, wouldn't you still be in the country somewhere, eating gruel and turning into a lump? What can you say to that? Nothing, I'll wager!''

"I stand corrected," said the manager.

"You do have your good points, though," Matsuemon went on. "There's hope for you yet, Manager! But you'll never get ahead in this world if you go around thinking the only way to keep warm is with charcoal, instead of wearing a good, thick, padded kimono. Just keep telling yourself that, once the padding's worn thin, it's all over for you. And you, Hachibei, your old mother's alone now, so be very good to her and don't cause her any trouble. You know the story about that Chinese what's-his-name that went out in the dead of winter to find bamboo shoots for his poor old father, and dug up a gold pot instead!''[71]

"Well," Hachibei said, "I'm pretty good to her, but probably not good enough to rate a gold pot! I do give her some sweet *sake* now and then, but the pot they bring it in is only brass!''

"Well, that's all right," Matsuemon said. "This playboy we're talking about, now even though he came into that huge fortune, he was unfilial, and that's why he wound up the way he did. At his father's funeral—you won't believe this—when it came time for him to light the incense, he came slouching in in full formal dress, looking for all the world like some actor. You could pretty well guess that he wasn't a very solid sort from the way he didn't seem in the least bit sad at losing his father, and, sure enough, it turned out we were right. Geishas here and jesters there—you name it, he brought 'em home and whooped it up with 'em. Or he'd go out and lurch and slide from teahouse to whorehouse and back again. The bills he piled up, both at home and away, kept getting bigger and bigger, his friends stopped having anything to do with him, and finally he used up the last bit of fat on his poor father's bones. But he's still snotty as you please—he looks down on everybody, and calls them blind and vulgar. He's very stuck-up about his social accomplishments, too—he built who knows how many tea-ceremony rooms. Such a dilettante! Anyway, it pays to watch yourself."

Sansuke,[72] a bathhouse attendant recently arrived from the countryside, had come in at some point carrying a shovel full of hot coals, and had been listening to the conversation.

"You boys say you got to lay up some money," Sansuke interrupted, "but you don't want to be a speculator, no sir. When I was still down home, there was one of those, what do you call 'em, freaks of nature, you know? There was this—what do you say in these parts, I wonder? Back home, we call 'em 'yams.'"

"They're 'yams' in Edo, too," everyone answered in chorus.

"Well, anyway," Sansuke continued, "this yam, boys, turned into an *eel!*"

"You don't say!" came another chorus.

"'Course it didn't quite have all its parts. Half of it was a yam, and the other half was an eel. A hunter found the thing, and was he surprised! He reckoned it was some kind of warning from the god of the mountain, or maybe a python. Pythons when they aren't pretending to be pythons are devils, you know, that's for sure. Anyhow, he could have killed it easy right then and there, but seems he didn't like to kill things that weren't half dead already, so what does he do? He goes to the village for consultations. Now, boys, there's this man in the village named Sonemura no Matsu-no-jō that knows about everything from Empress Jingū's time on down. Nothing he doesn't know, all the way right back to when this world began. Anyway, this Matsu-no-jō turned his neck around like a goose, and looked and looked at the thing. Didn't do anything except think and think, until you could hardly stand it anymore. Finally he says, 'This is an eel.' And then he says, 'If I am wrong, may I be separated from the god who watches over us here, and forced to leave this village where generations of my house have lived. But it looks like a yam has turned into an eel. Or perhaps an eel has turned into a yam. It's both things at once.

You don't have to have some priest do a divination, or get a sorceress in to do a purification. It's just an eel. And it's certainly not a python. Boys, that much I know. But I must say, even though there are things in books about sparrows diving into the sea and turning into clams, I've never seen anything in the *Teikin no ōrai*[73] or Imagawa Ryōshun,[74] or in any of the miscellanies or chronicles, either, about a yam turning into an eel.' That's what he told us, boys.

"Anyway," Sansuke continued, "there was this speculator there. Now, he had good ears, and heard about everything right away, and so, when he had found out the whole story, he talked things over with the right people, and paid twenty-four *ryō* in gold to buy the thing. That twenty-four *ryō*, by the way, went for cloudy *sake* and rice cakes for everybody in the village—everything you need to do up the Third-Day New Year's[75] in real style. Well anyway, this speculator, what do you suppose he did then? He figured he'd take his little attraction and put him in a square box, and make a lot of money showing him to crowds at temples and the like. So he got everything all set up, ready to go, and what do you think happened?"

"What? What?" cried the listeners.

"Well, we all like to busted a gut, it was so funny. Boys, that damned yam we thought was half eel, while that old speculator was getting ready to show it, went and stopped being a yam at all, and turned completely into an eel! That old half-yam had up and turned itself the rest of the way into an eel, and there it was, squirming around this way and that. If you tried to catch it, it just squeezed through your fingers, all wiggly and slippery like any regular old eel! Course, that wasn't surprising—any eel knows that if somebody grabs it too hard, it'll die. You know, if you buried an eel, it would certainly die, but I figure it just *might* turn into a yam. But once it turned into a yam, it sure wouldn't turn back into an eel!"

"Ah ha ha ha ha ha, ah ha ha ha ha," everyone laughed, over and over.

"Anyway," Sansuke began again, "since you couldn't tell what that little old performer really was anymore, there wasn't much to gawk at. That speculator sure had it figured wrong! He was out a good thirty *ryō* all told, what with putting up a stall and all. Wasn't a damned thing he could do about it, though, so he just grilled the eel and ate it. That figures out to be something like three *ryō,* two *bu* and then some a skewer. Pretty expensive eel! Thirty *ryō*'s worth of eel that man ate, all by himself! But that old eel had really skinned him, so it was right for him to skin the eel, but I'll bet it was tough![76] Ha ha ha ha ha."

Just as Sansuke was finishing his story, voices were heard in the bath crying, "Looks like he passed out from the heat! . . . Hey, Manager, there's somebody here that fainted. He passed out from the heat!"

"Somebody passed out?" said the manager. "Terrible, terrible!"

A crowd of bath attendants carried the man out. He turned out to be the palsy victim, Butashichi, who had fainted in the steam and heat.

"Who is he?"

"It's the spastic, Butashichi."

"If he's still sick, he shouldn't have stayed in the bath so long!"

"Splash some water on him."

"Put the lavatory sandals on his face!"

"No, stupid! That's for a fit! You're supposed to write 'horse beans' on his back, aren't you?"

"Hoarse? He isn't hoarse, he's passed out!"[77]

"Butashichi! Oh, Butashi-i-i-chi. Where ar-r-re you? Boom, boom, boom, bong, bong, bong."[78]

"Come on! This isn't funny. We have to bring him around. Wake up! Wake up!"

In the midst of all the commotion, the water they had thrown in Butashichi's face began to revive him.

"How are you, Butashichi? Butashichi! Can you hear me? Can you hear me?"

"Are you all right?"

"Unh-unh-ugh . . ." Butashichi grunted. "F-Fine, I'm f-fine. Wh-wha' happen' . . ."

"YOU PASSED OUT FROM THE HEAT!" someone told him in a loud voice.

"Huh? Huh?"

"YOU PASSED OUT FROM THE HEAT!"

"P-Passed . . . ou' . . . f-from the h-hea'? Unh . . . s-stupid thing . . . All righ' . . . I-I-I'm f-fine now. I p-passed b-back, passed b-back *in!* Unh . . . I was d-dreaming. F-Fine now. P-Pass' b-back in! F-Fine . . ."

*   *

It was lunchtime, and a water boy had come in and sat down at the counter in the manager's stead. Outside peddlers could be heard hawking their wares:

"Dumplings, du-u-mplings . . ."

"Sweet cowpeas . . ."

"Bean curd . . ."

"Broiled eel, very good! Broiled eel . . ."

"Fix your pots? Got any broken pots?"

"Hey, you—pot man! I've got a water urn that I need fixed."

"Ah, go on!" retorted the pot man.[79]

*   *

NOON-TIME SCENES

"Cool it off. Cool it off, huh? It's too hot!" someone called out from the bath as he pounded the side of the tub, *thump, thump, thump.*

"Don't make it any cooler! It'll be nothing but cold water!"

The manager said to the water boy, "There's more hot water now. Get the rinse buckets ready."

"Yes, sir," said the boy, leaving with a bucket.

*   *

An old man, clearly a busybody, was in the dressing room. Pushing aside with his foot a pail that someone was using to soak a towel, he grumbled, "Look here, you youngsters, get that drain board good and clean. It's dangerous for old people. It's easy for them to slip and fall. And what are all these buckets here for? You can hardly get past. Watch there's not too much water in the tub. Now look at that! Somebody's split open a soap bag. These people! What kind of pigs are they! And now somebody's old plaster's got stuck on my foot! Pfui. Disgusting. Ugh. Ugh. They spit all over. They pick off scabs and leave them lying about. Ugh. What a mess! Hail the Lotus Sutra!"

The old man bent over and peered through the pomegranate door. "Good Heavens!" he cried. "What an enormous rear end! Excuse me. Excuse me, please, but that's very rude, you know— get into the bath. You're blocking the door, and no one can get in after you. It doesn't do you any good, just sitting on the edge of the tub, you know. Aye! Old man coming through!" He settled into the tub. "Ah! This is nice! Anybody who complains about this being lukewarm would have to cuddle right up to the hot water pipe to get any hotter, or better yet, take off the grill and crawl right into the boiler! Ah, perfect, perfect! Hail the Lotus Sutra."

Someone in the bath began to sing, "'Lord Kiyomori had a fever. We . . .'[80] Hey, Grandpa! If you're going to cuddle up with some hot little thing,[81] make sure they don't get the duns after you! If you're too hot, just stick in your pickle and swish it around![82] Ah! There! It's started to boil. Terrific. Feels good on the old louse bites. It's sort of nice, really, when you have bites all over—you wind up all speckly, just like a fawn. Guess lice aren't totally bad!"

"'Came a lantern, creeping near,'" someone began to sing. "'"Igo, is that you?" she called. "Who did darling Yoshimatsu sleep with? If he slept with his Papa, that's fine, that's fine . . ."'"[83]

Someone else started another song. "'If only I could live with him, in Sangen'ya or Yamanaka . . .'"

"Ah! There you go! Sonuvabitch, that's the one I want to hear! Keep going. Do it up right!"

"'. . . Ah, lo-o-ove. Love without end!'" continued the singer, in the *Itako-bushi* style.[84]

Someone added a bad imitation of a *samisen* as accompaniment: "Teko-ten-ton, teko-teko-ten-ten, tsun-pon-pon."

"Hey, keep down the splashing, huh? Your *samisen*'s all wet as it is!"

"Oh, sorry!"

One of the men started to clamber out of the tub. "I'm getting out. Sorry, I have to step over you. Excuse me . . ."

"Wow!" cried the man who had been stepped over. "Did you see the size of his nuts? They were bouncing all over the place! He just calmly smacked me in the head with them. Now, *that* takes *balls*, wouldn't you say?" he joked after the man left. . . .[85] "Well, I'm getting out. Make way! Make way for a country boy!"

*   *

A man from the western provinces, on his first visit to Edo, had entered the bathhouse. He did not know the customs of the place, and so he at first stood rooted to the floor looking confused, until he spotted the bucket used for rinsing out underwear. In it, a new loincloth with string ties was soaking in hot water.

"Now there's something!" the man exclaimed. "They put out a nice bucket of hot water for you, with a towel already in it!"

He wrung out his own towel and draped it over the rack usually used for drying loincloths. He took the new loincloth with the ties out of the bucket and started to wash his face with it.

"This water really smells!" he exclaimed. "Whew, what a stink! Huh! That's funny—it looks like somebody's used this towel already, too. There's some kind of greasy stuff on it. Ecch. Disgusting. It looks like a whale's been washing with it, it's so slimy. What a funny smell! I'll dump out the bucket."

He poured out the water and took the bucket over toward the waterboys' station to refill it.

A waterboy, assuming he wanted to wash his loincloth, said, "You shouldn't bring that bucket over here. Leave it over there, and use one of the small buckets to fill it," he explained.

"Fine, fine," said the man from the western provinces. Following instructions, he took the bucket back and carefully used a smaller pail to fill it up with hot water.

"If it's a clean towel, why does it have dirty places all over it?" he asked himself. "It's amazing—looks like somebody's dragged it through the mud."

Spreading out the cloth, he noticed the strings attached to the ends.

"I suppose the strings on either end are so that when somebody puts the towel on his head while he's in the tub he can tie it around his chin," he said.

He wound the strings around his wrist, and crushing the cloth into a ball, began to scrub himself with it. Just then, a man who hailed from the Kamigata region [86] came toward him out of the bath, stopped next to the underwear bucket, and looked around uneasily.

"Hey! What's going on?" he said. "What happened to the loincloth I left here a little while ago to soak? It doesn't make any sense for something you haven't even washed yet to disappear! It's got to be somewhere, for Heaven's sake!" Spotting the man from the western provinces using the loincloth as a towel to wash his face with, he said angrily, "What the hell! That's not your towel, is it?"

"No, of course not," said the man. "I found it in this bucket. I hung up my own over there."

"Good grief!" cried the man from the Kamigata. "What a damned idiot! That's not a towel! It's my loincloth! Washing your face with a loincloth, indeed—how can you be so stupid? Have you been bewitched by a fox? Or are you just crazy? What are you *doing?* Give it back right away and rinse yourself off! The idea!"

The man from the western provinces had been getting more and more angry. "No wonder I thought it was all greasy!" he exclaimed. "So you let it sit for a while and then wash it! Damn! It sure smelled! When I think about it—ooh, sonuvabitch!" He tossed the loincloth back into the bucket and went on into the bath.

"Ah, ha ha ha ha ha," laughed the man from the Kamigata. "That certainly takes the cake! He could have at least waited until I'd washed it! . . . Ha ha ha ha ha!"[87]

The Bathhouse of the Floating World: A Burlesque
Book I, Part 1

Conclusion

When my previous effort, "The Men's Bath" of *The Bathhouse of the Floating World,* appeared, it attracted readers enough to fill a tub to overflowing, and bathed the publisher in the warm glow of success. The blocks from which it had been printed, however, were soon after lost in a fire,[1] turned to ash as surely as the coals in the bathhouse manager's brazier. Alas! They are gone, as prematurely and as wastefully as the fee one pays to enter the bath near closing time, only to have the drain plug pulled as he steps into the tub! Be that as it may, let the reader plunge back into this second bath, before the warmth of the first has faded. The requests for its appearance have been as eager as the impatience of the twice-daily bather awaiting the reopening of the bathhouse after its monthly day of rest; but the writer's brush, like the bath attendant's ladle, dribbles lazily about its ever-unfinished business, seemingly always behind schedule, an iris bath on the sixth, a peach-leaf bath in the waning days of summer.[2] "Aren't you through *yet?*"—such is the complaint of someone sent to fetch a bather fond of a good long soak, and likewise of a publisher impatient for a manuscript. But a writer's meager bag of tricks is not a scrub bag full of soap; squeeze it as you will, writing is still a long and dirty business. Easy though it may be to wring a 12-copper offering out of a festival-goer,[3] not so the draft of a book from an author.

The women's bath is a world of its own, and, though it can, of course, be imagined, no peeking is allowed. The present two-volume book, therefore, can only be like a quick glimpse through the bamboo pipe used to fill the wash buckets in the bath.

By way of preface to a fee increase, the management of the bathhouse will say, "Due to the present high cost of firewood . . ."; I have frugally gathered up the chips and scraps left over from my previous essay in literary carpentry, and use them now to fire the boiler for "The Women's Bath," a bit later, as in life, than "The Men's."[4] Plunge in and let it wash over you for a while!

Written, in response to urgent requests,
in the five days before and after the
9th day of the 9th month,
    By the Edoite withdrawn from
    Affairs of State,
        Shikitei Sanba

ADDENDUM[5]

One quickly discovers, in raising a child, that medicine is bitter and candy is sweet. In literature, the Three Histories and the Five Teachings[6] are the bitter medicine, and novels and popular histories are the sweet candy. Thus it is that, while there is no shortage of books written for the edification of the female sex, the woman or girl is rare indeed who genuinely enjoys the bitter flavor of such works as *The Greater Learning for Women*[7] and *The Woman's Imagawa Ryōshun.*[8] The present "Women's Bath," of course, is merely a light amusement; but, though it be sweet and easy to swallow, if read with close attention it will yield naturally an understanding of good and evil, deviance and rectitude. As the conventional wisdom has it, identifying the good and the evil in one's own behavior by observing that of others is a sure shortcut to true moral learning. Youth may turn a deaf ear to stern admonition, but will always sit still for instruction that is entertaining, and take it to heart. Even the most trifling of books, when read with care, will demonstrate once again that it is often in things of little value that the greatest profit is to be found. . . .[9]

The Bathhouse of the Floating World: A Burlesque Book II, Part 1 The Women's Bath

BY THE EDO DILETTANTE, SHIKITEI SANBA
SCENES FROM EARLY MORNING TO THE FORENOON

The neighborhood was filled with the chirping twitter of mendicants:[10]

"Purify all living beings, leave no filth behind. Pollutions, be no more. Let the jeweled wall, within and without, be clean, be pure . . ."

"May all Creation and the Four Seas come to the Miracle of the Law. Praise the name of the Founder, the *bodhisattva* Nichiren. Praise the Sutra of the Lotus of the Law . . ."

"May the blessings of piety be extended to every sentient being. Amida be praised. Amida be praised . . ."

The Pure Land Sect and the Nichiren, the Eight Sects and the Nine,[11] were represented in the crowd entering the women's bath in all their conflict and diversity.

*   *

A woman slid open the *shōji* door to the bath, complaining about the cold and shivering. She was a girl of seventeen or eighteen with unblackened teeth, and must surely have been an entertainer who called herself something-*moji* or *Toyo*-something.[12] She carried a robe in the latest style, dyed in a pattern that formed an old-fashioned rebus that meant "hearing good news."[13]

"Ah, Otai!" she cried. "Good morning! Things got a little lively last night, didn't they!"

"I should say so," answered Otai, who looked as if she worked in a restaurant. "You must have been pretty tired. That boozer certainly stays up late, doesn't he?"

"He certainly does," said the first girl, whose name turned out to be Osami, "but he behaves himself, anyway. He's a good drunk. At least he's not like Kasubei, who really gets out of control when he drinks. Anyway, he offered to take me home. It took a while, what with him slipping at every corner and all, but he saw me all the way to my gate."

"My, that was nice of him," said Otai. "The old fellow certainly likes to fuss over other people, doesn't he? Anyway, he's better than Donsuke, with his stupid games with his fingers, and Inroku, who's such a terrible drunk. They really frighten me."

"I know what you mean. And Shukō—he makes such a scene with his little *Jinku* songs!"[14]

"And then he always winds up just snoring away when he's done. Oh—speaking of 'done'—you got your hair done, didn't you?"

"Yes. Okushi came by this morning, first thing," answered Osami. "Who did you get to do yours this time?"

"Osuji," Otai said.

"It looks nice."

"Really? This Osuji who came this morning is new, and she was a little awkward, so it somehow feels funny."

"It's always that way," said Osami, "when you get a different person. Even if she knows what she's doing, it doesn't seem quite right. Turn around and let me see. Oh! It's a really good job!"

"Don't you think the back part's a little too high?"

"No. It's just fine," Osami reassured her.

"Well," said Otai as she stepped into her sandals and started toward the door to the street, "have a nice bath, now."

"Why don't you drop by sometime?" Osami said. "We've got a nice old lady, you know. Well, 'bye now!" Without waiting for Otai to answer, she hurried into the bath.

Soon after, another woman arrived. She was about thirty years old, and seemed to be in the same line of work as Osami; her teeth, too, were not blackened. Wrinkles had begun to accumulate above her eyebrows, and the creases on either side of her nose were deepening. Her skin color was somewhat dark, and her white teeth were, in fact, slightly yellowed; her eyebrows were bristly and sparse, but they gave her a proud air that helped to disguise the other shortcomings of her appearance. Kicking off her hinged sandals with a lively clatter on her way in, she greeted the mistress of the bath and tossed down her robe. As she untied her sash, she turned toward the bathroom. "Osami! Hey, Osami!" she called in a piercing voice, but Osami did not hear her. "OSAMI!" ARE YOU DEAF?"

From the bath, Osami at last answered, "Oh! Is that you, Obachi? Nice to see you so early in the morning."

"Early? It's hardly *early* by *now*. Why must you rub it in? You always do just as you like, don't you? Why should I care if you don't know the first thing about getting along with people? Didn't I ask you to wait just a little longer this morning?"

"Well, yes," Osami answered, "but you always take forever over your breakfast . . ."

"I guess that's because I'm such a big eater. I'm sorry. I suppose you're right," said Obachi as she slipped into the bath water. "I stopped by your place just now, and your Mama[15] said you'd just left, and that you'd been waiting for me right up to a few minutes before. She said you were a heartless child, to leave like that! She makes everyone feel so good. Honestly, your Mama is a smooth one! She really knows how to get along with people. Now the Mama at our place, she's always complaining and nagging at us. I can hardly bear it."

"Well, still," said Osami, "your Papa[16] is nice, and that sort of makes up for it, doesn't it?"

"Sometimes I think he's a little *too* nice," Obachi said. "Mama does nothing but scold him day and night. Now, I'm not taking Papa's side, you understand, but really, it's hard to stand by and just grind your teeth. Hey. Did you have any big drinkers last night?"

"Ye-e-s, Ma'm," answered Osami, using the affirmative favored by knowledgeable young girls in the trade. "And you?"

"I had an Ebisu Festival party, you know? They didn't leave until exactly two in the morning."

"Me too. I was all over the place, and got back just before two."

"Look at my eyes," Obachi said. "This is what happens when they make you drink with them. They're still puffy."

"You're right. And the color's bad, too."

"Ooh, this water's hot!" Obachi cried.

"Hot? You're too soft!"

"Soft, nothing! I'll bet it's a little hot for you, too. You're such a phony. You're just too proud to give in. Add a little cold water, won't you?" Obachi called out, thumping the side of the tub.

The water boy joked, "I just *did.* I can't add any *more!*"

"Well, even if you did, I still can't stand it," Obachi said. "It's still too hot. Add some more, you stupid Sansuke!"[17]

"If you call me 'Sansuke,' I won't add any at all!"

"All right. I beseech the Great God Sansuke, then!"

The boy began to run cold water into the tub. "All right, swish it around," he told the women.

"Oh no! You expect *me* to swish it around? Come on, Osami, sink yourself down over here, where the cold water's coming in. There. That's the way I like it. Listen, Osami. Tell me exactly where it was you went the day before yesterday."

"The theater," Osami said.

"Oh, really! Did somebody take you?"

"Come on! I paid my own way."

"Well, then who'd you go with?"

"The invitation was from Neko-moji's place, so I went with Ozuru and Toyotabo. We sent somebody over to your place, but they said you'd gone to Hori-no-uchi with Shatsū."

"That's right," Obachi said. "Listen. I haven't seen that play yet. Who's in it that's good?"

"Kinokuniya[18] was the best," Osami answered.

"That's no surprise. It makes me sick—I missed the last show, too."

"Anyway, after the show was over, we dropped in at the Marusabu and said hello to Sabu, and then when we were leaving, guess what happened? We heard somebody going 'ahem, ahem' up on the second floor, and when we looked up, there were a bunch of people sticking their heads out to look at us, you know? Yashichi, the one who does actors' voices, you know, and Noshimatsu, both of them shouted down at us, but who else was up there, I don't know, because we ran away good and fast. My, it still seems to be a little hot in here. What do you say we get out?"

Osami first, and then Obachi, got out of the tub onto the rinsing platform. The attendant who did the rinsing filled a pair of buckets and came over to rinse their backs.

"All right, Obachi, let's have your back," he said, and began to scrub.

"Will you look at that!" Osami cried. "Even though I got out first!"

"What difference does it make? You'll be leaving together anyway," protested the rinse man, who was probably going to be promoted to manager in a year or so. Since he had been with this bathhouse a long time, perhaps four or five years, he had learned to get along well with the women, and could get away with using rude and impertinent language.

"Come on! Be nice, won't you? You're always so rude!" Obachi complained. "You just give us a couple of quick rubs, splash on a little water, and quit!"

"Well, that's good enough. You're here every day—there can't be that much dirt!"

"Oh, skip it. You have such a mouth," Obachi said.

"So! She wants another fight, does she?" said the rinser. "Whoa! Let's not have a splashing contest! What a racket you make, you two girls! All right, that'll do for you. Osami, let's see your back."

"Huh? You're already seeing it! Wash it, will you? And don't be so rude, old man!"

This sort of banter continued for a long while; we shall omit the rest.

*   *

A merchant-class housewife of thirty-three or thirty-four entered through the street gate, accompanied by a girl of about seven and carrying a baby of barely two.

"Ooh, it's cold, it's cold," said the mother. "I'll bet you're cold, aren't you, Bō?" she asked the baby. Turning to the mistress of the bath, she said, "How have you been, Mistress?"

The mistress was sitting on a raised platform. "Ah, good morning! It's been damned cold the last couple of days, hasn't it! Oh! Osugi, you're here today, too! Oh ho ho ho ho! You're always full of beans, aren't you, Osugi-bō! Otama, do you have a vacation from school today?"

"No, Ma'm," answered the little girl.

"Aha! A lazybones, eh?"

"Just look at her, will you?" said the mother. "The minute my back is turned she thinks she can skip school. Today she completely fooled her Papa and got him to let her take the day off. Papa is so much trouble. He's just too nice, I'm afraid. She simply ignores everything I say."

"She's bound to be that way for a while yet," the mistress reassured her. "You know, it's funny, but it's always the father that dotes on a little girl. Ah ha ha ha. What's that you've got there, Osugi? A sweet potato? Oh, isn't that a nice thing to have! Oh ho ho ho. She's at her absolute cutest right now. What a good baby. You can tell by her face even now that she's got a terrific future. Oh-ho! You're smiling all by yourself! Oh, Osugi, you're a good little girl, yes you are!"

"Otama, when you get your clothes off, put them over there," instructed the mother. "Whoops! Don't fall over. Let's take your socks off, Osugi-bō. There! Now we undo your undershirt . . . Huh? Rin certainly has a funny way of tying this thing. I can't get the ties on your undershirt undone, Bō. Ah! There we are. It's all right. Let's hurry up and get in the tub and warm up! Go, go, go, go!"

Suddenly another little girl of about seven slid open the *shōji* and cried in from the street, "Ma! Ma-a!"

A woman came out from the bath and said, "What? Is that you, Ouma? What did you come here for?"

Ouma answered, "Well, I, um, Papa, um. Somebody came to visit, and, um, Papa says to finish up your bath quick, and not to, um, go anyplace else, and come straight home right now."

"All right, all right. I'll come right home, tell him. Who's there, I wonder? Wouldn't you know it! Just when I finally get out to go to the bath, he sends somebody right over to get me to go back. What a bother! Say—aren't you supposed to be at school? What did you come back for?"

"Today we, um, we do our good writing, you know? So, um, I came back to get my good notebook," Ouma explained.

"Oh. Well, that's all right, I guess. But go back right away."

"Oh, and Mama? Papa says, um, for a special treat, I can take my lunch."

"Oh, no! Not that again! Listen. You don't need to take your lunch unless it's raining."

"But, um . . ." Ouma sniffled. "Um, Mama? Please let me eat there. Come on. Papa said I could, Mama."

"All right. Be quiet. If he said so, then you can take your lunch. But you don't get to be picky about what's in it."

"Yes, Mama," Ouma said, and left.

A woman nearby, a Mrs. B.,[19] commented, "Everybody has the same problem about lunch, you know!"

"I do know," said Ouma's mother, Mrs. A., "but it still drives me crazy the way she's always whining at me about it. And then, if for some reason it isn't ready in time in the morning, she comes home to get it, and then takes it all the way back to the teacher's to eat it."

Mrs. B. laughed, and said, "Sure, it's fine for them to take a lunch if it's windy and rainy, so they don't slip and fall or whatever on the way home and back, but then they make such a fuss about wanting this or that to go with their rice. And then it's, 'Buy me a flower to stick in my water holder.' 'I want some cassia bark.' 'Gimme some oil of cloves, Mama.' 'I want to make clove water.'[20] Honestly, they just wear you out nagging you for things."

"I guess it's the same for everybody," said Mrs. A. "They ask you for gilt paper, or that lovely colored paper with the designs done on it in mica powder, and then they just waste it. They cut it all up and throw it away. And then there are those things they call 'switch pictures'[21] or whatever they are, the ones you fold one way or the other to change the pictures, you know, to make an actor do quick costume changes for instance. Anyway, my children buy them one after another, and then put them in a box. You wouldn't believe how packed that box is! And then my third one, the oldest boy, buys those—what are they? *gōkan*—those little illustrated novels, anyway, and *they* pile up in a *basket.* 'Toyokuni's the best!' 'Kunisada's the best!'—they even learn the names of all the illustrators! Children these days are up on simply everything!"

"They certainly are! When *we* were little," said Mrs. B., "we couldn't imagine anything more wonderful than a 'red-cover'[22] of some old story like 'The Mouse's Wedding.'"

"Well, everything changes, I guess. It seems like it was just a little while ago that people started wearing whalebone clips in their sidelocks. And before that, everybody . . ."

"Yes!" interrupted Mrs. B. "Everybody did their hair up in tight little buns. And then, when those handy little pins and paper strings came in, you could do your hair up yourself. And what about those 'quick Shimada' forms![23] Just like an actor's wig, I swear! All you do is put it on top of your head, and zip! You've got your hair done up. Now that's really clever."

"And we used to have a big topknot up on top," Mrs. A. continued. "But now we're back to the tiny little old-style Shimada again. Of course, now we're starting to get people that like the Kamigata style, too. Sometimes I just can't believe how quickly things change, really!"

"Yes, and people are always going on about the Kyoto style, or Kyoto pins and what not. I think Edo people should just stick with Edo things and be done with it, don't you? Say. This is a different subject, but did I hear that you finally got your oldest daughter taken care of?"

"Yes, we did. We found just the match for her, and managed to get it all settled."

"It must be a relief to get one of them taken care of, anyway," observed Mrs. B.

"What is it my husband always says? 'Girls are money-gobblers.' Honestly, he does nothing but complain!" said Mrs. A.

"Will she have a mother-in-law there?" Mrs. B. asked.

"Yes, and she's still young, too."

"Oh, dear. The girl may be in for a lot of hard work!"

"No, I don't really think so," Mrs. A. said. "The mother-in-law is very good-natured. Not only that, but the groom—he's settled down now, but he evidently used to be something of a playboy, so he's a very knowing sort of person. They certainly get along very well, anyway."

"Well, that's the important thing," Mrs. B. observed. "Even if the mother-in-law is a little difficult, things will work out if the two of them really get along with each other."

"She put on the maternity sash[24] last month, too!" said Mrs. A.

"Really? Oh, my goodness!" Mrs. B. exclaimed. "Nothing but one happy event after another. You must be sure she avoids anything that's bad for her. Nothing much can happen after the fifth month, but certainly don't let her have any sting ray or anything like that. It blocks up the nipples. You've had children, so I assume you won't forget to make sure she takes the pills she should, like 'Real Mother' and 'Queen.'"

"Oh, yes! Both of those worked so well for me, too. But there's another one that's good, too, the medicine for female complaint they sell at the *tabi* shops in Koami and Kofuna.[25] There aren't any signs up for it, but a lot of people know about it. It's really very good—it keeps you from getting dizzy. I know a lot of people that it's helped, so I tell people about it whenever I get a chance."

"Now, didn't I hear about a medicine of some kind, that if you use it for the first seven days, it keeps the milk coming? It keeps the nipples soft, too, and opens them up. Now what was it? I've suddenly forgotten. Where did I see it?"

"Oh," said Mrs. A., "that must be that 'Hiramatsu Black' compound they sell in Owari-chō.[26] That's good medicine. Anyway, you can be sure we've borrowed all sorts of lucky things from people, like a bear's sash,[27] and charms for easy childbirth, and one of those dolls from the Kurishima Shrine[28]—you know, that sort of thing. Even though I've had a lot of children myself, I still can't help worrying when a baby's due. I always just feel sort of uneasy."

"Well, that's natural," said Mrs. B. "Listen. When the baby comes, be sure to fill up a bottle with some of the water it's washed in, and bury the bottle along with the afterbirth. It's a charm to keep Baby from having trouble with its milk. My. We don't have any babies to take care of at our house, and that's no good at all. Oh, how I envy you!"

"Well, I don't know—you should be happy with just one child. At least he's a boy. We have three girls and two boys, and let me tell you, those girls are going to be a plague from cradle to grave."

"Oh, come!" protested Mrs. B. "Girls are good to have. They're a real pleasure. My! If you have two sons, you're in a perfect position to get the younger one adopted into some other family as an heir, aren't you? Now *my* son, he's nothing but trouble, let me tell you! He's driving me crazy. I'm really sorry now we didn't apprentice him out somewhere. But then, he's our only child, and a boy at that, and we spoil him terribly. Still, no matter how clever and intelligent someone is, he won't amount to anything unless he sees a little of the world. He'll certainly be good at spending money, but he won't know a thing about making it."

"Well, I don't know," said Mrs. A., "but he's in the prime of his youth. A little loose living is normal, don't you think? Now our second boy, he says being out in the world is like a tonic for him. We sent him out to apprentice in a book shop."

"My, already a grown-up apprentice!" said Mrs. B. "If a person doesn't know what it's like to eat someone else's rice, how can he ever hope to understand other people, you know? Especially if some day he's going to have his own apprentice! 'If you don't pinch yourself, you'll never know another's pain,' you know. It's really true that someone who never leaves his parents' side will never understand pain, or even an itch, for that matter! You were very wise to send your boy out, anyway."

"Yes. Well," said Mrs. A., "right now he's just doing the best he can. My husband is very strict, you see. He told him that he wasn't to come home except when he's supposed to have his visit, and so, even if they send him to our neighborhood on an errand, he won't stop by home."

While Mrs. A. was talking, a maid came running into the bath-house. "Ma'm" she cried, "Mr. Umatarō from the Shikite-ya is at the house, so won't you please come back?"

"All right, all right! I'm coming right away," Mrs. A. told the maid. She turned back to her companion. "There. You see? That's what—the second or third person he's sent for me? Really! I can't even take a bath in peace. Ho ho ho ho ho," she laughed. "Oh, Kiyo," she called to the maid. "Please get everything set up for tea."

"Yes, Ma'm," answered the maid, and left.

"Well, goodbye now," said Mrs. A. "Have a nice, quiet time."

"Goodbye. My regards to your husband—tell him we're sorry we haven't been in touch," said Mrs. B. as they parted.

*   *

Two old ladies were squatting just outside the tub gumming at each other as they wrung out their rice-bran filled scrubbing bags.

"Are you finishing up, Auntie?" asked one, a Mrs. C.

"Oh! It's you, Auntie. You're early. When did you get here?" said the other, Mrs. D. She was about the same age as Mrs. C.; each one greeted the other as "Auntie," so it was quite impossible to tell who was whose aunt.[29]

"I haven't been out and around much lately, Auntie," said Mrs. C.

"I've noticed. Haven't you been feeling very well?" Mrs. D. inquired.

"That's it, exactly. I suppose it's just old age. My eyes are bad, and my legs and my back bother me, but what can you do? 'Only the bride is happy.'"

"What? You're not *that* old!" protested Mrs. D.

"How old do you think I am?"

"Well, you are a little older than me, I guess," Mrs. D. said.

"Oh! A *little*? I certainly am older, by a full zodiac cycle, I'm sure," said Mrs. C.

"Eighty?"

"Ooh, Heaven help me! Don't be nasty now, Auntie," Mrs. C. cried. "I'm seventy."

"My, my. Well, actually, I was fifty-nine last year, they tell me, and now I've gone and put on another one, so I'm sixty. Now they're going around saying I'll be sixty-one next year!"

"Oh, you always say such funny things. You really do seem very young and full of life, you know."

"Well, I *am* young!" cried Mrs. D. "'There was an old lady of forty-nine years, who married a man from Shinano . . .'"[30] she sang. "But it's pretty much all over when you're sixty, I guess!" she said, laughing heartily.

"My, it's nice that you're always in such a good mood. You'll always be young at heart, even if your hair turns gray."

"You never get anywhere being unhappy, I always say. I just don't let things bother me. It might be nice, though, to dye my hair and live it up one more time! Listen, Auntie. If I should happen to have a chance to be a bride again, will you act as go-between? Even the Devil was sixty once,[31] and this old lady's still in her prime! Ah ha ha ha ha," laughed Mrs. D. again.

"Ha ha ha ha ha. My! Your next life is sure to be a good one!"

"Next life? What about this one! Let the chips fall where they may after I'm dead, I say. I hardly understand this world. How can I know anything about the next one? It's heaven enough for me to have a little nip of *sake* at bedtime, and get a good night's sleep!"

"See? There you are," said Mrs. C. "All you need is a little *sake* to cheer you up, but nothing like that works for me. I just get more and more depressed by the year. It's really disgraceful. I must say, I'm heartily sick of this world."

"Come, come, Auntie. What good does it do to be sick of the world? Who knows what the next life is going to be like! Isn't it better to live to be a hundred right here?"

"Oh! What a horrible thought! No, I'm thoroughly fed up. I can hardly wait for Nyorai to come and get me,[32] let me tell you!"

"What are you saying?" asked Mrs. D. "Don't you have any spirit at all? I don't think anybody that goes around saying 'I want to die, I want to die' ever really wants to. When Nyorai's messengers come, I'll bet you'll be begging them to wait a little longer!"

"No, no I won't," protested Mrs. C.

"Once you're dead, I'm sure you'll be wishing you were still alive. I must say, that will be like praising the wife you've sent away and criticizing the new one that came in her place. People always want everything their own way. When it's summer, they say they like winter better, and when winter comes, summer's better.

"Now, what I always tell my son and his wife," Mrs. D. went on, "is that they should give me lots of nice things now, while I'm still alive, or they'll regret it after I'm gone. Why line up a lot of offerings on the altar, I say. Sure, everybody eats sweet potatoes and bean paste, but who knows whether or not they eat anything after they've become Buddhas? And forget about fast days, too, I tell them—instead of putting a piece of fried bean curd on the altar for me, or giving me rice cakes or the Seven Offerings after I'm dead, isn't it a lot more virtuous to give me a bite of the first bonito of the season and a shot of *sake* while I'm still alive? What do you think, Auntie? Isn't that so?

"Maybe because that's the way I am, my son is very good to

me, and he works very hard in the business, besides. Every day on
the way home from work, he buys a little something wrapped in a
bamboo leaf, and says, 'Here, Mama, have one,' and offers me a
cup of *sake*." Mrs. D's eyes glistened with tears of happiness. "He
used to be something of a playboy, you know, but now he seems
to have settled down a little, and I must say, he's become very
serious and hardworking. I think losing his father so early has
made him steady, too. Believe me, Auntie, it was hard work, taking
on the job of bringing him up all by myself. It certainly wasn't
easy, I must say. Still, if he'd been born bad, he'd probably still
be out playing around even now, and no good to anybody. He
learned to be responsible very quickly, though. I suppose that's
partly thanks to me, and partly to him. And oh, his wife is a dear,
too. She's always looking after me, and believe me, that's a com-
fort. And to think she came to us practically out of the blue—that
Ashiemon of Dragon Alley [33] was the go-between. But you know,
it's already been three years, and I would so like to have a grand-
child! Somehow they just haven't managed so far. I guess it just
isn't right for them yet. That's something you simply have to wait
for, no matter how eager you are. If it doesn't happen, it doesn't
happen, does it, Auntie?"

"You're absolutely right," said Mrs. C. "You can't do a thing
about it. Now at our place—I'm really not very well, you know,
and I shouldn't have to look after children, but they all came
along less than a year apart. Honestly, it's almost got to the point
where I'd like to give them away. His first wife left us three when
she went away, and the new one has had two more, right in a row.
And would you believe it? Now she's going to have another! It
would be all right, I suppose, if she was at least willing to work
hard, but all she does is guzzle *sake* and loaf around, sometimes
for three or even five days at a stretch. As you can imagine, that's
terrible for the family business. Really, the other people in the
building call her a slut. She ignores her own children, and does
nothing but fuss with her hairdo. And not only does she make her
husband wear rags, she throws down dirty diapers just anywhere,
all covered with whatever, and won't wash a single one. When she
finishes eating, she pushes back her tray and makes one of her
poor little kids take it away. We don't have any help at all, of
course, so I'm the one that winds up having to clean up after her.
She just sits back and expects to be praised for having lots of

children, even though she obviously doesn't give a damn about taking care of her family. Whoever said you have to have a lot of children? She really is—she's actually *proud* of having children as often as she wants. I've stopped being surprised by now, let me tell you. Just look at her! You'd feel the same way, if you were in my position. She does her hair up like a fancy lady, and won't wear anything but her one decent kimono, which she's going to wear out completely. My goodness, Auntie, if she'd only take proper care of herself, she could always have clean clothes to wear, nice and crisp, fresh from the laundry. Not doing the laundry is one thing, but sewing, too! She doesn't even know how to hold a needle. I thought that since she used to be a courtesan, she wouldn't be able to have children, and I could gradually teach her something about housework, but it turns out she really can't do a thing. Except have children, which I thought she couldn't! I can't even get her to turn a few hems to make dust cloths! Give her a needle, and she starts stabbing away with it like a *tatami*-maker sewing on a border strip. And oh, her mouth! She yatters on and on, with a ten-word comeback for everybody else's one. Oh, I tell you, it drives me simply mad. And listen! She grates dried bonito on lacquer trays, and knocks out her pipe on the door sills, and if she feels like taking a nap, she'll grab any old thing to use for a pillow, and fall sound asleep right in front of everybody. Sometimes she'll sit there spitting in the brazier, and rolling the gobs around in the ashes. I get so angry when I come around later and have to scoop out a bunch of little round lumps. Really, it's like spitting on hearth and home! She's started staying up late, too, and then sleeping late the morning after, so when they have people over they go on and on with their stupid stories about the theater until all hours, and so then, of course, she gets cold and wants hot noodles. She slurps them up, and then she goes to sleep and starts snoring away. Combine that with my son talking in his sleep, and her grinding her teeth, too, and it gets so noisy I simply can't get a wink of sleep. And in the middle of all that, one of the babies will wake up and start screaming, and then all of them start crying at once. But you know, even then she won't get up. She doesn't even *wake* up! So there I am, night after night, in the middle of all that racket. It's just too much to take, Auntie."

"Well, nevertheless," Mrs. D. said, "as long as the two of them seem to get along, it's really none of your business. Leave them alone! You're too much of a busybody!"

"Well, I don't care," said Mrs. C. "If a couple gets along well, they shouldn't fight, but when these two aren't having a set-to with the children, they're going at each other. Then, as if she didn't share at least part of the blame, she goes and tells *him* to get the hell out! She just sits there and sulks, looking superior to everybody else, and then takes it all out on some blameless thing like the lamp. Even if it's perfectly fine, not dim at all, she'll say, 'This damned light is too dim,' and give the wick a good yank, and there goes all that expensive oil! Then, of course, my son being the way he is, *he* flies off the handle, and grabs some pot or dish that's handy, and breaks it. It happens every time. We're some of the best customers the pottery-mender and the lacquer man have, I tell you! But really, it's a shameful sort of thing. I simply don't have a quiet moment."

"Now listen!" said Mrs. D. "It's your own fault if you waste so much energy on that kind of thing. You can have your quiet moments if you really want to, you know. Don't think about the next life—just make this one heaven itself! You upset the whole household when you let yourself get steamed up. It's no wonder you feel like you're suffering the torments of hell! Even when you watch yourself, like I do, you run the risk of being called a meddling mother-in-law. You were twenty once yourself, you know, fifty years ago. Just pretend it's fifty years ago, and you're the new bride, and treat her as if she were your mother-in-law. It'll save you a lot of trouble! If you want a peaceful household, it's best for a mother-in-law simply to beat a retreat once she's found her son a bride. Anyway, I know that once a mother-in-law opens her mouth, there's never any peace. You keep saying you want to die. Well, just tell yourself you're already dead, and none of this will bother you!"

"Auntie!" Mrs. C. cried. "Are you taking her side, too?"

"What? Who's taking sides? You're just being silly. I may be a woman, but I think like a man, and I don't like it when people are silly. Why don't you stop talking that way and try going out to a sutra dedication or something instead? It's because you're home all the time that things are so bad. Just start pounding on your gong and march right out the door—'I praise the Buddha daily, yes I do, yes I do.' You know what I mean. You'll feel incredibly much better, I promise you. You'll live forever! Just forget about all that other business. It's not doing anybody any good. My goodness! I'm cold. Are you going to leave? Why don't you drop by during the Ten Nights? I'm sure a lay helper will be by with some tickets."

"Well, thank you. I think I'd like to do that," Mrs. C. replied.

"'I think I'd like to,' nothing! Just get yourself out of the house!" said Mrs. D., as she got into the tub.

*   *

A married woman of about thirty, with a long upper lip and a generally refined appearance, was scrubbing her temples.

"Oh!" the woman, a Mrs. E., cried out. "Can that be Onabe? It really hasn't been very long since I've seen her, but she's grown so much, hasn't she! How old is she this year, may I ask?"

"She's eight, thank you," answered Onabe's mother, Mrs. F., laughing.

"Is this her home visit?"

"Yes indeed, it is. She's been given three nights with us."

"My, isn't that splendid!" Mrs. E. exclaimed. "How wonderful for her dancing that you could get her taken in while she was still small. How old was she when she started?"

"She was accepted into service the fall she was five," Mrs. F. replied.

"My, that must have been difficult for you!"

"Yes, indeed. We sent her nurse with her, though, and so her apprenticeship has been going very well. Still, we are a bit concerned because she has always been a little disobedient."

"Some willfulness is perfectly all right, I'm sure. But I suppose it isn't easy for the nurse, all the same. What are the arrangements for her dancing practice, by the way?" asked Mrs. E.

"Well, of course, since we sent her into the Fujima household,[34] she can practice right there, in the compound," Mrs. F. explained.

"Ah! That's very fortunate, isn't it? I should imagine she's very good by now."

"Well, she seems to have some problems still, but the child enjoys it, so she learns quickly," said Mrs. F., and laughed politely.

"I should imagine she pesters you to take her to the theaters when she's home."

"Oh, yes. We've taken her to two already, but today we're making a temple visit. Whenever we have her home, I can't seem

to apply myself to anything. I can't get any of my chores taken
care of properly. We have to take her back tomorrow, though,
bright and early."

"My goodness!" said Mrs. E. "Why don't you ask for special
permission for her to stay with you for a few more days? What do
you think of that, Onabe? Oh ho ho ho ho. Perhaps you could
come visit us. I insist! She would be a perfect playmate for our
Okama."

"Well, thank you! Okama is very grown up, too. She's so good
about going to her practice every day."

"Well, yes, I suppose she is, but . . . She certainly has grown,
but I really can't say she's grown *up!* She practices, but only after
I've told her to, over and over again. She's really very lazy, I'm
afraid. It's true, my dear, isn't it, that without the right kind of
luck it's difficult to arrange an apprenticeship. If I find a house I'd
like to have accept her, they aren't willing to take her. And I always seem to have some sort of reservation about the households
that do like her. My goodness, how many places we've gone for
interviews! But there is always something that keeps it from working out. Oh ho ho ho ho. This sort of thing certainly keeps one
busy!" said Mrs. E., laughing once more.

"Don't be concerned," Mrs. F. said. "It's all a matter of luck, so
just be patient. But an apprenticeship is very much worth it, I
assure you. Without really being taught manners, they just naturally learn how to behave properly. If they're at home, they simply
won't straighten out, no matter how much you scold them. But
when you send them off to live in a good household, everything
begins to change. And let me tell you, my dear, this household of
Onabe's, I suppose because the lord's stipend is so good, is very
well off. The gifts they give her, whatever, everything is quite
sumptuous. And furthermore, the lady Onabe is assigned to is extremely kind. She treats her like her own child and goes to all sorts
of extra trouble with her, so she's willing to work very hard. And
the lord's wife has really come to be fond of her, too—instead of
calling her by her name, she uses a friendly little nickname for her
when she summons her to bring tea, and I gather she always puts
in a good word for her when there are guests present. My goodness, that's kind of her! I shall never forget, as long as I live, how
much we owe them for being so good about taking her in when
she was little. The only thing is, not only do they dress very

elegantly there, you know, but Onabe's things that she's been wearing are getting to be too small, and we'll have to replace them all with a lot of grown-up clothes. So I have a lot of headaches still ahead of me!"

"I can well imagine!" said Mrs. E. "But you can pass her old things down, can't you, to her little sister. That way they won't go to waste. But still, that certainly is hard on her Papa's wallet! Oh ho ho ho ho. Really, you must come by for a visit. I shall have our Okama play accompaniment, and Onabe can dance. I would so love to see her."

"Well, thank you," said Mrs. F. "What do you say, young lady?"

"Thank you, Ma'm," Onabe answered.

"Okama plays the *koto,* doesn't she?" continued Mrs. F.

"Yes, she does. We had been having her go to Ikuta, but lately we've been able to get her in with Amata.[35] She already has her intermediate certificate, by the way."

"Really! That's wonderful. I'll tell people, if I have the chance."

"Thank you! We'd be very grateful," said Mrs. E. as they parted.

*   *

Next there appeared a lady from the Kamigata region, short and pudgy, with fair skin and thick lips. The rims of her eyes were shaded with rouge, and her heavily applied lip rouge was dark and glistening. Her thick hairpins were carefully wound with white paper to keep the steam in the bath from warping the tortoise shell of which they were made.

"My, Oyama, it's cold, isn't it?" said the Kamigata lady in a sweet voice. "You know, for some reason lately I have been having a good deal of stomach trouble. It was becoming so annoying— stomach aches night after night—that I thought perhaps coming for hot baths would help. I've been here ever so many times now. Goodness, Oyama! Look over there! Look at the child standing next to that lady. What color is that robe of hers?"

"That?" Oyama asked. "I suppose you could call it a sky blue with crimson highlights."

"My, it's very nicely dyed, isn't it!"

"It has a sort of purplish cast to it that's very smart, don't you think?" Oyama commented.

"It certainly is very chic," said the lady from the Kamigata. "I must say, I adore the purples one sees in Edo. I would certainly like to wear something like that. Here, Oyama, turn around."

"Oh! Are you going to wash my back? Oh really, you need-n't . . ."

"Now, now. It's no trouble," interrupted the Kamigata lady. "Say, you're nice and plump."

"Ooh, don't say that!" Oyama cried. "I simply loathe being fat. I would really like to go on a vinegar diet or something."

"Come, come! It's good to be a little plump, don't you think?"

"Then why do people always talk about being as slender and supple as a willow?"

"Well, they do, don't they?" said the Kamigata lady. "But I just thought they meant that sort of person couldn't stand up straight in a wind! Now, somebody like me can always win a footrace by lying down and rolling!"

"Ha ha ha ha ha," Oyama laughed. "My goodness, it's already struck ten, hasn't it?"

"What? It certainly has, and a long time ago, too. It's nearly noon."

"Really? The day seems so short, doesn't it!"

"It surely does," the lady from the Kamigata agreed. "Why don't you come home with me when we're through here and have something to eat? I've told myself a thousand times I'd like to make myself some round the way we do in the Kamigata, but my husband won't stand for it. Today I said to myself, 'I'm going to cook up some round,' and round it's going to be, for lunch."

"What in the world is 'round?'" Oyama asked.

"You people here call it snapping turtle. Wouldn't you like to try it?"

"Oh, no! I couldn't bear it!" cried Oyama. "I can't even stand to look at turtles. When you said 'round,' I pictured round things of some sort, like whole barley grains in rice or something, but you meant turtle? Ooh, that sounds awful. In Edo, you know, we call turtles 'lids.'"

"What? Lids? That's certainly silly!" said the Kamigata lady. "Why in the world do you call them lids?"

"Well, they look like lids, so they're lids. Why do you call them rounds?" Oyama asked.

"Their shells are round, so we call them rounds."

"Well, that's just as far-fetched, isn't it?"

"I suppose so. Here, people always talk about 'boiled turtle,' don't they? When I thought about how you must prepare it, I realized you mean what we call *koroiri* in the Kamigata. That's not a soup at all, for Heaven's sake! And it's too salty altogether. It's just terrible! The way we make it, it's not that tasteless sort of thing at all. You use a light soy sauce for the soup base, so it's absolutely delicious as something to eat with *sake*. I love it, I really do. And what you people insist on doing with eel! It's terrible—it's always so limp. If you want to know what real Kamigata eel is like, the only places to go, I suppose, are the Kami-no-Ikesu in Kyoto, and the Daishō in Ōsaka. There are a lot of other restaurants that do fresh-water fish, but I think those are the best. I think what they usually do is grill them on skewers, and then, oh yes, after they're cooked, they cut them up in small pieces for you, and serve them up on a nice covered platter, so you don't have to worry about them being cold."

"In Edo, you know," Oyama interrupted, "people aren't so stingy. Real Edo eel they plop on a plate while it's still steaming hot, and if it happens to cool off while you're still eating, you put it aside and have them cook up another serving. That's what a real native does. Some people wrap up the part that's gotten cold in bamboo leaves and say they're going to take it home to feed to the cat, but that's only the really stingy ones."

"Really? Isn't that just like you Edo people! You're actually proud of letting things go to waste. You know, in the Kamigata, they think Edo people are terrible, the way they go on and on about how wonderful it is to be from Edo. It's always bad to be so proud of yourself. That's why we say Edo people are foolish."

"Well, then I'd just as soon be foolish," said Oyama. "The best thing about Edo people is that, from the day they're born till the day they die, they never leave their birthplace. People like you, you're born in Kyoto, and then live in Ōsaka or someplace, and then after you've moved all over the place, you still wind up in good old Edo. And you're still living here, aren't you? That's why we call you 'Kamigata sneaks.'"

"What's *that* supposed to mean?" the Kamigata lady asked. . . .

"It's just as well you don't know," Oyama told her. . . .[36]

"There! How do you like that?" asked the Kamigata lady.

"Ooh. Ow, ow, ow! That hurts! You got carried away and scrubbed my back so hard that it hurt. That's enough!" Oyama cried.

"Ha ha ha ha ha!" the Kamigata lady laughed. "I did get carried away, I guess! Ah, I'm tired."

"All right, now you turn around," Oyama said.

"Now, don't do anything to try to get even!" the Kamigata lady said warily. "How's this, Oyama? Ooh! Ouch! Don't be mean! Really, if it's too much trouble, you don't have to. Oww! What are you doing? I can't stand pain. I have a moxa burn back there, besides. Just rinse me off! Ouch, ouch, ouch!"

*   *

A young nursemaid, having for a time given over the care of her mistress's child to another, sat near the clothes lockers. She had spread out a child's kimono, and was picking lice from it. Near her was playing a group of four or five little girls about five years old, led by another girl of six or seven. They had set up a little folding screen made of shells, a souvenir of Enoshima,[37] and on top of a small incense box had spread out a doll's clothes. One doll they had covered with a quilt and put to sleep, but they had others to play with: a "big sister" doll made of bundled grass, a young woman with a full Shimada hairdo made of tightly crinkled paper, a middle-aged lady with her hair in a simple round bun, a woman with a "quick Shimada," and another "big sister," this one with her hair simply pinned up. Using matchsticks for hair ornaments, and scraps of red hairdressing ribbon for sashes, they were playing house and bickering with each other.

"There, little Bō," a little girl named Oharu was saying. "Be a good girl and go to sleep. When you get up in the morning, I'll give you a sweet potato before breakfast. Oh, oh! Are you awake again? Why don't you go to sleep? Onatsu! Onatsu! (Oh, no! She's supposed to be the lady next door!) My, my. Our little girl, you know, is driving me simply mad with her crying!"

"Well," Onatsu answered, "then you should give her a moxa treatment."

"Perhaps we should. Ooh, Bō! That's scary! Moxa! Isn't that scary? Now why don't you just hurry up and go to sleep! Ooh, the bogey man's coming! There. Bō's gone to sleep!"

Among the girls was a nasty one, roundly disliked, the sort of girl who made the younger ones cry, and started fights between children who had previously been getting along happily together. The girl was universally acknowledged to be a chatterbox, and was known as "Oniku with the big pockmarks"; but she was the leader of this little group of girls.

Wiping some greenish mucus from under her nose with a sideways flick of her hand, then wiping it on her lap, Oniku cried out,

"Hey! Hey! I don't like that. I don't like that! You're so selfish, Oharu. *You* aren't a housewife. Onatsu and me are the mothers, and you're the maid. Isn't that right, Oaki?"

"Wishy-washy Oaki" was the one most eager to please among the girls. "She's right, Onatsu," she said.

Onatsu, the cleverest among them, hesitated: "Oh, really? I don't know a thing about it."

"No, no, no!" Oharu protested. "That's not the way it was! We decided before that I was supposed to be a housewife. This isn't any fun. I'm not going to play with you.

Ofuyu, a "two-faced sticking plaster" who always tried to see both sides, said, "All right. Who cares? We don't mind if you don't play, do we, Oniku?"

"You're right," Oniku said. "I don't care at all."

"Oharu, why don't you just be patient and play with us?" Onatsu urged. "Even if you're the maid for a while, we'll all take turns, so it'll be all right. You can be a housewife later."

"No!" Oharu cried. "That's just what Oniku and Ofuyu were saying!"

"What did I say?" Ofuyu asked.

"You *did!* You said—" Oharu started to reply.

"All right. Forget it. We don't care about somebody like her," Oniku intervened.

"Okay, then you can give back what I gave you," said Oharu.

"Here! You can have it. Why would I need a dirty old thing like that, anyway?" said Oniku as she tossed back a little scrap of gold brocade.

"And Ofuyu can just give back what I gave *her* before, too!" Oharu said.

"All right," said Ofuyu, and pulled something from her sleeve, bringing with it some bits of sleeve lint. "What did you think I wanted an old *samisen* string for, anyway? Isn't that so, Oniku?"

"Okay. From now on, if you ever ask me for anything, I won't give it to you. I don't care!" said Oharu.

"Nyaah, nyaah, nyaaah!" Oniku said, pushing her face forward and scowling.

"Quit being mean!" Oharu cried.

"Crabby old lady, crabby old lady!" Oniku and Ofuyu chanted. "Rob-bers, rob-bers, robbers everywhere this year!"

"When was I ever a robber?" asked Oharu.

"Granny's got no teeth, let her drink some tea! Granny's got no teeth, let her drink some tea!" the other two taunted.

"Even if I didn't have any teeth I still wouldn't take anything from *you!*" Oharu said, pushing her lips into a pout. "Come here, Oaki! I'll give *you* this cloth!"

"Thank you very much," said Oaki.

"Let's just us play together," Oharu suggested. "Shall we play house?"

"Okay."

"Look at that!" Oniku interrupted. "That stupid Oaki! Onatsu and Ofuyu, don't you go over there. Play with me. What shall we do?"

"Um. Let's play bounce the ball," Ofuyu suggested.

"Good. Now we can play house together by ourselves," Oaki said.

"That's right. We don't want to play with those dummies anyway, do we, Oaki?" agreed Oharu.

"Oka-a-ay!" Ofuyu called out. "*We're* going to play *ball!* Let's go!"

"Let's be friends. It's not worth fighting about," Onatsu interrupted.

"All right," said Oniku. "Sing please. Everybody sings. 'One-two, three-four, five-six, seven-eight, nine and ten and twen-ty, thir-ty, for-ty, fif-ty, six-ty, seven-ty, eight-y, nine-ty-nine-and-luck-be-mine, right be-fore your eyes—a hundred!' Okay, now I bounce the ball. 'One-two, three-four, five-six'—oops! I dropped it . . ."

The girls finally chose their turns.

"All right, you're first, and I'm second. Ofuyu goes third," Onatsu announced.

"Hmm. Which one shall we do?" Oniku asked herself. "I know. I'll do 'By the Great Gate,' okay? 'By the Great Gate, Teahouse Lane. Mi-ura, Taka-ura, Kome-ya-no-kimi. See the girls, on parade, pretty, pretty, pretty. . . .'"[38]

"There! That's a hundred!" Oniku finally cried.

"Ah! You dropped it! Now *I'll* do 'Faces White,'" said Onatsu. "'Fa-ces white. White, white, white. Okoma of the Shi-ro-ki-ya. . . .'"[39]

"You dropped it!" Ofuyu cried. "'E-E-Enshū, pret-ty ba-by. . . .'[40] Ah, phooey! I dropped it. That makes me mad."

"This is fun, isn't it?" Oharu was saying to Oaki.

"Why don't you just shut up, you babies!" Oniku barked out. Turning back to Onatsu, she said, "Now listen, this time let's do 'Kyō-Kyō-Kyōbashi, Nan-Nan-Nakahashi,' you know? That song."

"Okay. That's a good one," Onatsu replied.

In the meantime, the other two girls were playing "Neighbors."

"Oh! How nice of you to come by. My, my. Come in, come in!" Oaki cried.

"I have some red bean rice here. It's nothing, really, but I'd like you to have it."

"Why, you've done a *lovely* job with it!"

"Please—I hope you'll want to eat a lot of it," Oharu said. She had slid her sash around, and tied a stuffed monkey to her back, to which she now began to sing a lullaby. "My Bō is something of a crybaby," she finally said. "I hope she won't bother you. Hmm. Why don't I go take you up to see the hill, Bō, and let you go pee-pee? Oh, look! The hill is just covered with trees and flowers, isn't it? There we go! Good! Let's cross the bridge. Boom, boom, boom! All right, this is where we turn around after we see the hill. Good, Bō! Do a good job—pss-s-s-s . . ."

"Oharu? I mean—neighbor? Did you go home?"

"No! We haven't gone home yet! We're up on the hill, flower-viewing!"

Oniku, still playing ball, glanced over at the others. "Just look at that," she exclaimed. "Nyaah, nyaah! Look at the little girl pretending she's a mommy! Look, Ofuyu—she busted off some broom straws to use for chopsticks, and now she's got a cup of dirt and she's pretending it's 'wed bean wice.' Aww! Hey, Mommy! Dat's a tewwible thing fow 'oo to do!" Thrusting out her lips, she imitated the smaller girl.

The young nursemaid, unable to sit by and watch any longer, finally broke in: "Now, Oniku, don't be nasty. You always tease the little ones. Why don't you all make up and play nicely together? The reason you get into fights is because you play separately. Play together!"

"All right," cried Oharu and Oaki.

"Who needs your advice?" Oniku said. "It's none of your business, you bitch!"

"*What?* What a disgusting child! That's why the boys always pick on you. You're exactly what people mean when they talk about nasty little girls."

"Well, so I'm nasty. So what!" Oniku snapped back. "Ptoo!" She spat at the nursemaid, ran three steps toward the door, and burst into tears. She ran off for home at top speed, but stopped crying on the way. When she turned the corner into the alley where her house was located, however, she started wailing once more.

Back at the bathhouse, Oharu was saying, "Why doesn't everybody come back to my house?"

"Yeah, let's go!" Onatsu agreed.

"Oharu? Can I be your friend, too?" Ofuyu asked.

"Sure. You come, too."

So it was that Two-faced Ofuyu, Wishy-washy Oaki, Clever Onatsu, and Silly Oharu raised their voices in squawky unison: "'Home we go,' cried the frogs, 'go-HOME, go-HOME! Home we go, go-HOME.'"[41]

Notes to the Translation

Translator's Note

The following notes to the translation are based, unless otherwise indicated, on the annotations to the relevant passages in the two principal modern editions of *Ukiyoburo,* those edited by Jinbō Kazuya (Kadokawa Shoten, Kadokawa bunko no. 2497, 1968), cited in the notes as "Jinbō, *UB,*" and Nakamura Michio, *Nihon koten bungaku taikei* series LXIII (Iwanami Shoten, 1957), hereafter cited as "Nakamura, *UB.*" Abbreviated citations of these editions that contain no page numbers are meant to refer to the annotations to the original passages corresponding to the English version.

I have not specified my sources for basic definitions and identifications of people, places, and things, which consist mostly of the standard reference works—dictionaries, biographical and literary dictionaries, encyclopedias and the like—that are used by any translator or student of premodern Japanese literature. I have, of course, noted sources for other than such basic information.

Notes to "The Men's Bath"

1. Jinbō, *UB,* p. 359, notes that this passage, like many others in this introduction, paraphrases the introduction to Santō Kyōden's *kibyōshi, Irikomi sentō shinwa* (1802), which he and earlier scholars have identified as a major literary source or inspiration for *Ukiyoburo.* I have not specifically noted every such echo of Kyōden's work.

2. Gonsuke and Osan were personal names often used generically for "male servant" and "female servant" respectively.

3. A satirical allusion to a passage in *Gobunshō* (or *Ofumi*), a popular collection of didactic letters addressed to his parishioners by the priest Rennyo (1415-1499): "Cheeks reddened with makeup in the morning turn to white bones by nightfall."

4. This passage contains a pun on *shōji*, meaning either "life and death" or "paper-covered door."

5. A phrase from the introduction to the tenth-century *Kokinshū* by Kino Tsurayuki (likewise "fierce warrior" above), in which the claim is made that poetry soothes all such untameables.

6. "Yajirō in the thicket" refers to someone who indulges in private in disreputable behavior. Jinbō, *UB*, cites the proverb *Usotsuki Yajirō yabu no naka de he o hitta* (The liar Yajirō farted in the thicket).

7. A short passage has been omitted here, since it consists of untranslatable punning allusions to popular medicines advertised on placards at the entrance to the bathhouse.

8. Rules governing the operation of the bathhouse were posted near the entrance. A typical list of such rules, dating probably from the 1830s, is reprinted in Kitagawa Kisō, *Morisada mankō*, ed. Muromatsu Iwao, part 2, p. 209, and reproduced in Nakamura, *UB*, p. 309.

9. The bathhouse closed early during periods of strong wind as a precaution against fire. See Kitagawa, *Morisada mankō*, part 2, p. 205.

10. An allusion to the proverb, "Regret gnaws at the navel," which is in turn based on a passage in the *Taiheiki*.

11. 1809.

12. 1769–1825. *Ukiyo-e* artist and illustrator of many of Sanba's works.

13. Active in the revival of the art of *rakugo* in Edo in the Bunka and Bunsei eras; d. 1833.

14. An allusion to a passage from *Lun-heng*, a Han-dynasty moral treatise by Wang Ch'ung (A.D. 27–96): "In a peaceful realm, one day of wind in five, one day of rain in ten."

15. New Year's housecleaning: a ritual cleaning carried out on the 13th day of the 12th month to mark the beginning of preparation for the New Year celebrations—one of a number of festival days on which patrons were expected to make a special "gift" to the bathhouse of 12 *mon* in lieu of the regular fee. Five Impurities: pollutions of the flesh arising from sexual desire, speech, and the senses of smell, taste, and touch.

16. Six Passions: desires or cravings arising from the "six roots" of desire, the eyes, ears, nose, tongue, body, and will. Gift Day Bath: on the 16th day of the 1st and 7th months, the bathhouse receipts went to the servants as a sort of bonus. Kitagawa, *Morisada mankō*, part 2, p. 205.

17. The apprentice misreads the characters for "Cash Bath," a reference to the cash fee paid by patrons who did not make special arrangements to pay on a periodic, flat-rate basis. The young scholar reads as *fuyu o shinobu yu*, "Bath of Escape from Winter," the characters properly read *suikazurayu*, "Honeysuckle or Woodbine Bath," a medicinal bath.

18. An allusion to the story, contained in Book 35 of the *Taiheiki*, of Aoto Fujitsuna, who, after dropping a 10-*mon* coin in the Nameri River one

night, spends 50 *mon* on torches so that his retainers can dive in and search for it in the dark.

19. The sixteen *rakan* (Chinese *lo-han*, Sanskrit *arhat*, *arahat*), introduced here simply in a play on their number, were "worthies" who reached enlightenment through others' teachings.

20. In the *jōruri* play *Kanadehon chūshingura*, En'ya Hangan is forced to commit *seppuku* as punishment for drawing his sword against the evil Kō no Moronao, who has attempted to seduce Hangan's wife, Kaoyo.

21. A reference to the *Analects* of Confucius, 4.25: "Virtue will not be alone, but will always have a neighbor (companion)."

22. In Japanese folk belief, images of Binzuru if rubbed had curative powers. (Hence the reference below to salve.) The bathhouse master's customary seat was on a raised platform just inside the street door. See diagram in Kitagawa, *Morisada mankō*, part 2, p. 207.

23. The bathhouse rented out for a nominal fee rough cloth bags into which the bather poured rice bran or a mixture of bran and soap powder. (Kitagawa, *Morisada mankō*, part 2, p. 212.) The natural oils in rice bran were regarded as good for the complexion. The rice-bran scrubbing bag (*nukabukuro*) has been nearly superseded by modern soap and cosmetics, but is still used to scrub and polish fine wood floors. See Miyao Shigeo and Kimura Senhide, *Edo shomin no fūzokushi*, pp. 212–215.

24. The passage alludes to the Book of Rites (*Li-chi*) which prohibits the mixing of the sexes after the age of 7, and to a passage in Mencius (T'ang Wen Kung, 1.4) that prescribes a separation of functions between man and wife.

25. According to folk tradition, Empress Kōmyō, consort to Emperor Shōmu (r. 724–749), personally bathed a thousand of her subjects. The last to appear was a particularly loathesome, pus-covered old beggar. The Empress cleaned his sores and bathed him, whereupon he revealed himself to be an incarnation of the Buddha Ashuku (Sans. Akṣobhya).

26. The title of a *nagauta* song first performed on the *kabuki* stage in 1756.

27., 28. Fixed, conventional lines heard in "old" (pre-Chikamatsu) *jōruri*.

29. A variety of Edo *jōruri* song, also known as *Katō-bushi*, most popular in the late seventeenth century.

30. A variety of *nagauta*.

31. A type of folk song that accompanied the folk dance known as *Ise-odori*, dating originally from the late Muromachi period.

32. A line from the Nō play *Shōjō*, part of the *waki* role's self-introduction (*nanori*).

33. This onomatopoeic rendering of the sound of a *samisen* echoes the sound of the verb *neru*, "to recline," filling out the progression, "Some sit, some stand."

34. *Yuiri* can suggest both "shooting with bow and arrow" and "entering the bath." Kitagawa, *Morisada mankō*, part 2, p. 204, reproduces a drawing

of a similar sign representing a drawn bow and arrow. The same drawing appears in Ishii Ryōsuke, *Edo no yūjo sono ta*, p. 76.

35. Presumably a nickname: *buta*, "pig," plus *shichi*, "seven."

36. This was apparently a kind of palsy with a sudden onset.

37. In Butashichi's speeches, Sanba tries to reproduce as accurately as possible the speech of a semi-paralytic, glossing them with *kanji* and *kana* where necessary as an aid to comprehension. The reader can thus reconstruct Butashichi's *a-aiyane na beyabo da ze* as standard Edo dialect *asane na berabō da ze*, here, "Still asleep, the slobs!" The evidence of Butashichi's impediment may suggest he has a cleft palate.

38. "Phoenix" (*hōō*) was a slang word for courtesan. The speaker here appears to be making ironic reference to the shabbiness of the other's clothing.

39. A shrine to Konpira (the Hindu demon-god Kumbhira) located on Shikoku in modern Kagawa Prefecture. Konpira was usually worshiped as a patron deity of sailors.

40. The reference is to the Myōshōji, a temple in Hori-no-uchi, a neighborhood in Suginami-ku, a ward in the western suburbs of modern Tokyo.

41. Also known as *niwaka kyōgen*, one of several varieties of comic storytelling popular in Edo.

42. *Zakuroguchi*, a small, low opening at the rear of the dressing room through which one entered the bath room proper, so built to reduce drafts inside. The origin of the name is said to lie in a pun on the verb *kagamiiru*, "to stoop to enter," since the juice of the pomegranate was used in polishing bronze mirrors (*kagami iru*, "mirror shines").

43. Ishikawa Goemon (1558–1594) was a famous bandit who was captured and boiled to death in a large cauldron.

44. Honjo Yoshida-chō, a neighborhood in modern Sumida-ku frequented in Sanba's day by low-class streetwalkers.

45. The retired gentleman quotes a ditty which predicts the weather according to the hour at which an earthquake occurs. For another contemporary version of the ditty and speculations on its origins in Chinese astrology, see Yamazaki Yoshinari, *Kairoku*, pp. 172–173.

46. Pinsuke confuses the earthquake ditty with a similar one that computes the number of one's souls according to which of the 5 elements (wood, fire, earth, metal, water) appeared in the cyclical year of one's birth. Jinbō, *UB*, finds the song quoted in full in Kyōden's *kibyōshi* of 1790, *Shingaku hayasomegusa*; it appeared also in Sanba's earliest work, *Tentō ukiyo no dezukai*.

47. The original reads, "wind if six or two," allowing a confusion between *kaze*, "wind," and *kaze*, "common cold, influenza."

48. The Tokuganji was a temple located in modern Chiba Prefecture. The Ten Nights (*o-jūya*) was a period set aside for special devotions by members of the Pure Land Sect, when worshipers would spend the ten days and

nights between the 6th and the 15th days of the 10th lunar month reading sutras and chanting the *nenbutsu*, a prayer invoking the name of Amida.

49. An alternate name for the Buddha Amida.

50. The priest has altered the usual unflattering proverb, *Bōzu marumōke*, "Priests make all the money," to *Asa bōzu, marumōke*, "Priest in the morning, make all the money."

51. *Bō*, literally "priest," was a common affectionate nickname or diminutive suffix for small children's names, because, one assumes, of a fancied resemblance between an infant's relatively hairless head and a priest's shaven pate.

52. A line from a children's play song.

53. A town now part of the northern suburbs of Tokyo.

54. Well-known restaurant-teahouses, both established in 1799 near the entrance to the Inari Shrine in Ōji.

55. The road to the Yoshiwara licensed quarter, so called because the quarter was then still surrounded by rice fields.

56. Sanba perhaps had in mind the Yamaguchi-Tomoeya, a "go-between teahouse" (*hikite-jaya*) that a near-contemporary Yoshiwara guide book, *Tōto Yoshiwara saiken no zu* (Tsutaya Jūzaburō, 1819), places in Edo-chō 1-chōme in the quarter.

57. From the *jōruri* play *Hiragana seisuiki* by Takeda Izumo I, first performed in Osaka in 1739.

58. A troll-like creature that lives in streams and rivers.

59. The reference is not to a form of child abuse, but to a medical treatment, still occasionally practiced, in which small piles of *mogusa*, a powdered, dried herb, are burned on the skin at certain places on the body according to theories similar to those underlying the practice of acupuncture, which was also widely followed.

60. The pounding of the drum in this children's song may allude to neighborhood search parties (see note 70 below); the dog, perhaps, has run off.

61. The three physicians have affected professional names borrowed from famous Chinese physicians of the Han, T'ang, and Yuan dynasties.

62. T'ang dynasty medical treatises.

63. Sanba here executes a satiric triple play, having the physician Takuan voice an attack on doctors in general for their pretensions and hokum, mocking Takuan himself for his unwarranted sense of superiority over his fellow charlatans, and expressing his distaste for scholars of Chinese and their windy exegeses of Chinese texts. Takuan puns on the traditional Japanese reading of a well-known poem by Po Chü-yi and turns it into a nonsensical medical diagnosis by exploiting the tendency of a Chinese text to become a gibberish of homonyms when read in Japanese. The poem was a frequent object of parody. (Jinbō, *UB*.)

64. Takuan makes another little joke, alluding to the rule of *haikai* compo-

sition prohibiting the use of the same word in consecutive verses of a sequence.

65. Takuan's imaginary doctor insists on referring to chicken eggs as *keiran*, an affected reading of characters normally read *tamago*, and then directs his patient to eat *ahiru ran*, an incongruous combination of the Japanese word for "duck" and the Sino-Japanese reading of the character for "egg."

66. The Major Counsellor Fujiwara no Narimichi (d. ca. 1159), noted for his skill at *kemari*, the kickball game played by members of the Court.

67. Li Li-weng: writer and painter of the late Ming and early Ch'ing. Ku Yen-wu: Ch'ing scholar and philosopher. Huang T'ing-chien, Su Tung-p'o, Lu Yu: major poets of the Sung dynasty.

68. The same image appears in a *senryū* verse adduced by Jinbō, *UB:* "An old-fashioned man ties his loincloth with his chin." The reference appears to be to the old-style loincloth made of a single narrow strip of fabric about six feet in length.

69. A festival in honor of Ebisu, one of the seven gods of wealth, celebrated in merchant homes on the 12th day of the 10th month with sumptuous parties for family, employees, and friends.

70. Literally, "search with bell and drum." Search parties organized to find lost children would comb the neighborhood to the accompaniment of a lively clatter of gongs and drums, which presumably would attract small children.

71. Matsuemon is confusing two separate tales from the Chinese collection *Erh-shi-ssu hsiao* (Twenty-four filial children), which was widely known (and parodied) throughout the Edo period. In the first tale, Meng Tsung's aged father is seized by a desire for fresh bamboo shoots in the dead of winter; Meng Tsung's devotion is rewarded when Heaven allows him to find bamboo shoots growing (out of season) in the snow. In the second tale, Kuo Ch'en is too poor to care for his parents. In order to reduce the number of mouths to feed, he decides to bury his children alive, and in the process of digging their intended grave unearths a golden pot.

72. On Sansuke's name, see note 17 to "The Women's Bath."

73. *Teikin ōrai,* a primer in epistolary format dating from the fourteenth or early fifteenth century but still widely used in the late Edo period.

74. Imagawa Ryōshun (1326–?) was a general and poet, author of numerous poetic treatises and didactic works, among them *Imagawa jō* (1412), a textbook still used in the temple schools (*terakoya*) of late Edo. Sanba (or Sansuke) is making fun of the rustic "scholar" for his referring to this and *Teikin ōrai* as authorities.

75. The first two days of the new year were devoted to ritual observances and formal visits; the third was devoted to less formal revels.

76. Sansuke puns on the idiom *Yoku no kawa ga tsuppatte iru,* "The skin of greed is stretched tight" (i.e., "bursting with greed"), by saying, *Yoku no*

kawa o hippatte, "stripping off the skin of greed," and uses the dialect word *kowai* (standard *katai*) in both its senses, "chewy" and "difficult"; a punch line (*ochi*) typical of *rakugo.*

77. I have substituted a less elaborate English play on words for an untranslatable series of puns involving horse beans (written "sword beans"), epileptic fits, and angina pectoris.

78. The speaker imitates the sounds of a search party.

79. The "pot man" (*yakitsugi*) was an itinerant mender of small pieces of crockery. The request that he mend something as large as a water urn (*mizukame*) is clearly meant as a joke.

80. Evidently the first line of a popular song.

81. In the previous paragraph, the old man suggests "sinking down toward the hot water pipe," *teppō no hō e shizumu,* where *teppō,* also "musket," refers to the pipe that carried hot water from the boiler into the bath. (Kitagawa, *Morisada mankō,* part 2, p. 218.) In this paragraph, the speaker uses *teppō* in yet another meaning, "cheap whorehouse," turning *teppō e shizumu* into "submerge in a cheap whorehouse." The *teppō* houses charged on a time basis, and so to "submerge," or stay for a long time, meant a large bill. Hence the later reference to "duns" (*tsukinma*).

82. The reference is to the custom of finishing the meal with a rice bowl of hot water or tea, which is both cleaned and cooled by stirring around in it a slice of pickled vegetable with one's chopsticks. A lewd interpretation is clearly intended.

83. A line from a popular song derived from Act 10 of *Kanadehon chūshingura.*

84. A popular song form based on a folk song from Itako in modern Ibaragi prefecture that first gained currency in Edo in the 1760s.

85. A brief exchange of puns on genitals and the names of pieces and moves used in *shōgi,* Japanese chess, is omitted here.

86. The area around Kyoto and Osaka.

87. The man from Kamigata puns untranslatably on the proverb *Futoshita koto de mokke no saiwai,* "Unexpected good fortune comes suddenly": for *futoshita,* "sudden," *fundoshita,* containing *fundoshi,* "loincloth;" for *mokke,* "unexpected," *mokko,* a kind of basket from which the name of a loincloth with ties (*mokkofundoshi*) is derived. The resulting "proverb," *Fundoshita koto de mokko no saiwai,* makes no sense in Japanese, let alone English.

Notes to "The Women's Bath"

1. A reference to the great fire of the 1st month of Bunka 6 (1809), which destroyed much of the Ryōgoku and Nihonbashi districts of Edo, including the establishment of Ishiwata Heihachi, publisher of "The Men's Bath."

2. It was the custom on the 4th or 5th day of the 5th month, to bathe in

water in which leaves of the *shōbu* plant had been steeped. (Kitagawa, *Morisada mankō*, part 2, p. 205.) *Shōbu* is here translated "iris," although the leaves used were not from that familiar plant but the similar ones of *Acorus calamus,* calamus or sweetflag, which bears a dense, columnar bunch of tiny greenish-yellow flowers. *Shōbu,* however, is frequently used interchangeably in Japan with *ayame* (written with the same characters) and *hanashōbu* (flowering *shōbu*), both of them species of iris.

Peach-leaf baths were taken during the first hot days of summer in the 6th month in order to ward off prickly heat. (Jinbō, *UB,* and Kitagawa, *Morisada mankō*, part 2, p. 205.)

Thus, both "an iris bath on the 6th" and "a peach-leaf bath in the waning days of summer" are metaphors for dilatoriness.

3. Twelve coppers (*mon, zeni*) was a standard offering at a temple or shrine, but it was also the customary gift at the public bath on certain festival and special gift days (*monbi*). Sanba uses the word *hineru* here to speak of "wringing out" a plot, but the verb has reference also to the custom of presenting these 12-*mon* tips to the bathhouse in twisted paper packages called *o-hineri.* (Kitagawa, *Morisada mankō*, part 2, p. 205.)

4. The women's bath customarily opened for business in the morning slightly later than the men's.

5. Jinbō, *UB,* p. 368, finds a model for this prefatory addendum in a preface by Hiraga Gennai to an early *kokkeibon* by Hirabaraya (Hezutsu) Tōsaku (1726-1789) entitled *Mizu no yukue* (1765).

6. The Three Histories: *Shih chi* (The records of the historian), *Han shu* History of the Han), and *Hou han shu* (History of the Later Han). The Five Teachings: *Yi ching* (The Classic of changes), *Shu ching* (The book of history), *Shih ching* (The book of odes), *Li chi* (The book of rites), and *Ch'un ch'iu* (The Spring and Autumn annals).

7. *Onna daigaku* (1729), abstracted posthumously from a longer work by Kaibara Ekiken (1630-1714).

8. *Onna Imagawa* (1700), a moral treatise for women modeled on the *Imagawa jō* of Imagawa Ryōshun.

9. This preface is followed by a brief advertisement regarding the reprinting of the first volume of *Ukiyoburo:*

> The first volume of this work suffered the wrath of Chu-jung, the god of fire, early in the spring of Bunka 6, when the printing blocks met with total destruction. We therefore contemplate the publication of a new and expanded edition. If our loyal readership throughout the realm will be so kind as to buy it upon its long-awaited publication, the publisher's good fortune will be great indeed.

The second edition of the first volume of *Ukiyoburo,* different from the first only in minor details, finally appeared in the 11th month of the 3rd year of Bunsei (1820).

10. According to Jinbō, *UB*, the three mendicants are, respectively, a begging monk of uncertain sect, someone intoning a prayer of the Nichiren sect, and an Amidist reciting a passage from the Lotus Sutra.

11. *Hasshū*, referring originally to the eight sects of Heian Buddhism, had by this time taken on the more general meaning of "diversity." Building on this idea, Sanba uses the word *kyūshū*, "nine sects," probably a pun on *kyū-shū*, "enemies," to hint at both the mutual distrust that prevailed between the Amidist Pure Land and the Nichiren sects and the petty conflicts that naturally arise in human intercourse.

12. Entertainers of the Tokiwazu school of *jōruri* song took professional names that included the element *-moji* after the founder of the school, Toki-wazu Moji-tayū (1709–1781). Likewise *-toyo*, another reading for the character read *bu* in the name of Tomimoto Buzen-no-jō, founder of the Tomimoto school.

13. Tiny drawings of the elements of the rebus (*yoki*, a hand ax; *koto*, the musical instrument; and *kiku*, chrysanthemum) appear in place of *kanji* in the text, accompanied by the appropriate *furigana* to show how they are to be read.

14. A type of popular song based on a verse of 3 lines of 7 syllables and one of 5.

15. *Kakasan:* the term used by geisha to refer to the mistress of their house; likewise *tottsan*, "papa," for the master of the house.

16. *Tottsan:* to the *kana* for *sa*, Sanba adds a *handokuten*, the small circle ordinarily used to convert *h-* to *p-* syllables, in order to represent the Edo dialect tendency to substitute *-tsa-* for *-sa-* under certain conditions.

17. A derisive nickname applied to male bath attendants. According to Jinbō, *UB*, who cites a set of late seventeenth-century bathhouse regulations, women were originally employed as back-scrubbers (*akakakionna*), limited by the rules to three in number; he suggests that the *san* (three) of "Sansuke" derives from this earlier custom.

18. The *yagō* (acting "clan" name) of the actor Sawamura Shūjūrō; here the fourth bearer of the name is probably meant.

19. Here, for the first time in the text, it becomes clear that the names Sanba is giving his female characters should not necessarily be taken as real women's names, for the speeches of the woman called here "Mrs. B." are labeled *Mi*, "snake," the 6th of the 12 animals of the Sino-Japanese zodiac. Mrs. A. is "dragon," the 5th animal, Mrs. C. is "monkey," and so on. Else-where, Sanba gives his women fanciful or symbolic names. The little girls in the bathhouse are Onabe, "pot"; Okama, "kettle"; Ouma, "horse" (also a zodiac animal); and Oniku, "meat," or more likely, given her personality, "hateful." We find also "Spring," "Summer," "Fall," and "Winter." The women who appear earlier have "names" connected with their trades: the geisha Osami (from *samisen*), Obachi (from the plectrum used to play the

samisen), and Ozuru (*jōruri* slang for *samisen*), and the hairdresser Okushi (comb).

20. Cassia-root bark and oil of cloves were used to make a simple sort of scented toilet water.

21. *Kawari-e:* pictures issued as single sheets or as illustrations in bound books that were designed in such a way that when cut or folded at certain points, part of one picture could be juxtaposed against part of another to create a new scene, or to give a figure a new costume, sometimes with intentionally funny or surprising results. Jinbō, *UB,* suggests that the actors' *kawari-e* mentioned here may be a reference to an 1809 production by Toyokuni.

22. *Akahon,* "red book," an illustrated book usually regarded as children's literature and bound with red covers; popular in Edo from the 1680s through the mid-1700s. Many *akahon* were retellings of folk or fairy tales.

23. The reference is to a simplified version of the Shimada hairstyle called *Shimada-kuzushi* that was popularized on the *kabuki* stage in the 1770s and 1780s, and was current among older women of the lower and middle classes in Sanba's time. The hair was done up over a form constructed either of papier-mâché or of iron wire covered with lacquered paper and stuffed with cotton. See Kitagawa, *Morisada mankō,* part 1, p. 360.

24. An *obi* of bleached cotton worn under the clothing for extra abdominal support after the fifth month of pregnancy.

25. Neighborhoods near Nihonbashi, modern Chūō-ku.

26. Near the modern Ginza 4-chōme, Chūō-ku.

27. *Kuma no haraobi:* perhaps a reference to the white cotton sash worn by bear cubs exhibited by street entertainers, believed to be a charm for safe delivery because of a belief that bears in some way lessened the severity of smallpox and measles.

28. Charms for a safe delivery issued by the Kurishima Shrine in Kada in the old province of Kii (modern Wakayama Prefecture).

29. The women call each other *obasan,* the direct-address or honorific term for "aunt," customarily used also to address a woman of a certain age older than oneself but not obviously older enough to warrant *obāsan,* "grandmother." Mrs. C. and Mrs. D. are thus not necessarily related to each other; Sanba is mocking them gently for using the term at their ages.

30. Both editors adduce a children's ball-bouncing song as source for this line. Nakamura, *UB,* also quotes a *haikai* verse of similar import by Kobayashi Issa (1763–1827).

31. Mrs. D. converts to her own uses the proverb, "Even the devil was once eighteen, and even coarse tea has its first infusion."

32. Adherents of the Amidist sects believed that, at the moment of death, Nyorai came from the Pure Land, riding on a purple cloud, to greet the deceased.

33. Tatsu no Kusojinmichi: neither editor is able to locate or explain this peculiar name, which means something like "New Dragon-shit Street."

34. Jinbō, *UB*, thinks this may be a reference to the contemporary head of the Fujima school of dance, Fujima Jinbei III (?–1821).

35. Both Ikuta and Amata were schools of *jōruri*-style *samisen*.

36. A passage of considerable length is omitted from the translation here in which the two women argue the relative merits of their respective dialects. The passage is virtually untranslatable, although Margarete Donath-Wiegand does admirably by it, giving Oyama and the Kamigata lady widely divergent German dialects to speak. Clearly, the dialects of American English are insufficiently distinct to permit a similar attempt here.

37. Then as now a popular resort area near Kamakura, south of Tokyo.

38. Because of the difficulty of maintaining a rhythm appropriate to a ball-bouncing song (*temariuta*) beyond a few lines of translation, I have omitted most of this song and of the following ones from the main body of the text. In literal paraphrase, this song might be rendered as follows:

By the Great Gate [to the Yoshiwara], in Ageyamachi, how magnificent the parade of the girls [*kimi*] of the Miuraya, Takauraya, and Komeya houses! Cast a glance around and see Hanamurasaki, Aikawa, Kiyokawa [famous courtesans of rank], dyed with the blush of new love, brocade upon brocade, like the Tatsuta River [in poetry, usually filled with a "brocade" of fallen autumn leaves]. *Anose, konose, yakkonose* [rhythmic refrain suggesting "over here, over there"]. Look there, at the Shinkawa [a canal running from Nihonbashi to the Sumida River]: two sailboats lined up! In those boats ride a great courtesan, a lesser courtesan. From behind, a covered pleasure boat overtakes them. "Hey, stop! Captain, stop the boat! When it stops we'll give you all five *shō* [of *sake*; one *shō* equals about 1.8 liters]." "We don't need five *shō*, we don't need three *shō* or five: we will be yours. The day is coming to a close, the day is coming to a close, the moon is rising. Ah, how kind you are, good sir!" There's a hundred, there's two hundred, there's three hundred . . . [elision in the original] . . . stopping, stopping, I've given you a thousand.

Having successfully completed one song (interesting in that it shows that even little girls were well aware of the details of life in the Yoshiwara), Oniku begins another, not at all clear in its meaning:

Osumi of the dyer's shop, and the Master, and Caihachi, too: when in Kyoto, it's Kiyomizu and the Rokkakudō [famous temples]. In the shelter of the pines, by the latticed windows, they see someone speak. There's a hundred . . .

39. Onatsu's song is based on the *jōruri* drama *Koimusume mukashi Hachijō*, first performed in 1775, the love of whose heroine, Okoma, for a hairdresser named Saiza is thwarted by the evil shop manager, Jōhachi. Jinbō, *UB*,

p. 369, provides the full text, but Onatsu drops the ball after the following few lines:

White makeup, white, white: Okoma of the Shiroki [white tree] -ya, and Saiza; but inside the shop, Jōhachi practices his calligraphy.

40. Ofuyu's song, also terminated abruptly, is as follows:

Enshū, what a pretty girl! And the unspeakably dashing youth, who is called "the grandson of the oil millionaire," who wears *tabi* even in summer, and sandals with braided laces, and shuffles carelessly along . . .

41. Literally, "Let's go home. The frogs are croaking! Let's go home. The frogs are croaking!" This little song, chanted by children going home from play in the evening, turns on the word *kaeru,* both "to return home" and "frog."

Bibliography
Glossary
Index

Bibliography

Except where otherwise noted, all works in Japanese in this bibliography were published in Tokyo (formerly Edo). Edo-period works are listed here only when available in modern printed editions; publication data for other works of the period may be found in the notes.

Modern editions of Edo-period literary works are cited in abbreviated form in annotations to the entries for those works. A key to these abbreviations precedes the notes to the chapters on p. 113 above.

WORKS IN JAPANESE

Asō Isoji 麻生磯次 . "Kokkeibon no honshitsu" 滑稽本の 本質 (The fundamental nature of the *kokkeibon*), *Kokugo to kokubungaku* 4.4:663–677 (April 1927).

Ebara Taizō 頴原退蔵 . *Edo bungei ronkō* 江戸文芸論考 (Essays on the literary arts of Edo). Sanseidō, 1937.

Engei Chinsho Kankōkai 演芸珍書刊行会 , ed. *Engeki bunko* 演劇文庫 (Drama library). 3 vols. Gannandō, 1973; reprint of the 1915 edition.

Fujimura Tsukuru 藤村作 . *Kamigata bungaku to Edo bungaku* 上方文学と江戸文学 (Kamigata literature and Edo literature). Shibundō, 1923.

Fujusanjin Suiōken 不濡山人翠応軒 . "Shidōkenden hyōron nantōshi" 志道軒伝評論難答誌 (A hard-to-answer critique of the biography of Shidōken). 1766. Ed. Jinbō Kazuya 神保五弥. In Hamada Giichiro 浜田義一郎, ed. *Tenmei bungaku: shiryō to kenkyū* 天明文学 : 資料と研究. Tō-kyōdō, 1979, pp. 301–328.

Furuya Chishin 古谷知新, ed. *Kokkei bungaku zenshū* 滑稽文学全集 (Complete collection of humorous literature). 12 vols. Bungei Shoin, 1918.
> Cited in this book as *KBZ*.

Futabatei Shimei 二葉亭四迷. "Yo ga genbun itchi no yurai" 余が言文一致の由来 (On the sources of my view of language reform), *Futabatei Shimei zenshū* V, 170–172.

Hakubunkan 博文館, ed. *Sanba kessakushū* 三馬傑作集 (Collected masterpieces of Sanba). *Teikoku bunko* series XIII. Hakubunkan, 1893.

Hamada Giichiro 浜田義一郎. "Kyōka" 狂歌, *Kōza Nihon bungaku* VIII, 17–33. Sanseidō, 1969.

———. *Ōta Nanpo* 大田南畝. Yoshikawa Kōbunkan, 1963.

Hayakawa Junzaburō 早川純三郎, ed. *Zatsugei sōsho* 雑芸叢書 (Miscellaneous arts collection). 2 vols. Kokusho Kankōkai, 1915.

Hiraga Gennai 平賀源内. *Fūrai Sanjin-shū* 風来山人集 (Collected works of Fūrai Sanjin). Ed. Nakamura Yukihiko 中村幸彦. *NKBT* LV. Iwanami Shoten, 1961.
> Fully annotated.

Hisamatsu Sen'ichi 久松潜一, ed. *Shinpan Nihon bungakushi* 新版日本文学史 (History of Japanese literature, new edition). Vol. V: *Kinsei II*. Shibundō, 1971.

Honda Yasuo 本田康雄. "Kokkeibon to wagei" 滑稽本と話芸 (The *kokkeibon* and *wagei*), *Kōza Nihon bungaku* VIII, 113–136 (Sanseidō 1969).

———. *Shikitei Sanba no bungei* 式亭三馬の文芸 (The literary art of Shikitei Sanba). Kasama Shobō, 1973.

———. "Ukiyomonomanemekitaru esemonogatari no koto" 浮世物真似めきたる笑せ物語のこと (On *ukiyomono-mane*-like fictions), *Kinsei bungei* 8:61–67 (1962).

Imaizumi Genkichi 今泉源吉. *Katsuragawake no hitobito* 桂川家の人々 (The people of the house of Katsuragawa). 3 vols. Shinozaki Shorin, 1968.

Ishii Ryōsuke 石井良助 . *Edo no yūjo sono ta* 江戸の遊女
その他 (The courtesans of Edo, and more). Shiji Nippōsha Shup-
pankyoku, 1971.
Iwamoto Keiichi 岩本堅一 . "Sanba no kokkei to sono fukasa
ni tsuite" 三馬の滑稽とその深さに就いて (On Sanba's
humor and its depth), *Kokubungaku kenkyū* 22:33-40 (Autumn
1949).
Iwamoto Sashichi (Darumaya Kattōshi) 岩本左七 (達磨屋
活東子). *Gesaku rokkasen* 戯作六家撰 (Six selected
sages of *gesaku*). [Preface dated 1857.]
      Reprinted in *Enseki jisshu* 燕石十種 I, 371-407. Ed. Iwa-
moto Sashichi. 3 vols. Kokusho Kankōkai, 1907.
———. *Gesakusha shōden* 戯作者小伝 (Brief biographies of
gesakusha). [1857?]
      Reprinted in *Enseki jisshu* I, 339-370. Ed. Iwamoto Sashichi.
3 vols. Kokusho Kankōkai, 1907.

Jinbō Kazuya 神保五弥 . "Kaseido Tenpōki no Edo shōsetsu
no sakusha to dokusha" 化政度天保期の江戸小説の
作者と読者 (Edo fiction of the Bunka, Bunsei, and Tenpō eras: authors and readers), *Bungaku* 26.5:95-108 (May
1958).
———. "Makki Edo shimin no warai: Shikitei Sanba ni okeru"
末期江戸市民の笑ひ：式亭三馬における (Late Edo
urban humor in Shikitei Sanba), *Kokubungaku kenkyū* 26:26-
36 (Autumn 1951).
———. "Shinrotei to Tamenaga Shunsui" 振鷺亭と為永春水
(Shinrotei and Tamenaga Shunsui), *Kinsei bungei* 7:39-50
(March 1962).
Jippensha Ikku 十返舎一九. *Tōkaidōchū hizakurige* 東海道中
膝栗毛 (Shanks' mare on the Tōkaidō road). 1802-1814.
Ed. Asō Isoji 麻生磯次 . *NKBT* LXII. Iwanami Shoten, 1958.
Jōfuku Isamu 城福勇 . *Hiraga Gennai no kenkyū* 平賀源内
の研究 (Studies on Hiraga Gennai). Osaka, Sōgensha, 1976.

Kenshōkaku Shujin 献笑閣主人 . *Gekka yojō* 月花余情
(Echoes of moon and flowers). Osaka, Harimaya Sahei, 1746.
      Reprinted in *NMZ* XII, 25-38.
Kimura Mokurō 木村黙老 . *Kokuji shōsetsu-tsū* 国字小説
通 (Connoisseur's guide to fiction in Japanese). [1849.]

Reprinted in *Zoku enseki jisshu* 続燕石十種 I, 248-257.
Ed. Kokusho Kankōkai 国書刊行会. Kokusho Kankōkai,
1908.

Kitagawa Kisō (Morisada) 喜田川李荘　(守貞). [*Ruijū kinsei
fūzokushi*] *Morisada mankō* [類聚近世風俗志] 守貞
漫稿 (Morisada's idle notes: A classified compendium of Edo-
period customs). Ed. Muromatsu Iwao 室松岩雄. Enomoto
Shobō, 1927.

Kōdō Tokuji 莘堂得知, ed. *Kibyōshi hyakushu* 黄表紙百
種. *Zoku teikoku bunko* series, no. 16. Hakubunkan, 1901.

Koike Tōgorō 小池藤五郎. *Santō Kyōden* 山東京伝. *Jinbutsu sōsho* series no. 72. Yoshikawa Kōbunkan, 1961.

Konta Yōzō 今田洋三. *Edo no hon'ya-san* 江戸の本屋
さん (Booksellers of Edo). Nihon Hōsō Shuppan Kyōkai, 1977.

Maeda Ai 前田愛. "Kinsei shuppan kikō no kaitai" 近世
出版機構の解体 (The dissolution of the Edo-period
publishing industry), 2 parts, *Kinsei bungei* 9: 54-65 (1963),
10: 45-54 (1964).

———. "Shuppansha to dokusha: kashihon'ya no yakuwari o chūshin to shite" 出版者と読者・貸本屋の役割を中心
として (Publisher and reader: the role of the commercial lending library), *Kokubungaku kaishaku to kanshō* 26.1: 124-135
(January 1961).

———. "Tenpō kaikaku ni okeru sakusha to shoshi" 天保改革
における作者と書肆 (Author and bookseller in the Tenpō
reforms), *Kinsei kokubungaku: kenkyū to shiryō* 近世国文
学：研究と資料, pp. 258-284. Ed. Shuzui Kenji 守隨
憲治. Sanseidō, 1960.

Mantei (Kannatei) Onitake 曼亭（感和亭）鬼武. *Kyūkanchō*
旧観帳 (The old subscribers' register). 4 vols. 1805-1809.
　　Reprinted in Mitamura, ed., *Kokkeibon meisakushū*, pp. 628-
704. Partially annotated.

Matsushima Eiichi 松島栄一. *Chūshingura* 忠臣蔵. Iwanami
Shoten, Iwanami shinsho no. 541, 1964.

Mitamura Engyo 三田村鳶魚, ed. *Kokkeibon meisakushū*
滑稽本名作集 (Masterpieces of the *kokkeibon*). *Hyōshaku
Edo bungaku sōsho* series, no. 10. Dai Nippon Yūbenkai Kōdansha, 1936.

Partially annotated texts of *Hizakurige, Kyūkanchō,* and *Ukiyoburo.*

Miyao Shigeo 宮尾しげを and Kimura Senhide 木村仙秀 *Edo shomin no fūzokushi* 江戸庶民の風俗誌. (Customs of the Edo commoner). Chiba Shuppan, division of Tenbōsha, 1970.

Miyoshi Ikkō 三好一光. *Edogo jiten* 江戸語事典 (Edo dialect dictionary). Seiabō, 1971.

Mizuno Minoru 水野稔. *Edo shōsetsu ronsō* 江戸小説論叢 (Essays on Edo fiction). Chūō Kōronsha, 1974.

―――. *Kibyōshi, sharebon no sekai* 黄表紙・洒落本の世界 (The world of the *kibyōshi* and the *sharebon*). Iwanami Shoten, 1976.

―――, ed. *Kibyōshi sharebonshū* 黄表紙洒落本集 (*Kibyōshi* and *sharebon* collection). *NKBT* LIX. Iwanami Shoten, 1958.

Fully annotated.

―――, ed. *Kibyōshi-shū I* 黄表紙集 一 (*Kibyōshi* collection, Vol. I). *Koten bunko* series, no. 264. Koten Bunko, 1969.

―――. "Kusazōshi to sono dokusha" 草双紙とその読者 (The *kusazōshi* and its readers), *Kōza Nihon bungaku* VIII, 87–112. Sanseidō, 1969.

Muchūsanjin Negoto sensei 夢中山人寝言先生. *Tatsumi no sono* 辰巳之園 (The garden of the southeast). 1770.

Reprinted in Mizuno, ed., *Kibyōshi sharebonshū. NKBT* LIX, 295–318. Fully annotated.

Nakamura Michio 中村通夫. "Sanba arekore" 三馬あれこれ (This and that about Sanba), *Nihon koten bungaku taikei geppō* 5: 6-8 (September 1957).

Nakamura Yukihiko 中村幸彦. *Gesakuron* 戯作論 (On *gesaku*). 2nd ed. Kadokawa Shoten, 1970.

―――. "Yomihon no dokusha" 読本の読者 (The readership of the *yomihon*), *Bungaku* 26.5: 74-82 (May 1958).

――― and Nishiyama Matsunosuke 西山松之助. *Bunka ryōran* 文化繚乱 (Cultural chaos). *Nihon bungaku no rekishi* series VIII. Kadokawa Shoten, 1967.

Nakano Mitsutoshi 中野三敏, Jinbō Kazuya, and Maeda Ai,

eds. *Sharebon, kokkeibon, ninjōbon* 洒落本・滑稽本・
人情本 . *NKBZ* XLVII. Shōgakkan, 1971.
　　Fully annotated.

Nihon Meicho Zenshū Kankōkai 日本名著全集刊行会　 , ed.
and publ. *Kibyōshi nijūgoshu* 黄表紙廿五種 (Twenty-
five *kibyōshi*). *NMZ* XI. 1926.

————. *Kokkeibonshū* 滑稽本集 (*Kokkeibon* collection).
NMZ XIV 1927.

————. *Sharebonshū* 洒落本集 (*Sharebon* collection). *NMZ* XII
1929.

Nobuhiro Shinji 延広真治 . "Tenmei kansei ki no Utei Enba"
天明寛政期の烏亭焉馬 (Utei Enba in the Tenmei and
Kansei eras), in *Inoura Yoshinobu-hakase kakō kinen ronbunshū: geinō to bungaku* 井浦芦信博士華甲記念論文集 ___
芸能と文学 , pp. 117-140. Kasama Shoin, 1977.

————. "Utei Enba" 烏亭焉馬 , in *Rakugo no subete* 落語の
すべて , pp. 93-99. Ed. Kokubungaku Henshūbu 国文学
編集部. Gakutōsha, n.d.

Noda Hisao 野田寿雄 . "Kokkeibon no keifu to shokeitai"
滑稽本の系譜と諸形態 (The derivation and forms of the
kokkeibon), *Kokugo to kokubungaku* 38.4: 25-34 (April 1961).

Okitsu Kaname 興津要 . *Edo shomin no fūzoku to ninjō* 江戸
庶民の風俗と人情 (Customs and psychology of the
Edo commoner). Ōfūsha, 1979.

————. *Nihon bungaku to rakugo* 日本文学と落語　 (Japanese literature and *rakugo*). Ōfūsha, 1974.

————. *Rakugo to Edokko* 落語と江戸っ子 (*Rakugo* and the
Edokko). Sangensha, 1973.

Ozaki Kyūya 尾崎久弥 . *Kinsei shomin bungaku ronkō* 近世
庶民文学論考 (Essays on the popular literature of the Edo
period). Ed. Nakamura Yukihiko 中村幸彦 . Chūō Kōronsha,
1973; a reprint of the 1950 edition.

Ryūtei Rijō 滝亭鯉丈 . *Hanagoyomi hasshōjin* 花暦八笑人
(Eight laughers: A blossom calendar). 1820.
　　Reprinted in *NMZ* XIV, 749-930.

Santō Kyōden 山東京伝 . *Keiseikai shijūhatte* 傾城買四十八
手 (Forty-eight ways to successful whoring).

Reprinted in Mizuno, ed., *Kibyōshi sharebonshū. NKBT* LIX, pp. 387–416. Fully annotated.

————. *Kokei no sanshō* 古契三娼 (Three old loves). 1787. Reprinted in Sasakawa, ed., *Sharebon kusazōshi shū*, pp. 585–612. Partially annotated.

————. *Seirō hiru no sekai nishiki no ura* 青楼昼之世界錦之裏 (The world of the brothel by day: The other side of the brocade). 1791. Reprinted in Mizuno, ed., *Kibyōshi sharebonshū* (*NKBT* LIX), pp. 417–440. Fully annotated.

————. *Shikake bunko* 仕懸文庫 (Library of courtesan's wiles). 1791. Reprinted in *NMZ* XII, 541–565.

————. *Shingaku hayasomegusa* 心学早染草 (Quick introduction to *shingaku*). 3 vols. 1791. Reprinted in Mizuno, ed., *Kibyōshi sharebonshū* (*NKBT* LIX), pp. 197–216. Fully annotated.

Sasakawa Shurō 笹川種郎. Introduction to *Jippensha Ikkushū* 十返舎一九集, pp. i–xxxi. Ed. Seibundō. *Kindai Nihon bungaku taikei* series XIII. Seibundō, 1933.

————. "Sanba kenkyū" 三馬研究 (Studies on Sanba), *Nihon bungaku kōza* 10, 265–296. Shinchōsha, 1931.

————, ed. *Sharebon kusazōshi shū* 洒落本草双紙集 (*Sharebon* and *kusazōshi* collection). *Hyōshaku Edo bungaku sōsho* series VIII. Dai Nippon Yūbenkai Kōdansha, 1936. Partially annotated.

Shikitei Sanba 式亭三馬. *Chaban kyōgen hayagatten* 茶番狂言早合点 (Shortcuts to success in amateur theatricals). Illustrated by Utagawa Kuninao. 2 vols. Nishimiya Shinroku, 1821–1824. Reprinted in Hayakawa Junzaburō, ed., *Zatsugei sōsho* II, 68–102.

————. *Chūshingura henchikiron* 忠臣蔵偏痴気論 ("The treasury of loyal retainers": A crackpot view). Illustrated by Utagawa Kuninao. 2 vols. Tsuruya Kinsuke, 1812. Reprinted in Engei Chinsho Kankōkai 演芸珍書刊行会, ed., *Engeki bunko* 演劇文庫. 3 vols. Gannandō, 1973; reprint of the 1915 edition. Vol. III, book 5, part 5, pp. 1–20, 1–37.

————. *Daisen sekai gakuya saguri* 大千世界楽屋探 (A

look at the "green room" of the Thousand Realms). Illustrated by Utagawa Toyokuni. 3 vols. Tsuruya Kinsuke, 1817.

Reprinted in Hakubunkan, ed., *Sanba kessakushū*, pp. 807-863.

————. *Gejō suigen maku no soto* 戲場粹言幕之外 (Theater chic this side of the curtain). Illustrated by Utagawa Kuninao. 2 vols. 1806.

Reprinted in *KBZ* V, 65-108.

————. *Hayagawari mune no karakuri* 早替胸機関 (Quick changes of heart). Illustrated by Utagawa Toyokuni. Nishimura Genroku, Ishiwata Risuke, Ishiwata Heihachi, 1810.

Reprinted in *NMZ* XIV, 393-422, and Hakubunkan, ed., *Sanba kessakushū*, pp. 627-659.

————. *Hitogokoro nozoki karakuri* 人心覗機関 (A mechanism for peering into the human heart). Illustrated by Utagawa Kuninao. 2 vols. Chōjiya Heibei, 1814.

Reprinted in *KBZ* III, 509-592, and Hakubunkan, ed., *Sanba kessakushū*, pp. 661-695.

————. *Ikazuchitarō gōaku monogatari* 雷太郎強悪物語 (The story of the villainous Ikazuchitarō). Illustrated by Utagawa Toyokuni. 10 vols. in 2 parts. Nishimiya Shinroku, 1806.

Modern edition: see following entry.

————. *Ikazuchitarō gōaku monogatari*. Ed. Suzuki Jūzō 鈴木 重三 and Honda Yasuo 本田康雄 . Kinsei Fūzoku Kenkyū-kai, 1967.

————. Introduction to *Keiseikai futasujimichi* 傾城買二筋 道, by Umebori Kokuga 梅暮里谷峨 . 1798.

Reprinted in Mizuno, ed., *Kibyōshi sharebonshū* (*NKBT* LIX), p. 442.

————. *Ippai kigen* 一盃綺言 (One cup and they're on their way). Illustrated by Utagawa Toyokuni. Ishiwata Risuke, 1813.

Reprinted in *KBZ* IV, 211-236.

————. *Kanadehon kuraishō* 仮名手本蔵意抄 (Gleanings from the copy-book storehouse). Illustrated by Utagawa Kunisada. Nishimura Genroku, 1813.

Reprinted in *NMZ* XIV, 637-686.

————. *Kokon hyakubaka* 古今百馬鹿 (A hundred fools, ancient and modern). Illustrated by Utagawa Kuninao. 3 vols. Tsutaya Jūzaburō et al., 1814.

Reprinted in *KBZ* IV, 175-210; *NMZ* XIV, 717-748; and Hakubunkan, ed., *Sanba kessakushū*, pp. 289-426.

————. *Kusazōshi kojitsuke nendaiki* 稗史憶説年代記 (*Kusa-zōshi:* A burlesque chronicle). Illustrated by the author. 3 vols. Nishimiya Shinroku, 1802.

Reprinted in Sasakawa, ed., *Sharebon kusazōshishū*, pp. 223-240. Partially annotated.

————. *Kyakusha hyōbanki* 客者評判記 (Critiques of theater patrons). Illustrated by Utagawa Kunisada. 3 vols. Tsuruya Kinsuke, 1811.

Reprinted in *NMZ* XIV, 423-510, and Geinōshi Kenkyūkai 芸能史研究会 , ed., *Nihon shomin bunka shiryō shūsei* 日本庶民文化史料集成 VI. San'ichi Shobō, 1973, pp. 481-529.

————. *Kyōgen kigyo* 狂言綺語 (Mad words, beguiling prose). 2 vols. 1804.

Reprinted in Hakubunkan, ed., *Sanba kessakushū*, pp. 757-806.

————. *Mashin gigen* 痲疹戯言 (A whimsical discourse on the measles). Yorozuya Tajiemon, 1803.

Reprinted in Hakubunkan, ed., *Sanba kessakushū*, pp. 923-939, as *Hashika no kami o okuru hyō* 送痲疹神表 .

————. *Namaei katagi* 酩酊気質 (Portraits of drinkers). Illustrated by Utagawa Toyokuni. 2 vols. Kazusaya Sasuke, 1806.

Reprinted in Nakano et al., eds., *Sharebon, kokkeibon, ninjōbon*, pp. 201-254, fully annotated; *KBZ* VI, 313-350; and Hakubunkan, ed., *Sanba kessakushū*, pp. 865-921.

————. *Ningen banji uso bakkari* 人間萬事虚誕訂 (In human affairs, nothing but lies). Illustrated by Utagawa Kuninao. Igaya Kan'emon, Sekiguchi Heiemon, 1813.

Reprinted in *NMZ* XIV, 599-622, and *KBZ* IV, 237-284.

————. *Sendō shinwa* 船頭深話 (Profound tales of a boatman). 1806.

Reprinted in Hakubunkan, ed., *Sanba kessakushū*, pp. 535-598.

————. *Sendōbeya* 船頭部屋 (The boatman's quarters). 1807.

Reprinted in Hakubunkan, ed., *Sanba kessakushū*, pp. 599-625.

————. *Shijūhachikuse* 四十八癖 (Forty-eight nasty habits). Illustrated by Utagawa Kuninao, Yanagikawa Shigenobu, and Utagawa Yoshimaro. 4 vols. Tsuruya Kinsuke, 1812-1818.

Reprinted in *KBZ* IV, 43-174.

————. *Shikitei zakki* 式亭雑記 (Shikitei's jottings). [1810-

1811.] In *Zoku enseki jisshu* 続燕石十種   I, 44-82. Ed. Kokusho Kankōkai 国書刊行会 . 2 vols. Kokusho Kankō-kai, 1908.

Sanba's diary or commonplace book for 1810-1811.

―――. *Shirōto kyōgen monkirigata* 素人狂言紋切形 (The archetypal amateur theatrical). 2 vols. 1814.

Reprinted in *KBZ* V, 109-172, and Hakubunkan, ed., *Sanba kessakushū*, pp. 941-1005.

―――. *Tatsumi fugen* 辰巳婦言 (Women's words from the southeast). Illustrated by Kitagawa Utamaro. 1798.

Reprinted in *NMZ* XII, 567-602; Sasakawa, ed., *Sharebon kusazōshishū*, pp. 659-696, partially annotated; and Haku-bunkan, ed., *Sanba kessakushū*, pp. 497-534.

―――. *Tentō ukiyo no dezukai* 天道浮世出星操 (The heavenly puppeteers of the floating world). Illustrated by Uta-gawa Toyokuni. 2 vols. Nishimiya Shinroku, 1794.

Reprinted in Kōdō, ed., *Kibyōshi hyakushu*, pp. 845-859.

―――. *Tōsei nanakuse jōgo* 当世七癖上戸 (Seven habits of modern drunks). Illustrated by Utagawa Kunisada. 3 vols. Nishi-mura Genroku, Nishimiya Yohei, Nishimiya Heihachi, 1810.

Reprinted in *KBZ* IV, 1-42.

―――. *Ukiyoburo* 浮世風呂 (The bathhouse of the floating world). Illustrated by Kitagawa Yoshimaro and Utagawa Kuni-nao. 9 vols. Nishimura Genroku, Ishiwata Risuke, Ishiwata Hei-hachi, 1809-1813.

For modern reprints, see following entries.

―――. *Ukiyoburo.* Ed. Jinbō Kazuya 神保五弥 . Kadokawa Shoten, *Kadokawa bunko* no. 2597, 1968.

Fully annotated.

―――. *Ukiyoburo.* Ed. Nakamura Michio 中村通夫 . *NKBT* LXIII. Iwanami Shoten, 1957.

Fully annotated.

―――. *Ukiyodoko* 浮世床 (The barbershop of the floating world). Illustrated by Utagawa Kuninao. 5 vols. Tsuruya Kin-suke, Kashiwaya Hanzō, 1813-1814.

For modern reprints, see following entries.

―――. *Ukiyodoko.* Ed. Nakanishi Zenzō 中西善三 . *Nihon koten zensho* series. Asahi Shinbunsha, 1961.

Fully annotated.

————. *Edo no rakugo: Ukiyodoko.* Ed. Ono Takeo 小野武雄 . *Edo fūzoku shiryō* series V. Tenbōsha, 1974.
   Partially annotated; includes text of Book III, a continuation by Ryūtei Rijō.

————. *Ukiyodoko.* Modern Japanese translation by Kubota Mantarō 久保田万太郎 . In Hisamatsu Sen'ichi et al., eds., *Edo shōsetsu-shū I*, pp. 271-309. *Nihon no koten* series XXV. Kawade Shobō, 1974.

Shimizu Shigeru 清水茂 . "Shikitei Sanba to Futabatei Shimei: ketsuron no nai nōto" 式亭三馬と二葉亭四迷：結論のないノート (Shikitei Sanba and Futabatei Shimei: Some inconclusive notes), *Tsubouchi Shōyō, Futabatei Shimei* 坪内逍遥・二葉亭四迷 , pp. 180-186. Ed. Nihon Bungaku Kenkyū Shiryō Kankōkai. Yūseidō, 1979.

Suwa Haruo 諏訪春雄 . *Shuppan kotohajime* 出版事始 (The beginnings of publishing). Mainichi Shinbunsha, 1978.

Suzuki Jūzō 鈴木重三 . "Gōkanmono no daizai tenki to Tanehiko" 合巻物の題材転機と種彦 (Tanehiko and the change in *gōkan* subject matter), *Kokugo to kokubungaku* 38.4: 57-71 (April 1961).

Takayanagi Mitsuhisa 高柳光寿 et al., eds. *Nihonshi jiten* 日本史辞典 (Dictionary of Japanese history). Kadokawa Shoten, 1966.

Takizawa (Kyokutei) Bakin 滝沢（曲亭）馬琴 . *Heiben* 駢（駢）鞭 (An excoriation of Sanba). In Takizawa Bakin, *Kyokutei ikō* 曲亭遺稿 , pp. 275-296. Ed. Hayakawa Junzaburō. Kokusho Kankōkai, 1911.

————. *Iwademo no ki* 伊波伝毛之記 (Record of things as well unsaid). [1819.] In *Shin enseki jisshu* 新燕石十種 IV, 185-203. Ed. Kokusho Kankōkai, 5 vols. Kokusho Kankōkai, 1913.

————. *Kinsei mono no hon Edo sakusha burui* 近世物之本江戸作者部類 (The book in recent times: Edo writers classified). [Preface dated 1834.] In *Onchi sōsho* 温知叢書 , Vol. V, part 3, pp. 1-191. Ed. Kishigami Misao 岸上操 . Hakubunkan, 1891.

Tamabayashi Haruo 玉林晴朗 . *Shokusanjin no kenkyū* 蜀山人の研究 (Studies on Shokusanjin). Hobō Shoin, 1944.

Tamenaga Shunsui 為永春水 . *Shunshoku umegoyomi* 春色
梅児與美 (Young love, a blossom calendar). Ed. Nakamura
Yukihiko. *NKBT* LXIV. Iwanami Shoten, 1962.
  Fully annotated.
Tanaka Shin 田中伸 . "Shikitei Sanba no hōhō" 式亭三馬の
  方法 (Shikitei Sanba's methods), *Kokubungaku kenkyū* 24:
  85–92 (Autumn 1950).
Terakado Seiken 寺門静軒 . *Edo hanjōki* 江戸繁昌記
  (Thriving Edo). 3 vols. Ed. Asakura Haruhiko 朝倉治彦 and
  Andō Kikuji 安藤菊二 . Heibonsha, 1974–1976.
Teruoka Yasutaka 暉峻康隆 and Gunji Masakatsu 郡司正勝
    Edo shimin bungaku no kaika 江戸市民文化の開花
  (The flowering of Edo urban culture). *Nihon no bungaku* series
  V. Shibundō, 1967.

Ueda Kazutoshi 上田萬年 and Higuchi Yasuchiyo 樋口慶千
  世 , comps. *Chikamatsu goi* 近松語彙 (Chikamatsu concordance). Fuzanbō, 1930.
Uesato Shunsei 上里春生 . *Edo shosekishō shi* 江戸書籍商
  史 (History of the Edo book trade). Meicho Kankōkai,
  1965; a reprint of the 1930 edition.

Yamaguchi Takeshi 山口剛 . Introduction to *Kibyōshi nijūgoshu*, pp. i–lxxvi. *NMZ* XI. 1926.
———. Introduction to *Kokkeibonshū*, pp. i–lxxv. *NMZ* XIV.
  1927.
———. Introduction to *Sharebonshū*, pp. i–clii. *NMZ* XII. 1929.
Yamazaki Fumoto 山崎麓 . *Kaitei Nihon shōsetsu shomoku
  nenpyō* 改訂日本小説書目年表 (Chronological bibli-
  ography of Japanese fiction, revised and corrected). Ed. Shoshi
  Kenkyūkai 書誌・研究会 . Yumani Shobo, 1977.
Yamazaki Yoshinari 山崎美成 . *Kairoku* 海録 (Record of
  the seas). Ed. Hayakawa Junzaburō. Kokusho Kankōkai, 1915.

WORKS IN WESTERN LANGUAGES

Aston, W. G. *A History of Japanese Literature.* Rutland and Tokyo,
  Charles E. Tuttle, 1972; a reprint of the 1899 edition.
Bellah, Robert N. *Tokugawa Religion.* New York, Free Press, 1967.

Blacker, Carmen. *The Japanese Enlightenment.* Cambridge, Cambridge University Press, 1964.

Brandon, James R. *Kabuki: Five Classic Plays.* Cambridge, Harvard University Press, 1975.

Donath-Wiegand, Margarete. *Zur literarhistorische Stellung des Ukiyoburo von Shikitei Samba.* Wiesbaden, Otto Harrassowitz, 1963.

Hibbett, Howard S. *The Floating World in Japanese Fiction.* New York, Oxford University Press, 1959.

James, Louis. *Fiction for the Working Man, 1830-1850.* New York, Oxford University Press, 1963.

Keene, Donald. *World Within Walls: Japanese Literature of the Pre-modern Era, 1600-1867.* New York, Holt, Rinehart and Winston, 1976.

———, trans. *Chūshingura: The Treasury of Loyal Retainers.* New York, Columbia University Press, 1971.

Kornicki, Peter F. "*Nishiki no Ura:* An Instance of Censorship and the Structure of a *Sharebon,*" *Monumenta Nipponica* 32.2: 153-188 (Summer 1977).

———. "The Publisher's Go-Between: *Kashihonya* in the Meiji Period," *Modern Asian Studies* 14.2: 331-344 (April 1980).

Neuburg, Victor E. *Popular Literature: A History and Guide from the Beginning of Printing to the Year 1897.* New York, Penguin Books, 1977.

Raz, Jacob. "The Audience Evaluated: Shikitei Sanba's *Kyakusha Hyōbanki,*" *Monumenta Nipponica* 35.2: 199-221 (Summer 1980).

Satchell, Thomas, trans. *Shanks' Mare: Being a Translation of the Tokaido Volumes of "Hizakurige," Japan's Great Comic Novel of Travel & Ribaldry by Ikku Jippensha (1765-1831).* Rutland and Tokyo, Charles E. Tuttle, 1960; a reprint of the 1929 edition published by subscription in Kobe.

Steven, Chigusa. "*Hachikazuki:* A Muromachi Short Story," *Monumenta Nipponica* 32.3: 303-331 (Autumn 1977).

Tillotson, Kathleen. *Novels of the Eighteen-Forties.* Oxford, Clarendon Press, 1954.

Turk, Frank A. *The Prints of Japan.* New York, October House, 1966.

Watt, Ian. *The Rise of the Novel.* Berkeley, University of California Press, 1957.

Glossary

The following is a selected list of Japanese terms, titles, and names that appear in the text and notes. Titles of works that appear in the bibliography are excluded, as are Chinese names, terms, and titles, and the names of people active after 1868.

akahon 赤本
Akogi monogatari
阿古義物語
ana 穴
aobon 青本
Asanebō Muraku
朝寝房夢楽
Azuma kaidō onna katakiuchi
吾妻街道女敵討

Bokusentei Yukimaro
墨川亭雪麻呂
Bokutei Tsukimaro
墨亭月麻呂
bunjin 文人

chaban kyōgen 茶番狂言
Chikamatsu Monzaemon
近松門左衛門
chōnin 町人

chūbon 中本
Chūshingura jinbutsu hyōron
忠臣蔵人物評論

daibon 台本
dangibon 談義本

Edokko 江戸っ子
Ejima (ya) Kiseki 江島(屋)
其磧
Ekitei San'yū 益亭三友

Fukagawa haiken 富賀川
拌見
Fukai Shidōken 深井
志道軒
Fukutei Sanshō 福亭三笑
Fukuzawa Yukichi 福沢諭吉
Fūrai Sanjin 風来山人

221

Fūrai Sennin 風来仙人
furoya 風呂屋

ga 雅
Gakutei Sanshi 学亭三子
genkin'yu 現金湯
gesakusha 戯作者
Gesakusha 戯作舎
Go taiheiki Shiraishibanashi
碁太平記白石噺
gōkan 合巻

Hachimonjiya Jishō
八文字屋自笑
hanamichi 花道
hanashibon 噺本
hankatsū 半可通
hanshibon 半紙本
Hara no uchi gesaku shubon
腹之内戯作種本
Harasuji ōmuseki
腹筋逢夢石
Haratsutsumi heso no shitakata
腹鼓臍噺曲
Hatakenaka Kansai 畠中観斎
Hatsumonogatari 初物語
Hayagawari kufū no adauchi
早替工夫の仇討
Hayashi Shihei 林子平
henchikiron 偏痴気論
Hirabaraya (Hezutsu) Tōsaku
　平原（平秩）東作
Hōhiron 放屁論
Hōraisanjin Kikyō
蓬来山人帰橋
Horinoya Nihei (Gangetsudō)
　堀野屋仁兵衛（覩
月堂）
Hōseidō Kisanji 朋誠堂
喜三二

Ichikawa Danjūrō
市川団十郎
Ihara Saikaku 井原西鶴
Imayō heta dangi 当世下手
談義
Inaka shibai chūshingura
田舎芝居忠臣蔵
Iozaki mushi no hyōban
五百崎蟲の評判
Irikomi sentō shinwa
凌銭湯新話

Ishida Baigan 石田梅巌
Ishikawa Masamochi 石川雅望
Ishiwata Heihachi 石渡平八
Ishiwata Risuke 石渡利助
Itakobushi 潮来婦誌
Ittei Sanraku 一亭三楽
Ittei Sanshi 一亭三子
Ittei Sanshō 一亭三生

Jōkanbō Kōa 静観房好阿
jōruri 浄瑠璃

Kaikō Sanjin 蟹行山人
Kaikoku heidan 海国兵談
Kamiya Isaburō 紙屋
伊三郎
Kanadehon chūshingura
仮名手本忠臣蔵
kanzen chōaku 勧善懲悪
kashihon'ya 貸本屋
katagimono 気質物
Katakiuchi Adatarayama
敵討安達太郎山
Katakiuchi gijo no hanabusa
敵討義女英
Katakiuchi Shiraishibanashi
敵討白石噺
katakiuchimono 敵討物
Katsukawa Shuntei 勝川春亭

kawari-e 替絵

Keiko jamisen 稽古三弦

Ken'a Midabutsu
嫌阿弥陀仏

Kentei Bokusan 硯亭墨山

kibyōshi 黄表紙

Kikuchi Kyūtoku 菊地久徳

Kikuchi Mohei (Seiundō)
菊地茂兵衛（晴雲堂　）

Kikuchi Taisuke 菊地太助
（泰輔　）

Kikuchi Takehisa 菊地武幾

kinsei 近世

Kitagawa Utamaro
喜多川歌麻呂

Kitao Shigemasa 北尾重政

Kitao Shigenobu 北尾重信

kobon 小本

Kogawa Yoshimaro 小川美麿

Koikawa Harumachi 恋川春町

kokkeibon 滑稽本

Kokkeidō　滑稽堂

Kokontei Sanchō
古今亭三鳥

kokugaku 国学

kōshaku 講釈

kurobon 黒本

kusazōshi 草双紙（是草
紙　）

Kyan taiheiki mukō hachimaki
侠太平記向鉢巻

kyankaku 侠客

kyōbun 狂文

Kyōgen inaka ayatsuri
狂言田舎操

kyōka 狂歌

Kyōkakei 狂歌艦

Kyōkun mune no karakuri
教訓胸機関

Kyōkuntei Kinryū
教訓亭金竜

kyōshi 狂詩

Manjutei Shōji 萬寿亭正二

Manzōtei 万象亭

Matsudaira Sadanobu
松平定信

Morishima Chūryō 森島中良

mukō hachimaki 向鉢巻

mukō hikimaku 向引幕

Myōdai no aburaya
名代のあぶらや

*Naburu mo yomi to utajizu-
kushi* 嬲訓歌字尽

Nakazawa Dōni 中沢道二

nakihon 泣本

Nansenshō Somabito
南杣笑楚満人

Nansō Satomi hakkenden
南総里見八犬伝

Nihon-ichi ahō no kagami
日本一癡鑑

Ningen isshin nozoki karakuri
人間一心覗替繰

ninjōbanashi 人情話

ninjōbon　人情本

Nishimiya Shinroku 西宮新六

Nishimiya Taisuke 西宮太助

Nishimura Genroku 西村源六

niwaka 俄

Oka Sanchō 岡三鳥

okabasho 岡場所

Okamoto Mansaku 岡本万作

Ono no Bakamura usojizukushi
小野篶（馬鹿村　）
譃字尽

Ono no Takamura 小野篁

Ōta Nanpo　大田南畝
otogizōshi　御伽草子
otokodate　男達
Otoshibanashi chūkō raiyū
　落語中興来由
Oya no kataki uchimatakōyaku
　親讐胯膏薬

rakugo　落語
Rakutei (Rakusanjin) Bashō
　楽亭(楽山人)馬笑
Rakutei Seiba　楽亭西馬
rangakusha　蘭学者
Rokujuen　六樹園
Ryūtei Riraku　滝亭鯉楽
Ryūtei Tanehiko　柳亭種彦

Sakigakezōshi　魁草紙
Sakuragawa Jihinari
　桜川慈悲成
Sakuragawa Jinkō　桜川甚車
Sakurahime azuma bunshō
　桜姫吾妻文章
Sanshōtei Karaku　三笑亭可楽
Santei Goran　三亭五蘭
Santei Shunba　三亭春馬
Sato no Bakamura mudajizu-
　kushi　廓蕞費字尽
Seiyō jijō　西洋事情
sekenbanashi　世間話
senryū　川柳
sentō　銭湯
serifu　台詞
setsuyōshū　節用集
Settei Santō　雪亭三冬
Sharakusai　洒落斉
sharebon　洒落本
Shibai kinmō zui
　戯場訓蒙図彙
Shiba Zenkō　芝全交

Shikatsube no Magao
　鹿津部真顔
shikisanbasō　式三番叟
Shikisanjin　四季山人
Shinra Manzō (Banshō)
　森羅万象
Shinrotei (Kantōbei)振鷺亭
　(関東米)
Shokusanjin　蜀山人
Shōtei Sansei　匠亭三世
Shōtei Sanshichi　匠亭三七
Shuntei Sangyō　春亭三暁
Sono atomaku baba Dōjōji
　其跡幕婆道成寺
Sono henpō bakemonobanashi
　其返報怪談
suikazurayu　忍冬湯
Suwaraya Ichibei
　須原屋市兵衛

Tamenaga Masasuke　為永正輔
Tararirō　哆囉哩楼
Tentō daifukuchō　天道
　大福帳
Tōkaidō Yotsuya kaidan
　東海道四谷怪談
Tokutei Sankō　徳亭三孝
Tōrai Sanna　唐来三和
tōrimono　通者
Tōsei orimagai Hachijō
　当世織續紛八丈
tsū　通
Tsuruya Nanboku　鶴屋南北
Tsutaya Jūzaburō　蔦屋重三郎

Ueda Akinari　上田秋成
ugachi　穿ち
Ukiyo ayatsuri kumen jūmen
　浮世操九面十面

ukiyo-e 浮世絵
ukiyomonomane
浮世物真似
ukiyozōshi 浮世草子
Umebori Kokuga
梅暮里谷峨
uranagaya 裏長屋
Utagawa Kunimasa 歌川国政
Utagawa Kuninao 歌川国直
Utagawa Kunisada 歌川国貞
Utagawa Kuniyasu 歌川国安
Utagawa Toyokuni 歌川豊国
Utagawa Yoshimaru 歌川美丸
utajizukushi 歌字尽
Utei (Tatekawa) Enba 烏亭
（立川）馬馬

wagei 話芸
Wata onjaku kikō hōjō
綿温石奇効報条

Yadoya no Meshimori
宿屋飯盛

Yakusha gakuya tsū
俳優楽室通
Yakusha hiiki katagi
俳優家顧贔気質
yakusha hyōbanki
役者評判記
Yakusha kuchijamisen
役者口三味線
yomihon 読本
Yomo no Akara 四面赤良
Yomo no Utagaki 四面歌垣
Yorozuya Tajiemon (Rankōdō)
万屋太治右衛門（蘭
香堂　）
Yorozuya Taisuke 万屋太助
yose 寄席
Yūgidō　遊戯堂
Yūgidōjin 遊戯堂人
yuya 湯屋

zakuroguchi 石榴口
zashiki 座敷
zoku 俗

Index

Addison, Joseph, 12
Advertisements: by *gesakusha*, 35, 37–40, 54–55, 70–72; in *gesaku* works, 47, 93
akahon, 8, 27, 82, 202n22
Akogi monogatari, 53
ana, 69
aobon, 8, 82
Artists and illustrators, 11, 49. *See also* individuals
Asanebō Muraku, 64
Aston, W. G., 38, 123n22
Audience for fiction, 3

bakufu (shogunate), 8, 20, 23, 27, 29, 37, 42
Bokusentei Yukimaro, 16, 58–59
Bokutei Tsukimaro. *See* Kitagawa Tsukimaro
bunjin, 37

Censorship, 23, 27, 29, 30–31
Cervantes, Miguel de, 12
chaban kyōgen, 65
Chikamatsu Monzaemon, 12, 30
chōnin classes, 10, 49–51, 68, 70, 75
chūbon, 28, 60, 63, 70, 72
Chūshingura. See Kanadehon chūshingura

Chūshingura henchikiron, 72–73, 74
Chūshingura jinbutsu hyōron, 73
Commercialization of fiction, 3, 6–7, 10–11, 39–40, 43, 46–49, 55, 61. *See also* Publishing (Edo period)

dangi, 66
dangibon, 60–61, 65, 67; and oral storytelling, 66
Darumaya Kattōshi. *See* Iwamoto Sashichi
Dialects, 68, 71, 103, 104–106, 111
Dialogue in fiction, 13, 65–68; linguistic realism in, 13, 62, 65, 91
Dickens, Charles, 12, 47–48
Drama. *See jōruri; kabuki*
Dutch learning. *See rangaku*

Ebara Taizō, 14
Edo, 1, 7, 108–109
Edo period, 6, 114n4
Edokko, 7, 56, 111
Ejima Kiseki, 22, 28, 77–78, 80
Ekitei Sanyū, 52, 54

Fielding, Henry, 12
Formula in fiction, 6, 51
Fukagawa, 24, 25–26, 28, 59
Fukagawa haiken, 25